Hebron Journal

He has told you, O mortal, what is good;
and what does the Lord require of you but to do
justice, and to love kindness, and to walk humbly
with your God?
Micah 6:8

And the king will answer them, "Truly I tell you,
just as you did it to one of the least of these who
are members of my family, you did it to me.
Jesus, in Matthew 25:40

O ye who believe! Stand out firmly for Allah, as
witnesses to fair dealing, and let not the hatred of
others to you make you swerve to wrong and
depart from justice. Be just: that is next to piety.
Koran, Surah 5:8

Hebron Journal

STORIES OF NONVIOLENT PEACEMAKING

Arthur G. Gish

Herald
Press

Scottdale, Pennsylvania
Waterloo, Ontario

Library of Congress Cataloging-in-Publication Data
Gish, Arthur G., 1939-
    Hebron journal: stories of nonviolent peacemaking / Arthur G. Gish.
    p. cm.
    ISBN 0-8361-9168-4 (alk. paper)
    1. Arab-Israeli conflict—1993—West Bank—Hebron. 2. Conflict
management—West Bank—Hebron. 3. Intergroup relations—West
Bank—Hebron. 4. Palestinian Arabs—West Bank—Hebron—
Attitudes. 5. Israelis—West Bank—Hebron—Attitudes. 6. Christian
Peace Maker Teams. 7. Gish, Arthur G., 1939—Diaries. 8. Hebron—
Politics and government—20th century. I. Title.
    DS119.76.G57 2001
    956.05'3—dc21   2001039299

⊕ ∞™

The paper used in this publication is recycled and meets the minimum
requirements of American National Standard for Information Sciences—
Permanence of Paper for Printed Library Materials, ANSI 239.48-1984.

HEBRON JOURNAL
Copyright © 2001 by Herald Press, Scottdale, Pa. 15683
    Released simultaneously in Canada by Herald Press,
    Waterloo, Ont. N2L 6H7. All rights reserved
International Standard Book Number: 0-8361-9168-4
Library of Congress Catalog Card Number: 2001039299
Printed in the United States of America
Cover and book design by Merrill R. Miller

10 09 08 07 06 05 04 03 02   10 9 8 7 6 5 4 3 2

To order or request information, please call
1-800-759-4447 (individuals);1-800-245-7894 (trade).
Website: www.mph.org

To Peggy, my loving wife,
who has given so much
in the work for peace
and justice

Contents

Foreword

Christian Peacemaker Teams (CPT) was conceived in the mid-1980s when peace church people were seeking new ways to express their faith. Grass roots wars had broken out in many places including Central America, and in North America the U. S. government repeatedly was identified with the elite groups of outmoded oppressive systems. Emerging in that period was a consciousness that by using the creative energy of nonviolence, ordinary people could stand in front of the guns and encourage less violent ways for change to happen. People were learning that courageous faith could overcome cynicism.

In 1984 Ron Sider challenged the Mennonite World Conference in Strasbourg, France, with these words:

> We must take up our cross and follow Jesus to Golgotha. We must be prepared to die by the thousands. Those who believed in peace through the sword have not hesitated to die. Proudly, courageously, they gave their lives. Again and again, they sacrificed bright futures to the tragic illusion that one more righteous crusade would bring peace in their time, and they laid down their lives by the millions.
>
> Unless we . . . are ready to start to die by the thousands in dramatic vigorous new exploits for peace and justice, we should sadly confess that we never really meant what we said, and we dare never whisper another word about pacifism to our sisters and brothers in those desperate lands filled with injustice. Unless we are ready to die developing new nonviolent attempts to reduce conflict, we should confess that we never really meant that the cross was an alternative to the sword.

This call awakened vigorous conversations in churches across North America. In 1986 the discussions culminated in a late fall gathering in suburban Chicago and a call went out for Christian Peacemaker Teams (CPT) to be formed. Representative denominations appointed a steering committee to hammer out basic directions. In early fall 1988 I was invited to begin work as the first staff person.

By 1992 CPT had put together a series of delegations to Haiti, Iraq, and the West Bank. That experience helped to clarify the need for a trained full-time corps to work toward violence reduction in crisis situations. A goal was set to develop a Christian Peacemaker Corps of twelve full-time persons with a much larger number of reservists, available for up to two months each year. By 1998, with the achievement of a twelve-person Christian Peacemaker Corps, CPT was able to sustain two full-time projects and other less work-intensive projects. Among those projects were Haiti and Washington, D.C.

The CPT experience has demonstrated that teams of four to six people trained in the skills of documentation, observation, nonviolent intervention, and various ministries of presence—including patience—can make a striking difference in explosive situations. Full-time teams in places like Hebron are needed where the contending parties simply cannot be convinced to make changes in the distribution of power so that the road to peace becomes clear. Hebron typifies conditions in which one party has most of the power and the other has little. Until both parties have hope for a fair relationship at the negotiating table, the conflict appears unresolvable. CPT workers try to emphasize or encourage nonviolent methods for redress and get in the way of violence when they can.

CPT believes that similarly organized groups of trained peacemakers in urban and rural settings around the world can provide important intervention in local conflicts. Often these conflicts are accentuated by abusive behavior of law enforcement or other security forces. In other cases police and soldiers are the front end of fundamentally unfair policies.

CPT is a grassroots effort and most of its support comes from church members, congregations, and meetings. Full-time workers are compensated according to need. This pattern allows for enormous flexibility and financial frugality. The original call for Christian Peacemaker Teams was informed by the scriptural encouragement for creative public ministry and enemy loving in the Spirit of Jesus. The peace churches have brought an important gift to the table; namely, the absolute refusal to kill in situations of conflict.

As others join this movement to find ways for justice to happen without killing, they will bring their own special gifts to build the work. When Christians lay aside the weapons of destruction usually controlled by the culture of the mighty, the surprising power for transformation becomes a miracle available to redeem all of human kind and the earth itself.

The work in Hebron grew out of the experiences of a series of delegations in which CPT workers gained a base of relationships with Palestinians and Israelis concerned about the occupation of Judea and Samaria (the West Bank). Early in 1995 Wendy Lehman and Kathleen Kern, both experienced Peacemaker Corps members, spent several months exploring the possibility of a long-term project and were advised to consider the largely Muslim city of Hebron where there was little peacemaking or human rights presence. A very explosive situation existed in downtown Hebron where radical Jewish settlers had taken up residence. Discussions in Hebron culminated in a formal letter of invitation from Hebron's mayor and the beginning of a team of violence reduction workers in June 1995.

Art Gish's description of the work of the CPT team in Hebron describes some of the hard work that has been done to begin to realize the vision. Gish has described graphically the day-by-day life and dilemmas faced by one CPT team.

We are all grateful that he took the time and care to document his own internal struggle to do the right thing.

The style and approach of the team in Hebron have informed all the work of CPT, though the details of the work vary widely from project to project. The CPT framework includes disciplined and skilled people, an emphasis on spirituality and risk-taking combined with careful grassroots organizational work. If we sustain a spirit of unity in our purpose, the work of bringing this vision to life may be an important gift for the world in this new century.

—*Gene Stoltzfus, CPT director*

Preface & Acknowledgments

My special thanks to my wife, Peggy, who stayed home while I was away having all the "fun." She is the one who has made the most sacrifice, and deserves any credit. She has been fully supportive of my work, partly because of her own experiences with Witness for Peace in Nicaragua and with CPT in the West Bank.

Thanks also to the people of New Covenant Fellowship, the Christian intentional community near Athens, Ohio, that encourages me, sustains me, nurtures me, and is an important part of how I discern God's word for our time. I want my life to be an expression of the life we have together in community.

My thanks to all those active in Christian Peacemaker Teams and to Gene Stoltzfus, the director of CPT, who initially "twisted my arm" to go to Hebron and wrote the foreword. Without all the other saints in CPT with whom I worked in Hebron, none of this would have been possible.

I cannot mention all the people who contributed to this book by encouraging, supporting, and challenging me, all the people who read my original journal. I do want to thank Jake Kaufman, Trisha Lachman, Yeshua Moser-Puangsuwan, Don and Marge Foxvog, Jim Foxvog, Robert Whealey, Jim Phillips, Cliff Kindy, Irva Taylor, Gifford Doxsee, Joel Gish, Jamey Bouwmeester, Rich Meyer, Daniel Hertzler, and S. David Garber for their help in editing.

Any mistakes, misrepresentations, or insensitivities are my responsibility. Not everyone who has worked in CPT will agree with everything in this journal. What I have written comes out of my own perspective.

Finally, thank you to all the wonderful people of Hebron: to the Palestinians who have suffered so much, yet remain so open, loving, and hopeful; to all the Israelis who open their hearts to their Palestinians neighbors; and to the soldiers, police, and settlers who played their part in my experience in Hebron. I love all of you and pray for all of us one day to be reconciled.

—*Art Gish*

Introduction

Christian Peacemaker Teams (CPT) is part of a larger movement of nonviolence which has been building over the past 50 years. One of the most significant contributions of the 20th century is the conscious development of the theory and strategy of nonviolent direct action.[1] One immediately thinks of Gandhi and the independence struggle in India, Martin Luther King Jr. and the Civil Rights Movement in the United States, and the massive nonviolent revolution of 1989, when one third of the world's population experienced the nonviolent overthrow of totalitarian communism.

CPT is part of a growing movement of citizen intervention in situations of conflict, exemplified by groups like the Balkan Peace Teams, Peace Brigades International, Witness for Peace, and Nonviolence International.[2] These groups train ordinary people to go unarmed into situations of conflict. All over the world people are realizing that peace is too important to be left to governments or experts.

The work of CPT in Hebron is multifaceted. Our first, and perhaps most important purpose, in being in Hebron is to learn, to talk with every side in the conflict, to listen, and try to understand. When people feel listened to they begin to lower their defenses.

---

[1] Actually, there is a rich history of nonviolent action from the beginning of history. For a detailed history of nonviolence see Gene Sharp, *The Politics of Nonviolent Action* (Boston: Porter Sargent Publishers, 1973).

[2] For a thorough description of these groups and the concept of citizen intervention in international conflicts, see Yeshua Moser-Paungsuwan and Thomas Weber, *Nonviolent Intervention Across Borders* (Honolulu: University of Hawaii, 2000).

Second, we act as international observers, monitoring what is happening, and reporting what we see to churches in North America and to a worldwide network of concerned people. This involves monitoring human rights abuses, acts of violence against either Israelis or Palestinians, and abusive behavior by Israeli soldiers and police. We believe international observers have a violence-deterring effect. We call it "the grandmother effect." There are things no one will do if their grandmother, or anyone else, is watching. We try to tell the stories of people's pain and struggle, and identify signs of hope.

Our third objective is to be an active nonviolent presence in the midst of the conflict. We engage in nonviolent direct action. In order to achieve peace and reconciliation in places of conflict like Hebron, the imbalance of power must be addressed. For negotiations to be successful, both sides must be able to act somewhat as equals. A huge imbalance of power exists in Hebron. Nonviolent direct action can help balance the power equation by activists standing with the oppressed. We say that we stand on the side of whoever the gun is pointed at. This involves intense relationships with all sides. Any side may alternately see us as allies, obstacles, or enemies.

Reconciliation can happen only after injustices have been acknowledged. Often nonviolent direct action is needed to expose the oppression that exists, because it is often difficult for both victims and victimizers to recognize injustices. Nonviolent direct action is one necessary ingredient in any peace process. Mediation is a wonderful tool, but mediation can work only if both sides are open to mediation and a negotiated resolution to the conflict. If both sides are not open, then nonviolent direct action is needed to address the conflict.

CPT's approach is to work with those who are powerless. Our role in Hebron is not to act as mediators between the Israeli and Palestinian authorities, but rather to work with those on the bottom of the power equation and engage in actions that help set the agenda for those making decisions for Israeli/Palestinian relationships.

Fourth, we work with local nonviolent groups, both Israeli and Palestinian. We try to engage in actions together with, or in consultation with, Palestinians and Israelis. We could do little on our own without the support of our Israeli and Palestinian friends.

Fifth, we are a faith-based group, rooted in the nonviolent gospel of Jesus, and acting out of a spiritual center. Our times of group prayer and worship each day and personal prayer life are essential to our work. Prayer is a source of strength and courage to act in calmness and love. It is essential in discerning how to respond to difficult situations. We know that we ourselves cannot solve the problems of Hebron, but we have a vision of watering the miracle of peace, of being open to be part of God's reconciling and healing work in Hebron.

A basic way of confronting evil and injustice is to make ourselves vulnerable to that evil. This goes to the heart of a Christian understanding of nonviolence, the way of the cross. The New Testament presents us with an understanding that God's ultimate way of overcoming evil is the cross: nonviolent, redemptive, suffering love. It is not through worldly power, but rather through love, weakness, and vulnerability that we overcome evil.

Whether with an angry, alienated individual, or an unjust system, the only way to reconciliation and peace that I know of is for people to open themselves to the pain of the person or system, and through active suffering love to be agents of God's healing power. That is what we try to do in Hebron.

Our work in Hebron is rooted in the biblical tradition. The difference in the Hebrew sScriptures between true and false prophets was their willingness to speak the truth to power, or their willingness to support and defend the powers of injustice. Christian Peacemaker Teams is acting out of the belief that faith communities today also must be willing to speak truth to power and call oppressors to repentance.

The Hebrew prophets not only spoke the word of truth, they put those words into actions. Jeremiah not only spoke against those who said "Peace, peace," when there was no peace. He also proclaimed those words in public actions, walking around Jerusalem wearing a yoke, buying a new loincloth, and breaking clay jars by slamming them together. Isaiah walked the streets of Jerusalem naked and barefoot for three years to illustrate Israel's shame. Ezekiel lay bound on his side for 430 days, shaved his head, and burned portions of his hair. Daniel defied the Babylonian powers by praying in public.

Jesus followed the prophetic confrontational tradition by publically healing on the Sabbath, violating the rules in his relating to women, upsetting the tables of the money changers in the temple, and organizing a nonviolent march on a donkey into Jerusalem. In the book of Acts we read of the early church boldly confronting the powers that be, spending time in prison, and dying as martyrs rather than cave in to the demands of government and commerce. Are we called to less than this?

The five times during the past six years that I have had the privilege of being part of a Christian Peacemaker Team in Hebron have been the most intense experiences of my life. Here are some of the stories from those experiences. I hope these stories will serve as an example of the exciting possibilities of peacemaking. CPT has a vision of peacemaking that deserves to be studied as we work to find nonviolent alternatives to the failed military approaches to conflict resolution. CPT's experience in Hebron is a specific, concrete example of one approach to peacemaking.

The things CPT is learning are relevant not only to conflicts far from home, but are needed in every local community. In my home area of Athens, Ohio, we have a Ready Response Team trained in nonviolence and prepared to intervene in local conflicts.

As I reflect on why my experiences in Hebron were so powerful, I realize that it is in the process of struggle that we become most fully human. When we engage in serious dialogue across the lines of culture, gender, class, race, and religion, our whole beings are challenged. As we listen to each other and engage in deep conversation with those who are different from us, we have to either grow or retreat. When this happens in the context of putting our very lives on the line, the possibilities for growth are greatly increased.

It is out of this process that people like Gandhi, Fannie Lou Hamer, Martin Luther King Jr., and Dorothy Day emerge. With all the conflicts everywhere around us, the opportunities for engagement are everywhere. We can retreat and put up walls of defense, or we can open our lives to God's Spirit and to our neighbor, and engage in difficult conversation and struggle with those who are called our enemies, with those who are different.

To engage in the struggle, armed only with faith, hope, and love, is a wonderful opportunity. It is too good to turn down.

Hebron, a divided, troubled city

Hebron is no ordinary city. One of the oldest continually inhabited cities of the world, Hebron nestles, beautiful and picturesque, between four mountains in the Judean hills, about twenty miles south of Jerusalem.

Hebron has a long history that keeps intruding itself into the present. It is mentioned seventy times in the Bible. Hebron is the burial site for Abraham and Sarah, Isaac and Rebekah, Jacob and Leah. It was the site of King David's first capital. Over the centuries many battles have been fought in Hebron.

Hebron also has a long history of peace. Its name, in both Hebrew and Arabic, means "friend." When Abraham's wife, Sarah, died in Hebron, the Hittites sold the Cave of Machpelah to Abraham to bury her (Genesis 23:1-11). When Abraham died, both Ishmael and Isaac buried him there, indicating reconciliation between the two brothers (Genesis 25:9).

Herod the Great built walls around the Cave of Machpelah where Abraham and Sarah are buried. Queen Helena, the mother of Constantine, built a church building inside the wall, over the cave, which later became a mosque, then during the Crusades again became a church building, then became a mosque again, and is now part mosque (Ibrahimi Mosque) and part synagogue. It is a sacred place for Muslims and Jews.

During the Byzantine period almost everyone in Hebron was "Christian." Then the Hebronites converted to Islam. So the Muslims in Hebron have both Jewish and Christian ancestors. Probably most of them are not only descendants of Ishmael, but also of Jacob.

In the sixteenth century, Hebron Muslims welcomed Jews fleeing the Inquisition in Spain. For centuries, Jews and Muslims lived together peacefully in Hebron. In 1900 Palestinian Christians and Muslims were the majority population in Palestine, although there was a substantial Palestinian Jewish population as well. Relationships between the Palestinian Arabs and Jews were generally positive, I am told.

That peace was broken in the last century due in part to tensions which developed as a result of Zionism and the resulting large influx of Jews into Palestine. Zionism, with its call for Jews to return to Palestine, developed as a response to anti-Semitism in Europe and North America, and from a desire for a life of self-determination for Jews in their ancient homeland. In 1929, Palestinian Muslims brutally massacred 67 Hebron Jews. The Jewish community of Hebron then was temporarily disbanded.

The large-scale immigration of Jews to Palestine after 1900 created much fear in the Arab community. Among the results were violent clashes between Palestinians and the new immigrants, culminating in the war of 1948; the flight of 750,000 Palestinians from their homes; the partition of Palestine; and the creation of the state of Israel in 1948. In the 1967 war, Israel captured the rest of Palestine (the West Bank and Gaza) and has occupied this territory since then. This occupation has included the building of Jewish settlements throughout the West Bank and Gaza, and continual conflict.

Life in Hebron today is a microcosm of the larger Israeli-Palestinian conflict. Hebron's population of over 120,000 is all Palestinian Muslim except for a few hundred Israeli settlers who over the past 20 years have taken over four spots in the center of the old city and established small settlements in the historical Jewish Quarter. This small group of settlers is protected by 1,200 Israeli soldiers who maintain check-points day and night around the settlements. Kiryat Arba, a large settlement of approximately 6,000 Israelis on the eastern edge of Hebron is also a point of tension. Kiryat Arba was the first Israeli settlement established in the West Bank.

When CPT began our presence in Hebron in June 1995, the conflict between the settlers and the Palestinians was intense, with frequent clashes, stabbings, and shootings. In the two years of 1994-96, settlers and soldiers killed seventy Palestinians in Hebron. Palestinians also killed several Israelis. Both sides were throwing stones. This tension had reached a peak in February 25, 1994, when Baruch Goldstein, a settler from Kiryat Arba, killed twenty-nine Muslim men and boys as they prayed in the Ibrahimi Mosque.

The Israeli army killed at least that many or more in the demonstrations following that massacre. The Palestinians were put under curfew for 40 days. The main street through Hebron was closed to Palestinian vehicles. What had been the Ibrahimi Mosque became half mosque and half synagogue, with a steel wall dividing the two sides. The Palestinians are bitter about what they see as the injustice of their situation. Much of their land has been confiscated, their economy is in ruins, and they daily experience the humiliations of occupation.

The Israeli settlers are afraid, yet determined to *hang on* to what they believe was given to them by God. They see themselves as pioneers, laying claim to what they see as rightfully theirs. The soldiers have a difficult, thankless job, hated by Palestinians and settlers alike.

On June 1, 1995, Christian Peacemaker Teams, at the invitation of the Hebron mayor's office, began a continuing presence in Hebron. The situation was tense, a difficult and challenging place to try out an experiment in nonviolent peacemaking. Six months later, I arrived to join the team.

My interest in Palestinian/Israeli issues began in March 1960, when I visited the Holy Land on a three-week MCC tour. My wife, Peggy, was on a CPT delegation to the West Bank in February 1995. Part of the work of that delegation was to find a place for CPT to begin full-time work in the Middle East.

In the fall of 1995, Gene Stoltzfus called our community to ask that we send someone to join the team in Hebron in December. New Covenant Fellowship asked me to go.

THE JOURNAL
December 16, 1995—January 21, 1996

December 16, 1995, Saturday

After spending the night in Jerusalem, I got a taxi to Hebron this morning. It was exciting to see the beautiful countryside, to drive through Bethlehem. Soon I was at the municipal building in Hebron. Ahlam Muhtasib, the public relations person for the Palestinian mayor and CPT's contact in city hall, invited me into her office. Soon Cliff Kindy (a 50-year-old organic farmer from Indiana) and Anne Montgomery (a 70-year-old Catholic nun), both members of the CPT team here, arrived and we walked to our apartment in the old city.

The old city is in a valley surrounded by hills and ancient stone houses. Our apartment is on the second floor of a building at the edge of the old market, in a small street that used to be the glassmakers' street. Now it is known as chicken market. Each day the competing squawks of the chickens, turkeys, ducks, geese, and other creatures fill the air.

Our apartment is two doors from the corner of Shuhada Street, which used to be the main street through Hebron, but is now closed to Palestinian vehicles. Walk half a block up Shuhada Street and you come to a military encampment in what used to be the Palestinian central bus station. Go one more block up the street and you come to the Beit Hadassah settlement. Go two blocks up a steep hill to the left and you find the Tel Rumeida settlement. There is a Yeshiva school (Beit Romano) just below the military encampment. Go the other way on Shuhada Street about three blocks and you come to the Ibrahimi Mosque/Synagogue, also known as the tomb of the Patriarchs (and Matriarchs). Between our apartment and the mosque/synagogue is the Avraham Avinu settlement. There are military checkpoints in each direction. It feels like we are in the middle of the action.

Today was Saturday, the biggest day of the week for our team. Lots of settlers from all over the West Bank come to Hebron each Sabbath weekend to support the Hebron settlers. Many acts of violence have happened on Saturdays, due to the interaction of settlers, soldiers, and Palestinians on the street. Anne, Cliff, and I spent the day walking up and down the street. The most disturbing thing I saw was settlers walking back and forth with their automatic weapons.

Right away I began to learn CPT tactics from Cliff. We were in the park near the mosque/synagogue when two soldiers ran across the park, pretending to be attacking someone with their weapons. Soon another group of soldiers did the same thing. Cliff walked right up to them and talked with them about how dangerous it is to act that way in a tense situation where their actions could be interpreted as an attack. He talked to them about the need to be sensitive. I was impressed with his courage and gentleness. It had never occurred to me that one could actually confront soldiers about their actions.

Later we saw four Palestinian men standing up against a wall. We learned that two soldiers had taken away their identity passes and made them stand there for four hours because they had opened their shop during curfew. The market is closed as a collective punishment because two days ago a Palestinian was shot in front of the mosque/synagogue and left for two hours to bleed to death. He is reported to have stabbed two settlers after being harassed by settlers.

We approached the two soldiers and asked them about what was happening. They didn't want to talk with us, or give us their names. Cliff told them his name and said that since he wasn't ashamed of what he was doing, he wasn't afraid to give his name. We went to the police station and made a complaint about this incident. The policeman said he would contact the commanding officer.

This evening we visited the Abu Haikel family. The family has been harassed for years by the settlers in the neighboring Tel Rumeida settlement, because the settlers want the Abu Haikel land which adjoins the Tel Rumeida settlement. Settlers have attacked the Abu Haikels and damaged their property. We have been accompanying their young daughter past the settlement when she comes home from school, because she has been threatened by the settlers.

Last summer soldiers detained two CPT members for ten hours after accompanying a water truck up to the Abu Haikel home. The family had been without water and the settlers were preventing water trucks from passing the settlement. Because two North Americans were involved, this incident received international attention and raised awareness about the water problem in Hebron, where settlers enjoy well-watered lawns even as Palestinians lack water for basic

Israeli soldiers in front of Beit Hadassah settlement.

needs. Prime Minister Rabin even sent a fact-finding group to evaluate the water problem in Hebron. The publicity also helped ease the pressure on the Abu Haikel family.

On the way home we were stopped by six soldiers who wanted to see our passports. They told us they heard we had created a lot of trouble this afternoon. We had a good talk with them about what we are doing in Hebron.

December 17, 1995, Sunday

We got up early this morning and took Anne Montgomery to a taxi for her trip back to the United States. During the next week, Cliff and I will be the only team members here. Usually we try to have five or six people on the team. We took a taxi to Jerusalem and heard Naim Ateek preach at St. George's Anglican Cathedral. After that we spent a little time walking through the old city where we met a group of Palestinians who identified themselves as Christians. When they heard we are living in Hebron, they couldn't believe it. They informed us that Hebron is Muslim, and no Christian can live with Muslims. It seemed difficult for them to believe that we could be doing what we are doing. They were extremely pessimistic about the future, and want to emigrate to America.

In the taxi on the way back to Hebron, someone asked us who we were. This triggered a big discussion, especially when they found out we were Christians living in Hebron. They were all Muslims and couldn't believe any Christian would live in Hebron.

We got home this evening, ate a bit, and then heard singing outside. It turned out to be a group of over 50 settler men celebrating the beginning of Hanukkah. Extra soldiers patrolled the street. The settlers marched to the Avraham Avinu settlement and back. We watched and greeted them with "Happy Hanukkah" and chatted with a few soldiers. We heard one shot or firecracker that sent the soldiers running, but we never heard that there was any trouble.

I had to deal with a lot of fear this evening, especially when I walked past a settler in the dark with his machine gun. It was scary having him behind me. I came here knowing that it could mean my death. I have tried to accept that I may be killed here. That acceptance of death gives me a lot of freedom. If I am free to die, then I am free to live. I am free to take risks, free to be open and vulnerable, free to go anywhere. But I am still afraid.

December 18, 1995, Monday

This morning we had our time of worship in the park across from the Tomb of the Patriarchs and Matriarchs. Cliff read the story of Hagar and Sarah from Genesis 16. The struggle between Hagar and Sarah (Arab and Jew) manifests itself today here at Sarah's tomb.

Cliff and I met a Palestinian supporter of CPT and asked him about our seeking dialogue with the settlers. Our team has been wrestling with how to relate to the settlers. He was supportive of more dialogue, as long as we do nothing that would be seen as collaboration with the settlers. With him was a man who lives beside the Kiryat Arba settlement and has been harassed by settlers there for the past ten years. Windows have been broken, fires set in the house, and many stones thrown at the family. In the past our team members have stayed at the house to prevent settler attacks. It seems that settlers are less likely to attack Palestinians if North Americans are present. We still visit his family once a week.

After this conversation Cliff took me into the Ibrahimi Mosque which is built over the Cave of Machpelah. Since the massacre here in 1994, a wall has divided the building into a mosque and a synagogue. Muslims are not permitted on the Jewish side and Jews are not permitted on the Muslim side. Christians can enter either side, except for Palestinian Christians who are not permitted on the Jewish side. Israeli soldiers checked our passports and had us go through metal detectors at two separate checkpoints. It was sobering to pray where the massacre took place. I saw bullet holes in the wall at the front of the mosque.

After eating some lunch, we left to visit people Cliff thought I should meet. A family that CPT has been close to treated us royally. We then visited a group of journalists with whom CPT works. When there is trouble, they call us and we call them. They are on the front lines in reporting human rights abuses and often suffer for it. I learned a lot about the struggles in the Palestinian community and their fear that violence could happen soon in our neighborhood, started by either the settlers or the Palestinians.

We got home, started supper, and decided to walk Shuhada Street one time before eating. Everything was quiet, but we got into a long conversation with a group of soldiers beside their encampment. They hate being soldiers and wish they could see a way toward peace. We talked about how peace might be possible. We heard a lot of fear. They want-ed to know what we are doing and why. They seemed to

The Ibrahimi Mosque/Cave of Machpelah

appreciate our presence. They even invited us to join them in lighting the Hanukkah candle.

I am tired of seeing guns, tired of having automatic rifles pointed at me. It feels eerie to be surrounded by a dozen soldiers with their automatic weapons. As Cliff puts it, guns are stupid. Guns are useless. You can't build anything with them, you can't farm with them, you can't nurture children with them, you can't care for the sick with them. What can one do with a gun? They certainly do not bring anyone security, or peace, or freedom. The soldiers have lots of guns, but they are neither free nor secure.

December 19, 1995, Tuesday

This morning we went to visit Khalid Amayreh, an Islamist friend of the team. Islamists want to establish a Muslim society, based on Islamic ideals. They are disillusioned with secular nationalism. Hamas is the largest Islamic political party here in Palestine. Many of the of the bombing attacks on Israelis have been attributed to Hamas. Our friend shared his frustrations with Yasir Arafat's Palestinian Authority and voiced his opposition to the peace process, which he sees as a sell-out to the Israelis. He shared his vision of an Islamic society, a world in which there would be justice, equality, and no oppression, a society guided by moral values rather than by the notion that "might makes right." He talked about the relation of Christianity to Islam, and sees Jews and Christians as integral parts of Islam. The last words of Muhammad were, "be kind to the people of the book." He emphasized that there should be no compulsion in religion.

As we were leaving, a boy who recognized Cliff told us there was trouble down by the market. We went to investigate. When we got near home we saw a large group of soldiers and settlers on the street by our house. We heard from the police that a Palestinian had stabbed a settler woman. We talked with other soldiers who told us that the problem this morning resulted from a Palestinian throwing an ax and barely missing a settler girl.

Cliff and I walked down our street and talked to a group of Palestinians who told us that a settler girl had come down into the market and deliberately spilled some grain at one of the shops. They tried to stop her, the police were called, and a number of Palestinians were arrested. The Palestinians suspect that because today is a Muslim holy day, the settlers wanted to create a disturbance and thereby prevent Muslims from going to the mosque.

We headed toward the mosque/synagogue. A curfew had been called and all the shops were closed. Fresh produce lay on the ground in the market, thrown there, we were told, by settlers. A large group of settlers was milling around on the street. The Palestinians were mostly gone, and the settlers had taken over the street. They started directing a lot of hate toward us, calling us Nazis and anti-Semites. They said "All Christians are Nazis," "F— Jesus," and "Jesus is a son of a bitch." I told them that both Jesus and his mother were Jews. A young boy called me stupid. I asked him why he thought I was stupid. He just repeated that I am stupid. Maybe he is right. I just said "Shalom" to him.

We started talking to the soldiers, who were getting frustrated with the settlers. One soldier wanted to know if I had protested the Vietnam War. When I said yes, he was impressed. He said he wished he could have protested that war. He called himself a hippie in uniform.

We walked up to the police station by the mosque/synagogue where about 20 Palestinians were lined up against the wall. We stood nearby and watched, though the soldiers did not appreciate our being there. One by one the Palestinians were released.

There were a lot of journalists there. I thank God for their presence. The threat of exposure to the world deters the soldiers from doing anything they feel like doing. The journalists pay a heavy price for what they do. Most have been beaten and abused. They told us they got video footage of settlers stoning and hitting Palestinians this morning.

A soldier whom Cliff confronted on Saturday was here by our street, and apparently out of spite, would not let us go to our house. We learned that his name is Avri. He told us we had to go all the way around the block and come in through the market. We decided to take the long way around. In a nice way we told him we would walk around the block, that we enjoy walking.

Earlier this morning a soldier told me to move and I just ignored him, so he walked away. I am learning that I do not have to do everything the soldiers tell me to do. But I am also free to obey them, which is important too. This morning a soldier asked us to move away from the settlers in hope that the settlers too would then go away. We left, and then the settlers left.

This evening we went out to walk around a bit before supper and saw a crowd of settlers gathering on Shuhada Street. It turned out that the settlers were going to light their third Hanukkah candle here, where they claim an ax was thrown at a settler girl this morning. We decided to observe in case there was trouble.

We took a fair amount of abuse from the settler children who called us "stupid," "jackasses," and so on. One child asked me to bray like a donkey, so I decided to turn the whole thing into a joke. I did my hew-haw routine. The children laughed, I think, partly at the humor, and partly out of a spirit of ridicule. I wanted to break the spell of hate and hope I may have partially succeeded. They probably still think we are stupid Nazis, but maybe they might also see us as persons with whom they connected in some small way.

I am disturbed at the general unruliness of the settler children and the lack of concern from their parents. These beautiful children are being taught to hate and disrespect others. At one point they climbed up some Palestinian stairs and started banging on them. I went to the soldiers and told them that it didn't seem right for the children to be doing that, and that the settlers would never permit the Palestinians to do that on settler stairs. The soldiers talked briefly and then removed the children from the stairs. I thanked the soldiers.

A soldier asked us to leave when the children were harassing us. I told the soldier that I am a reasonable person and if someone has a concern and wants me to leave, I will certainly listen and consider the request. But when some people are causing trouble, it doesn't sound reasonable for us to be the ones to leave. I suggested he deal with the disturbances being caused by the children. We refused to leave and the soldier went away. As the children backed away, Cliff and I decided to do likewise. We watched the Israeli dancing and the lighting of the "candles," actually buckets of paper and kerosene.

When the ceremony was finished, Cliff and I decided to clean up the mess the settlers left in front of the Palestinian house. We decided first to ask Avri, the soldier who had earlier asked us to leave and the one Cliff had confronted on Saturday. He said no. We told him if they didn't clean it up, we would do it first thing in the morning. He doesn't seem to like us.

I feel for the soldiers. What a terrible job. We were told that Hebron is one of the worst assignments they can get. Their work here is boring, and their role ambiguous. They were trained as soldiers, but must act mainly as police. Sometimes they see the settlers as extremists and feel like traitors when they restrain their own people.

Yesterday, I heard that the Israelis just confiscated a big chunk of land near Bethlehem. In the two years since the Oslo Agreement, six times as much land has been confiscated as in the two years before the agreement. Is this peace? A large amount of Palestinian land, much of it the best farmland, is being taken in this area for new roads, to be used only by settlers.

December 20, 1995, Wednesday

This morning before breakfast, Cliff and I went down and cleaned off the sidewalk where the settlers had left their junk last night. At least the Palestinians will not have to deal with it. Much of the market is closed today due to what happened yesterday. We are still not sure what actually did happen.

We were near Beit Hadassah settlement when we met a settler from Kiryat Arba, an American who has been here 25 years. He seemed like an open person, and obviously has developed good relations with the Palestinians. We watched him as he walked through the neighborhood and was warmly welcomed by the Palestinians. Here is one Israeli who is not afraid to walk through the Palestinian neighborhoods. He has taken the time to establish relationships, and treats the Palestinians with respect. That impressed me. Relationships between Israelis and Palestinians are possible if based on mutual respect.

The Women in Green, a settler organization opposed to the Women in Black (an Israeli peace group), held a tour of Hebron today to show support for the Hebron settlers. Since we wanted to observe this group, we spent much of the day on the street. Soon we saw the first group walking up Shuhada Street. There were about 75 people, some obviously Americans. I found their marching and carrying Israeli flags through a Palestinian neighborhood arrogant and provocative. I compare it to a white power group marching through an African-American neighborhood carrying a confederate flag, or a Nazi group marching through a Jewish neighborhood with a swastika. It was difficult to watch. I can feel the anger of the Palestinians. I sensed a lot of hostility toward us from the tourists, so I assume that their settler guide told them about us.

I initiated a conversation with two of the tourists. They talked about how Jews have been victims over the centuries, but that they will never again allow themselves to be victims. I asked them if the only alternative to being victims was to oppress others. An older Jewish woman from Brooklyn said she considers the settlers here to be brave heroes facing impossible odds.

Cliff and I had a long talk with a soldier. We started asking questions and he told us he wouldn't hesitate to kill an Arab who was attacking an Israeli, but wouldn't kill an Israeli who was attacking a Palestinian. He admitted that this was a double standard, but said that is just the way it is. To him, nothing is more important than Israel. I told him that in the Hebrew Scriptures, the worst of all sins is idolatry. To put anything above God is a terrible act that leads to disastrous consequences. He said that he understood that, but that no matter what, Israel comes first.

After supper we walked out on the streets to patrol. We try to go on patrol around the city every evening. On the way back we met two yeshiva students who didn't know who we were. They thought we were Amish. We talked about the Amish, about nonviolence and peace, about living without being controlled by fear. We joked, we talked about CPT, and they invited us to come eat with them.

Then Anat Cohen, a Hebron settler, came and started talking to the students in a very serious tone. She was speaking in Hebrew, but we kept hearing the word, Hamas. She was telling them that we are Hamas (a militant Islamic group) and that they should not be talking with us. I said to her that we are not Hamas, that we are Christians who believe in nonviolence. It was obvious that the students were in a difficult situation, so we told them that we would leave so that we would not cause them any trouble. We said goodbye, Shalom, and happy Hanukkah to them. We also said Shalom and happy Hanukkah to Anat.

I thank God for Anat. What a catalyst she is. She brings all the hate and prejudice out into the open. I also consider her to be a challenge. I will not accept the wall she keeps putting up between us. I will try hard to break down, go under, above, around, or through that wall.

December 21, 1995, Thursday

This morning we saw a crowd of settlers and soldiers near our apartment. The settlers were trying to come down our street into the market, and the soldiers were preventing them. Anat was there and seemed to be at the center of the trouble. The settler story is that this morning a Palestinian assaulted a young settler near our house, and that is why the settlers are so upset.

We observed only briefly before we were approached by a policeman who confiscated our passports and said he wanted to talk with us at the police station. We didn't know what was happening. On the way to the station Cliff phoned support people. At the police station, the policeman gave us a fatherly talk about staying out of trouble, being careful, and advised that if there were any problems, we should call him. He then returned our passports and let us go. We don't quite understand what happened, but we think a settler made a complaint about us in order to have us temporarily removed.

When we got back home there was still a crowd at both ends of our street. A big group of settlers at the upper end was still being restrained by the soldiers, who had closed the gate to our street. Anat was arguing with the soldiers. All of a sudden a group of settlers broke through and headed down into the market. It looked like big trouble. Cliff went into the market and I stayed by the gate. The soldiers called the area a closed military zone and ordered the shops closed. The soldiers were trying to keep the rest of the settlers out of the market. The settlers kept trying to push through. Occasionally one would break through the soldier line and run down the alley with soldiers trying to catch him. Usually they got away. But poor Anat never did get through. She seemed really frustrated.

Noam Arnon, a leader and spokesman for the settlers here, came to the gate and began talking to me. He wanted to know who I am and what I am doing here. Other settlers listened suspiciously. I told him a little about CPT. He asked why we support the Arab side. I told him we want to listen to all sides. I told him we would like to talk with him, and that our main purpose would be to listen and try to understand. He seemed a bit taken aback by that. He never did give me an answer, but I felt like I had gotten through some walls.

Soon I was talking to another settler, an American from New York, who was raised Catholic, got involved in messianic groups, and then converted to Judaism. We had a long, intense talk through the gate. Several settlers tried to stop us, but we kept talking. He wanted to know who we were, so I told him about CPT.

We had a discussion about nonviolence and faith. He was very critical of CPT because we are seen not as neutral, but as taking the side of the Arabs. He wanted to know if we are Hamas. I said no, and told him that we want to reach out to all sides, but are cursed and turned away when we reach out to settlers. I asked him to help set up a meeting for us with the settlers.

He told me how terrible and violent the Arabs are and showed me a scar on his head which he claimed was from an attack by an Arab. He said the settlers feel as if they are in a cage, and are fighting back.

I learned that the settlers are angry with us not only because they think we side with the Palestinians, but because they think we put up signs that read, "Kill a Jew for peace." No wonder they are angry with us. I assured the former Catholic there is no way that we would have done that. I told him about some of my experiences confronting anti-Semitism in the past and risking my life facing the KKK and skinheads in the United States.

Cliff shared with me some things that an Israeli translated for our team last summer during a settler party at the end of our street. The speaker at the party said that the settlers should do things to make the Arabs angry, so that the Arabs will take foolish actions in response, making it possible to force the Arabs out of the city. How does that fit with what we have been experiencing the past few days? Cliff thinks the settlers' purpose was to close the market, thus punishing the Palestinians. If so, they succeeded.

I am impressed with how much energy the settlers put into these confrontations. Many of them were out on the street here today, including schoolchildren.

After lunch we heard noise outside. I went down and saw soldiers running down our street into the market. A soldier saw me and ordered me back into the house. Then Cliff came down and we went out into the street. Soldiers had some Palestinians lined up against the wall. We went right up to the soldiers and watched them. A soldier in a jeep used a loudspeaker to order us to leave the area. He gave the order to leave in both Hebrew and English, loud enough to hear a mile away. We pretended not to hear. The Palestinians were being treated very roughly, including having their legs kicked apart as they stood with their hands on the wall above their heads.

We told the soldiers to treat them with respect. That made them angry. The soldier in the jeep again ordered us to leave. "Can't you hear?" he asked. Cliff gently explained to them that if they were not ashamed of what they are doing, they wouldn't mind us watching. The soldier replied that it was none of our business. I told him we were international observers and had a right to watch. Again we told the soldiers to stop mistreating the Palestinians.

At this point the soldier jumped out of the jeep, grabbed his automatic rifle, and told Cliff to get into the jeep. Cliff asked if we were being arrested. The soldier said, "You are under arrest." Cliff for some reason didn't accept that. He asked why he was being arrested. The soldier replied that this was a closed military zone. Cliff asked to see the paper designating this area a closed military zone.

The soldier hesitated, then said it would be brought. He

again ordered us to leave. At this point they had finished roughing up the last Palestinian and had let them all go. We again reminded the soldiers that all people should be treated with respect. Since there was no longer a reason to stay, we decided to leave. The soldiers ignored us as we walked away.

My stomach was in knots.

We then walked down Shuhada Street and were stopped by the soldiers at the next checkpoint. They wanted to talk. They asked us who we are, what we are doing, and why. They agreed that the Border Police, the soldiers we had just encountered, are pretty bad. They said the Border Police have been through some rough times and are afraid.

I just finished reading Kathy Kern's book, *We Are the Pharisees*. I appreciated the warning of the danger of self-righteousness, and the story of the horrible effects of anti-Semitism. I need to keep both of these concerns in mind here. When I worked in the Civil Rights Movement back in the 1960s, I became aware of the racism in my own life and have tried to work on that ever since. Now I am realizing that I have been influenced by the anti-Semitism that pervades Western culture. I want to work at that with as much vigor as I have dealt with racism.

December 23, 1995, Saturday

I was sitting out on the street studying Arabic when I saw a young settler boy, maybe ten years old, talking with the soldiers across the street. It was clear they were talking about me, so I walked over to them and asked the boy if he wanted to talk with me. He asked me why I want to kill Jews, why I support the Arabs who want to kill Jews. We had a long, good talk. His answer to everything I said was that the Arabs want to kill the settlers. He brought up the 1929 massacre of Jews here. I told him that was terrible, that every act of violence is terrible. He mentioned that Christians had killed millions of Jews.

I got down on my knees before that boy and told him I

was sorry for what so-called Christians have done to Jews. I told him that over the centuries, Christians have treated Jews much worse than have Muslims. The boy and soldiers all agreed with me on that. I talked to the boy about what fear and hate can do to our hearts. I told the boy that he is very intelligent and that he needs to work at finding a creative answer to the problems here.

This was Saturday and we did a lot of patrolling up and down Shuhada Street today. We accompanied the Abu Haikel girl from school to her home by the Tel Rumeida settlement. We now do that only on Saturdays, when there is more chance of settler violence.

December 24, 1995, Sunday

This morning Cliff and I had a time of worship down by the mosque/synagogue, and then got a bus to Bethlehem for Christmas. When we got off the bus in Bethlehem, one of the first things we saw was Palestinian police. Redeployment was just two days ago, in Bethlehem, at which point the Israeli soldiers left and the Palestinian Authority took over. Yasir Arafat has been here the past few days.

We met Kathy Kern and Marge Ardgelan, who had just arrived. Now there are four in our team.

We went to the Lutheran Church building for a 5:00 p.m. Christmas Eve service that lasted two hours and was in Arabic, German, and English. A dramatic part of the service was the appearance of Yasir Arafat's wife, Suha, who sat in front right across from us. That was a circus. Photographers were everywhere. They took over. I felt sorry for Suha and was disgusted at the arrogance of the photographers, who showed no respect for her, or the meeting for worship. At one point I got up and quietly told one photographer to sit down.

I had mixed reactions to Suha being there. Since she is Christian it was appropriate for her to be there. I appreciate the way Arafat is reaching out to Christians. Her being there is an encouragement to Palestinian Christians. It bodes well for the future. But I was also uncomfortable with how much attention was given to her. Much support was given to Arafat in the prayers and sermons. I appreciated the clear commitment to justice and liberation that permeated the service. I also appreciated that there were no Palestinian flags in the building. It is important that the church not become captive to any political movement, that we understand that our kingdom is not of this world, that we see our calling as a counterculture, and that our prophetic role be maintained.

During the meeting for worship we heard loud explosions outside. That was quite unnerving until I realized that it was fireworks. After the meeting for worship, Cliff and I spent some time in Manger Square. It had a Fourth of July feeling. There was even cotton candy! It was a mass celebration of independence. There were continual fireworks. All were happy to again have control of their own city. There was a feeling of hope.

This was Christmas Eve, supposedly a Christian celebration. Christmas trees and even Santa were visible. There was a big stage with choirs from all over the world singing Christmas music. There was a clear Christian presence and witness there, but it was somewhat overwhelmed by the independence celebration. Most of the people there were Muslims, but Muslims and Christians mingled freely. They were in this together. Actually, since Muslims also recognize Jesus as the Messiah, they can also celebrate his birth.

December 25, 1995, Monday

This morning the four of us had a team meeting. It was mainly a sharing time, learning to know each other. We talked about our fears and about baggage we have brought with us that may be a hindrance to us here. We agreed that Cliff should be the team leader, with all of us being equal. We each have different roles in the team, but make our decisions by consensus.

We had lunch with Zougby Zougby and his wife, Elaine. Zougby is a veteran Palestinian activist and both are important friends of CPT. I initiated a conversation about our role in Hebron. They said that the question of whether the settlers here go or stay is not something we should get involved in. That is between the Israelis and Palestinians. Our role is to be a humanizing presence in the middle of this strife.

This would include relating to soldiers, building trust and understanding, and being a deterrent to their use of violence against the Palestinians. We can try to build some bridges of understanding between the settlers and us. We should be extremely careful that the settlers not use us or manipulate us. Zougby believes they may twist anything for their own purposes. He also urged us to be very careful around them, for they may not hesitate to kill us. Since the killing of Prime Minister Rabin this past fall, it seems the settlers may do anything.

On relating to the Palestinians, we should be talking and listening to everyone, not identifying with any faction, being an open, understanding presence among them. Their stories need to be heard. We can be a presence that will help deter violence against them by soldiers or settlers.

December 26, 1995, Tuesday

Kathy and Marge went to meet with Ahlam at the municipal building to keep the mayor's office informed on what we are doing. I heard a story about Ahlam today. Once as she was being threatened by an Israeli soldier who was screaming at her, she said to him, "You have beautiful eyes." The soldier was quite embarrassed and stopped his actions. By taking the initiative, Ahlam had won the struggle. She did not permit herself to be a victim.

This evening we had a long team meeting, talking about direction and focus, which we seem to lack. Some issues that arose include whether we should focus on Hebron or on wider justice issues. What should we be doing to prepare for redeployment, the turning over of authority here to the Palestinians? We agreed to reach out to settlers and work at deterring violence. We talked about facilitating contact between Israeli peace and solidarity groups and the people of Hebron, helping Israelis take responsibility for what is happening in Hebron, and helping Palestinians learn to trust Israeli activists.

December 27, 1995, Wednesday

This morning after our prayer time, we all went to Hebron University. I saw where our team, along with some Israeli friends from the Hebron Solidarity Committee, had opened the gate to the university last summer. Back then, if you were at the main entrance to the university, you had to take a fifteen-minute walk and enter at the rear, because the Israeli military had sealed the main entrance with a concrete block wall. The administration, faculty, and students suggested that CPT reopen the main entrance. Early one morning, the team and some Israelis took sledgehammers and simply broke down the wall closing the entrance. They were arrested, held three days, and released. When we got to the university, the students swarmed around Cliff, who had helped open the gate and was one of those arrested.

It wasn't long before I had a crowd around me, asking all kinds of questions. It felt like the old days back in the United States when I did street preaching on college campuses during the Vietnam War. They wanted to know what I thought about the peace process. We talked about the oppression the Palestinians have suffered, and America's role in that. I apologized to them for the horrible treatment Muslims have suffered from Christians. We talked about nonviolence. I did some listening, but mostly they kept questioning me.

Marge and I went to see the museum at Beit Hadassah. A friendly soldier told us just to go on in. We walked in and a young boy kept telling us to go away. We ignored him. We went downstairs and an older man met us and gave us a tour of the museum, which centers entirely on the massacre of 67 Jews in Hebron in 1929. I was deeply moved by the exhibition. What a tragedy. It helped me understand better the fear the settlers have, and also their determination to right those wrongs and never let that happen again. I apologized to him for the horrible things Christians have done to Jews over the centuries. One important omission from the museum is the story of how many Hebron Muslim families saved many Jewish lives during the massacre by hiding the Jews in their homes.

We went upstairs and met Noam Arnon, the settler leader I talked to last week on the street. I thanked him for the privilege of visiting the museum and said how horrified I am by the massacre. He said he didn't want to talk now, but I said I did want to briefly talk about the rumor that we had put up a sign, "Kill Jews for peace." I assured him that none of us would have done that. I even told him I would rather be shot than agree to write that. I told him we wanted to understand him better and hoped to have more conversations with him. I again asked to arrange a meeting for sharing with the settlers. He was noncommittal. I told him if he had concerns about CPT he should feel free to contact us, that we want to take their concerns seriously. He said that he felt that our presence is giving legitimacy to the Arabs who want to force the settlers out of Hebron. He said the settlers want to live in peace with the people of Hebron, that anyone should be free to live in Hebron.

After supper, Cliff, Marge, and I went for a walk around the area. We saw a soldier helping a Palestinian boy who fell off his bicycle and skinned his knee. We see many acts of cruelty and humiliation, but also expressions of love and kindness. Last Saturday we saw a Palestinian close the gate to the donkey pen at Beit Hadassah where the settlers' animals were getting out. The other day I got involved in a little soccer game on Shuhada Street with Palestinian boys and Israeli soldiers. These are all signs of peace.

December 28, 1995, Thursday

I went to the village of Beit Ummar to visit a student I met yesterday at Hebron University. We spent some time going around the town. I saw many homes that were demolished during the Intifada. U.S. President Jimmy Carter once came here to see the demolished homes. I was impressed again with how deeply the Palestinians have suffered, and their courage and strength. Many people from the village were killed by Israelis during the Intifada. I heard clearly from them that they want peace. I am challenged by their willingness to forgive. But they are deeply concerned about the expanding settlements around the village.

I was told that because of the strong resistance, Israeli soldiers no longer come into this village, and that there are no police. But things seem to be running smoothly.

On the way home, two men on the bus got into a big argument. The bus driver came back, quietly intervened, and put one man off the bus. I was impressed with how skillfully various people dealt with that conflict. They are already practicing nonviolent conflict resolution.

On the bus I again saw the new road cutting through prime agricultural land, displacing the Palestinians. The road will be only for Israelis. That is racist. That is apartheid. It is also stupid. If only Israelis are on the road, it is a "safe" target for violent attacks against Israelis.

When we were eating supper, we heard what sounded like an explosion out on the street. We went down Shuhada Street where there were lots of soldiers. They said that they found a suspicious object. The soldiers have a robot vehicle that goes up to suspicious objects and blows them up. This one was a burning tire, not a bomb.

There were lots of yeshiva students there waiting to get through the street. They seemed open to talk with us. Our talk began with them asking Cliff and me if we are Amish. Many Israelis have seen the movie, *Witness*, a story about Amish life. We told them that we are somewhat similar to

Amish. They wanted to know why we shave our moustaches. We told them the story of the connection between moustaches and militarism in the minds of many people in the nineteenth century and for that reason church members were encouraged not to have moustaches.

That led to a big discussion of war and peace. We listened to their story. They believe that everyone wants peace, except for the Arabs. They asked us what we think can be done for peace. We suggested that we need to be creative and try to look at things in a new way, find new responses, to try to see things through the perspectives of those we call our enemies. We explained to them that we, without guns or any form of defense, are free and safe to go anywhere in the city. Those with guns are less safe and less free.

I just heard this evening that a local settler has said the holocaust was God's punishment on the Jews for staying in Europe and not moving to Israel. Wow!

December 29, 1995, Friday

This morning we got into a conversation with some soldiers, one of whom was Avri. They agreed that things are calmer and the soldiers more relaxed now than a few weeks ago. Avri told us that he saw us as an obstacle to peace, rather than a help, because we are obstructing the soldiers from doing their job. Some soldiers may see us that way. We have sometimes obstructed them.

Avri then said that the soldiers never instigate anything, that they have never killed anyone except when necessary. They only respond to trouble. When there is trouble, they put both the Palestinians and the settlers under curfew. I asked him why it was that when Baruch Goldstein killed 29 people praying in the mosque, the Palestinians were punished with a 40-day curfew, but not the settlers. He said that was done only to prevent further violence. I told him we had never seen settlers put under curfew when there is trouble. At that point he became upset and told me I was not objective. That was the end of our conversation.

We walked back up the street and Cliff and Marge told me that maybe I pushed too hard. I then went back to Avri and apologized to him for being too pushy. In a noncommittal way, he said "Okay," and walked away.

This led to a good discussion among us about how to respond to talk about how pure and blameless the Israelis are. It is clear to all of us that mainly we need to listen. But at what point is listening interpreted as giving assent? At what point can we question their mythology? Was I wrong in challenging Avri? How can we break through their walls and help them see other alternatives? I may have said too much. If I had it to do over again, I wish I would have said only about half as much as I said. On the other hand, maybe he did hear me. Maybe he stopped the conversation at the right time for him.

This evening we went up to visit the Abu Haikel family. We talked about how the family saved seventeen Jews in 1929. Now they are being cursed and threatened by the settlers.

On the way up and back there were a lot of settlers on the street. We greeted them with "Shabbat Shalom." Some responded in a friendly way, some responded grudgingly, and some cursed us, spat at us, and pretended to vomit at us. One said, "screw you." Cliff received two death threats from settler children today.

December 30, 1995, Saturday

This morning I was having a wonderful conversation with a group of yeshiva students when some settlers came by and cursed me. They said, "Go to hell. May you die like Jesus." They spat at me. Then they scolded the students for talking with me. I politely told the students that I didn't want to cause them any trouble, and that I would leave. The students said "Shalom" to me.

That was the beginning of a long day walking up and

down Shuhada Street. There was a large group of Israelis out on the street today. Many were warm and friendly. We talked with some of them. Others cursed and spat at us.

This afternoon I met some Israeli musicians and had a good talk about the situation here and what could be done for peace. They said they were giving a concert this evening at 8:00 and very much wanted us to come. I said I didn't think we would be welcome. They said we would be their guests. Then a settler came by and told them not to talk to us. After the settler left, I explained that there was a lot of hostility from the settlers toward us. They still strongly urged us to come. I felt we should go.

Close to sunset, Marge and I saw a large group of Israelis marching up the hill to Tel Rumeida, singing and clapping. One of them invited us to join in. We waited for them to come back. On the way back some of them invited us to come with them to a party. I declined, but they insisted. I thought I would love to go to a party with them. What an opportunity! We started walking with them and I tried to explain that I didn't think we would be welcome. They insisted that we were welcome and they wanted us. These were not Israelis who live in Hebron.

Our conversation was then interrupted by some settlers who told them they should not be talking with us. There was quite a bit of conversation between them. Then, being very embarrassed, our new friends had to tell us that they could not invite us to eat with them after all. We told them we understood. We parted in peace.

It was getting late. We came back to the apartment, ate supper, and had a big discussion about whether we should go to the concert. Would that be too pushy, too much in their faces? Could it result in a big blowup that would only close doors? I felt if the door was open, we should go in, that the worst case was for a big blowup to happen and we would be in a position to listen and respond with love. Actually, I didn't think they would let us in, but felt we should try. We decided that Cliff and I should go, but that we would not go in without checking first and getting permission.

When we got to the settler gift shop near the Cave of Machpelah where the concert was to be held, we saw a large crowd waiting to get in. We waited a little bit to get a feel of the situation. Then we started asking people if we could go in. Everyone welcomed us. But it was clear that none of these people live in Hebron. Soon a local settler, who has given us trouble in the past, realized what was going on. He made it clear that we were not welcome and should leave. That resulted in a big discussion among the Israelis. There was a lot of disagreement among them. Cliff got into a conversation with an American Jew who was new to Israel and didn't speak Hebrew, but vigorously spoke up for us. He was quite upset with how we were being treated.

I got to talk with a group of students. They wanted to know why we raise money for Hamas, why we hate the Jews and support the Arabs. I tried to explain who we are. I reminded them of the Hebrew Scripture that says not to bear false witness. They seemed to take that seriously. We were being cursed and treated quite rudely by some. One teenager told me, "We can kill you."

At this point a soldier came and said he wanted to talk with us. Apparently he was asked by the settlers to remove us. He took our passports and asked us to come to the police station nearby. We explained that we had been invited to the concert and were checking to see if we were welcome, and that we now did not plan to attend. He gave us our passports and let us go.

I wish I could hear the conversations that are taking place because of our presence this evening. Some may call us troublemakers, but I am reminded of Martin Luther King's response to charges that he was stirring up trouble. He argued that he wasn't creating any trouble, but only bringing the hatred and fear to the surface where it can be dealt with. Cautious people need to read King's "Letter from the

Birmingham Jail." They also might read the Bible, especially the Gospels and Acts.

I am trying to understand the settlers. Their whole world, their future is being challenged. They must be experiencing a lot of fear. They are in an impossible situation. I can understand that they would see us as an obstacle to their dreams. As one person put it yesterday, "If you don't support Israel, you are an enemy of Israel." There is no middle ground. So we are seen as an enemy.

January 2, 1996, Tuesday

Jeff Heie appeared at our door this morning with his bicycle. It is good to have him as part of our team. Now there are five of us. Jeff was here this past summer and should help us to think of new ideas and new ways of looking at things.

I have been thinking about what our relationship should be with the police and courts. Back home I have been pretty clear about not using the power of the police and their guns to protect others and myself. I came here more open to reporting abuses to the police. But if a settler beats me up, do I want to go to the police, have the person arrested and put in jail? That doesn't seem nonviolent, loving, or even pragmatic. We should do something to hold the person accountable, to use that event to educate and reconcile. Police and prisons do not do that very well.

The Israeli police have asked us to help spy on the settlers. That doesn't sound like what our role should be. What is our role here in Hebron? Are we a solidarity group? Are we neutral? Are we conflict management mediators? Do we take sides? We come with a clear commitment to peace and justice, rooted in love. We are not neutral, but also not a solidarity group. We stand on the side of whomever the gun is pointed at, whoever is suffering injustice. We engage in the conflict, not as objective observers, but by standing in the middle. Our having an apartment right in the middle feels right. It reflects our role here, to be in the middle.

January 4, 1996, Thursday

This morning we all went to Jerusalem to visit the International Christian Embassy. We got there, picked up some literature, and watched a video. We then met with Faans Klopper, the chaplain at the embassy, who explained their work and beliefs. They believe that God is gathering all the Jews back to Israel so that God's Spirit can be poured out and then Jesus can return and destroy all who haven't accepted him as the Messiah.

He said that for too long we have condemned or tried to convert Jews. What we need to do is comfort them, which means support. In this way they will turn to Jesus. So they are channeling large amounts of money to Israel, especially for Russian Jews to come to Israel. I really tried to understand why it is so important for Jews to return to Israel. So Jesus can come back? So the rest of the world can get rid of the Jews? What does it mean to comfort? To help Israel displace and oppress more people?

We asked him how we should respond to settler hate. He said to always respond in love and to pray for them. That sounded good. I asked him about their relationship with Palestinian Christians. He didn't have much to say. He only used the word Arab, and said that we should work for unity with Jewish believers. We tried to talk about the suffering of the Palestinians, but couldn't get anywhere. His hope for Hebron is that it will come under full Israeli authority. I asked him about Ezekiel 47, where God commands the Jews coming back from exile in Babylon to divide the land fairly with the "strangers" living in the land. He responded that the "strangers" should be treated fairly, but that it is a terrible mistake to give any land back to the Palestinians. Everything belongs to the Jews, who are to rule over the Arabs, who are not God's chosen people. We had a cordial conversation, in which we mainly listened.

Christian Zionism is a perversion of biblical faith. God is not a real estate agent. Any understanding of land that claims exclusive rights and justifies displacing people from their homes is a denial of God's ultimate ownership of the land and is idolatry. To give unquestioned support for the nation state of Israel is to reject the prophetic tradition in the Bible, which is not afraid to proclaim God's judgment on Israel's acts of injustice. To both reject Arabic Christianity and affirm the superiority of Israel's claims over the rights of Palestinian Christians is treachery. The Christian Embassy's demonization of Islam must be rejected by all people who believe in any standard of fairness.[1]

It was difficult for me to be in that building, which was stolen from the family of Edward Said, a Palestinian Christian, professor at Columbia University, and recognized leader in the Palestinian cause. Martin Buber, a well-known Jewish philosopher, lived in that house. How can people like Buber so separate their philosophy from their lives? I know, we all do it. But we can stop it.

We then went to the Holocaust Museum. There I saw picture after picture, description after description, of some of the worst horror ever committed by humans. It was a sobering experience. The subject was hate, racism, oppression, dehumanization, murder, and death. How can people stoop so low? How can we become so brutal?

The killing of six million Jews was a horrible thing. I felt the pain of it all very deeply. I needed to be reminded again of what happened to the Jews, of the tragic effects of anti-Semitism and racism. I want to continue to oppose them in all their forms. The holocaust is more than an event in the past, however. Atrocities are still happening all around the world, and here in Palestine.

---

[1] For an excellent discussion of Christian Zionism and a biblical understanding of the issues raised by Zionism, see Donald E. Wagner, *Anxious for Armageddon* (Scottdale, Pa.: Herald Press, 1995).

I was struck by one of the captions to a horror picture which described Nazi ideology as a belief in a master race called by God to control the inferiors. Isn't that what I heard this morning from the people at the Christian Embassy? Isn't that what I hear from right-wing Israelis? That Jews are a special people who are called by God to rule over the "inferior" Arabs? Haven't many Israelis adopted the ideology of their oppressors? A sign at the entrance to the museum read that we should remember in order to become strong. Strong. Not compassionate, merciful, or kind.

As I saw all those Stars of David and the Nazi exhortations to "Kill the Jews," I remembered all the Stars of David spray painted on Palestinian homes and shops here in Hebron and all the graffiti that says, "Kill the Arabs." The parallel is too obvious to ignore. The Star of David is again used as a curse. Now it is "Kill the Arabs." Now it is the Arabs who are the "inferior people" who may be discriminated against. Isn't it all the same? Isn't fascism fascism?

When I saw the Nazi guns on display in the museum, I thought of the guns I see on the street every day here in Hebron, guns used to humiliate and oppress an "inferior people."

I have the feeling that the Holocaust Museum may be a hindrance rather than an aid to the goals of peace, justice, and reconciliation. Remembering the holocaust has been a bondage for Israel. It has closed their hearts, made them less able to be merciful, made them more fearful. A shameful tragedy has been transformed into a weapon, into a form of bondage.

If there is to be peace, both sides will have to give up their horror stories about the other side, be able to trust, and make a new beginning. Both sides are enslaved and imprisoned by their mistrust for the other side. The museums, the horror stories, are chains which enslave, which bind, which cut us off from new possibilities, which keep us from being open to the living God who wants to give something new. The enslaving, binding effects of holocaust memories are so visible here: the fear, the mistrust, the feelings of being victims, the belief that only by armed might and oppressing others can we be safe and secure. This is a paranoid delusion. It can only lead to disaster. It will destroy the soul of Israel and Palestine.

It seems to me that remembering the holocaust should cause us to examine ourselves and see whether any seeds of fear, hate, and racism are in our own hearts. Remembering should be liberating. It should help us move forward, not keep us trapped. If remembering causes us to become hard, calloused, and closed, maybe it would be better not to remember. More important than remembering is to look to God for our strength and salvation.

After we came home, Kawther, a Palestinian journalist, came to us crying. She had just been detained by Israeli soldiers for two hours. During those two hours she was humiliated. They ridiculed her for being a Palestinian, told her that she was no good, and stomped their feet like they were killing an insect. They spat at her. She said they did other horrible things. In the past Israeli soldiers have masturbated in front of her to humiliate her. I am thinking about the Holocaust Museum.

January 5, 1996, Friday

Last evening when Cliff and Jeff walked up to Beit Hadassah they saw a Palestinian girl with a bloody face. She had been hit by a rock thrown by settlers at Beit Hadassah. She required stitches. A number of other stones were thrown and flung with slingshots. Apparently the settlers were upset because the Al Atal family was pouring concrete and making improvements to their house, which is right behind Beit Hadassah settlement. Cliff said soldiers watched the whole incident and did nothing. I wonder if all the settlers will be put under curfew for a week for this, since that is what would happen if Palestinians had done it. Maybe the military will demolish Beit Hadassah for this.

I went with the others to visit the Al Atal family this morning. They told us that around thirty-five settlers threw rocks at them from two directions last evening. The fourteen-year-old girl was hit inside the house by a rock thrown through the window. The father was hit on the head and three others were also hit. I was impressed that in spite of their trauma, they were so full of warmth and love.

January 6, 1996, Saturday

This morning we went up to the vacant Palestinian gas station on Shuhada Street for our time of worship. It has been raining all night, the first rain since I came here. We could stand there under the roof. Jeff was reading something from Francis of Assisi when a young settler walked right by us and said, "I will kill you." There was something good about that. He was honest about *his* feelings, he put them right out in the open, and he displayed a kind of courage. *This guy* has been one of the most hostile of all the settlers. I hope we can somehow reach him and encourage him to step out of his bondage. We then sang "Be Not Afraid." How appropriate. We do not need to be afraid. Even if they kill us, God will be with us.

This is Saturday, so we were on the street all afternoon. We learned that Yihye Ayyash, a well-known Hamas leader, was killed by an Israeli bomb yesterday in Gaza. There is a three-day strike in honor of him, so the shops and market are closed. I sense a lot of tension. The soldiers seem tense. They fear a reprisal. The Palestinians are upset. What is our role in this situation?

It was a busy afternoon. The soldiers arrested three Palestinians here by our house. They had come to what we were told was a PLO office across the street and were arrested for going to the door. We heard that the soldiers had raided the office last night. We called journalists to alert them to what was happening. We later heard the men were released. Then the soldiers detained another young man who had knocked on the door to that office. Cliff and I, both at different times, went and knocked on that door, but we were ignored by the soldiers.

I met the young settler who this morning had said he would kill us. Again he said he would kill me and spat at me. I went up to him and asked why he wanted to kill me. He said, "Because I am Hamas." I told him I am not Hamas. He said, "You like the Arabs." I said, "Yes, I like the Arabs, I like the Israelis, I like the Russians, I like everyone." Again he said he wants to kill me. I told him, "Here I am. You may kill me, but I want to be your friend." He repeated that I support the Arabs, I hate the Jews. I kept responding in a gentle way. We talked as we walked up Shuhada Street. When we got to the entrance of the soldier camp he stopped threatening me.

The young boy with whom I had a long conversation two weeks ago was there at the soldier camp. He expressed a lot of hostility toward me, saying that I want to kill the Jews. It seemed like we had never had our previous conversation.

I shudder to think of what is happening to Israeli youth. These young boys experience so much fear, hatred, and violence. Last fall our team accompanied Moshe Zimmerman, head of the German department at Hebrew University and a recognized authority on the holocaust, around Hebron. He compares the settler youth to the Hitler Youth. That is what I see.

I think it is wrong to view the settlers here in Hebron, or people like Ygal Amir or Baruch Goldstein, as fanatics. If we call them fanatics we can dismiss them and not take them seriously. It would be more helpful to see these people as caricatures, as a sign of what Israel is becoming. In these settlers the future of Israel comes into focus. They are a sign of the future, the result of the decisions Israel has been making. Unless Israel turns from occupation, domination, and oppression, and decides to live in justice, equality, and peace with Palestinians, the settler mentality will be Israel's future.

I think back to my time in Edward Said's house, in which Martin Buber used to live. Martin Buber probably could not see the horrible consequences for the future of Israel of his living in a stolen house. Now they are becoming visible. How naive it is to believe that we can act unjustly and it will have no consequences for the future. What we sow we will reap. There is karma. All of our actions have eternal significance. The judgment of God is sure. We sow the seeds of our own destruction. Say it how you will. There is something true and real about the almost universal understanding that we ultimately cannot escape the consequences of our actions. How important it is that our first concern be to live justly, love tenderly, and walk humbly with our God (Mic. 6:8). Nothing else matters.

January 7, 1996, Sunday

We heard on the news this morning that the West Bank and Gaza are closed because of the death of Ayyash. Things are tense. Most of the market is closed.

I got a phone call this morning saying there was trouble at Baab iZawia. I headed up there and saw lots of soldiers. They had a menacing look. There were lots of Palestinians milling around. Things were very tense. The situation looked serious, so I decided to get involved. I went to the middle of the intersection and stood between the soldiers and the Palestinians. That felt scary, but also right. Every now and then groups of two or three soldiers would make quick forays into the crowd to intimidate and harass the Palestinians. Some of the soldiers were carrying big sticks as clubs. They seemed to be looking for trouble. I saw soldiers pushing people around and pointing their M-16s in their faces. I went up to one of the soldiers who had his gun in a Palestinian's face and calmly told him it was impolite to point a gun at someone like that. He seemed rather stunned, and walked away.

Soon Cliff and Marge showed up. We spread out. When a small group of soldiers went beyond our area, one of us followed them. When they detained someone, we stood by the person detained. I saw Marge squatting when Palestinians were forced to squat. We were in the soldiers' faces, telling them to treat people with respect. The soldiers obviously were not happy with us.

I played cat and mouse with one group of soldiers. They would go down an alley and I would show up in front of them at the other end, casually looking around. When they quickly left for another area a block away, I would be there in front of them. I monitored everything they were doing. After about ten minutes of this, they went back to the other soldiers.

After about an hour things settled down and most of the soldiers left. It was amazing how a very tense and dangerous situation was defused. Cliff said he never before saw an incident like this quiet down so quickly. These situations usually escalate. We would like to think that our presence made a difference. Many people thanked us for being there.

What was it that we did that made the difference in this situation? We claimed space in the middle of the street, in the center of the conflict. Our presence and our being in the face of the soldiers every time they acted inappropriately seemed to have a moderating effect on their aggressive behavior. Because of our presence, they didn't feel free to be as aggressive as they wanted to be. In all of our confrontations with the soldiers, we were calm, polite, and assertive.

Just standing on the sidelines as international observers may have had some calming effect, but being actively engaged seemed to be most helpful. Our actions of confronting the soldiers may have had a calming effect on the Palestinians as well. Since they saw that the soldiers were being confronted, they may have felt less need to react.

Late this afternoon we were again called over to Baab iZawia because of a new problem there. The soldiers had taken the identity card and driving permit of a man who apparently didn't move his car as the soldiers wanted. There was a group of men, all very excited, around the man and the car. I listened to their frustration. They are tired of being harassed, controlled, and humiliated. They feel the soldiers are trying to control more and more area and push the Palestinians back farther and farther. Then a soldier came and said the man had not moved his car. Apparently the soldiers are concerned to keep the area clear so they can see what is happening around them, because they are afraid of a bomb. Immediately after we listened to him, he gave the man back his papers.

My next step was to talk with the soldiers. I began by asking them what could be done to reduce the tension here. That led to a wonderful time of sharing. One of them told me that last night, on his time off, he had participated in a peace demonstration in Jerusalem where he was verbally attacked by a right-wing Israeli. This soldier seemed like a sensible person who really wants peace. He wants to come back to Hebron in the future with his children and be accepted and not be afraid. He is trying to build relationships with Palestinians and is ashamed of how many Israelis are treating Palestinians.

As we walked through the market this morning we noticed that part of a metal barrier in one of the old arches in the market was gone. We cleared away a few chunks of concrete left there so that people would not stumble over them. Later this morning Cliff and Marge went by the gate that was partially removed and saw Palestinians working to remove all of it. Later people recognized me when I went by the gate and wanted me to join them in tearing down more gates. I declined. I wanted team support and discernment. We heard that some Palestinians are planning to open more gates in the market tomorrow.

These gates or barriers in the four big old arches in the market were put up by the Israelis during the Intifada to make it easier for the soldiers to control or close the market. Only a narrow passageway was left open on one side for people in the busy market to pass through, single file. They no longer serve any real function and are badly deteriorated, so are only a daily nuisance for the local people. They are supposed to be removed according to the Oslo II agreement.

We invited some Palestinian friends over this evening to ask for their advice concerning our possible involvement in removing the barriers. Our friends told us it was a great idea, but it has to have mass support. We should not initiate anything, but it would be good to be involved as support.

Cole Hull came this afternoon. Now there are six in our team. Cole has come for three months, and has only been married for three months. I call that commitment. But shouldn't our commitment be as deep as that of soldiers?

January 10, 1996, Wednesday

I haven't written since Sunday because I have been in jail since then. I got home around noon today. So, I have a long story to tell. Some of this was written in my jail cell.

Monday morning after our time of worship by the mosque we walked through the market to check the gates. Everything was normal, but we were expecting people would work at opening the gates. So we milled around awhile in the market. If people decided to open the gates, we wanted to be there, but we didn't want to initiate anything.

At about 9:00 a small group started working on the lower gate. When I got there they had already started. Soon more people joined in. Before long it was a large crowd, all working together. We saw our role primarily as a nonviolent presence, in case the soldiers intervened. Our plan was that if the soldiers did intervene, we would stand between them and the Palestinians. Mainly we watched for soldiers, talked with people, and I think made the Palestinians feel safer. Apparently this was appreciated. People kept thanking us, bringing us coffee, tea, and things to eat.

It was a fantastic time. People were cooperating in an incredible way. All of a sudden, people spontaneously took control of their lives. This was democracy in action. It was a popular, nonviolent action that came from the grassroots. People were deciding together what the next steps should be. There was a sense of community, a spirit of liberation. Hundreds of people were involved. If people feel empowered, if they believe they can participate in shaping the future, they are less likely to resort to violence. This spirit can lead to peace if it is allowed to grow and flower. If this spirit is suppressed, then there will be no peace. There can be no peace if people are constantly frustrated, if they see no hope. Frustration will lead to violence.

About three-fourths of the way through opening this gate, a Palestinian grabbed me by the arm and forced me to go with him. I didn't know what was going on. It felt like I was being kidnapped. He spoke no English. I could only trust him. Where was he taking me and why? He took me to another gate that was being removed. Apparently he wanted the presence of one of our team there for protection.

Palestinians going through arch in the Hebron market where the gates were removed.

In about twenty minutes this gate was gone. I then realized that the gate at the end of our alley was being dismantled. I had been walking over there regularly to look up the street to the military checkpoint which is visible from there, and saw that the soldiers apparently still didn't know what was going on. It wasn't long, however, until the soldiers suspected something. Two of them casually walked down the street to investigate. When they realized what was happening, they walked back up to the checkpoint to call for reinforcements. Soon about ten soldiers were coming down the alley. By this time the last gate had been removed.

The soldiers grabbed one young man and arrested him. Immediately Cliff and I told the soldiers that if they arrested him, they would also have to arrest us. We had told people that if anyone was arrested, Cliff and I would also be arrested. So we walked with Hisham, the young man, up to the checkpoint by our house. At that point the soldiers would have been happy for us to just walk away and leave them alone.

A large crowd gathered around the checkpoint to watch and encourage us. Excitement was in the air. The other CPT members were milling around, helping keep things joyful. They were even throwing a foam football. I tried to dialogue with the soldiers, but their commander, Avri, wouldn't allow them to talk with us. He was very angry with us. He has been upset with us before. Noam came by but refused to look at me. Other settlers were hanging around. I don't know what this will do to our relationship with them.

After a while police loaded four of us into their van. At the last minute they decided to also take Cole in order to inspect the videotape in his camera to see if any incriminating evidence was there. There wasn't. Cole had wisely changed tapes just before the arrest. We were taken down to the police station at the mosque/synagogue for questioning. Officer Omri questioned us. We had a lot of fun with him. He is a friendly, jovial guy. Avri, our soldier friend, was there giving the police his story. He wanted us to be charged with serious crimes.

Soon we were taken to police headquarters in the civil administration building for more questioning. Things were beginning to feel more serious. They interrogated Hisham first and we learned that he was going to be detained ninety-six hours without charges. That is common here. Punish people by holding them without charges. No proof is needed. Then they took in Cole to check his tape, but found nothing on the tape, so they released him.

Next they questioned Cliff. We agreed that we would be cooperative, but admit to nothing without a lawyer present. When Cliff came out, he told us they were releasing him, but would be arresting me. He learned that I was the one Avri wanted to get.

Then it was my turn. Omri came out and told me I was under arrest for destroying military property and interfering with the duties of soldiers. I said good-bye to the others and assured them I was fine and not to worry. I was eager for what I would get to experience. I was taken back to an office for interrogation. There were three police in the office, with others going and coming. The police didn't quite know what to do with me. I obviously wasn't a hardened criminal, but the military wanted to bring serious charges against me. Immediate deportation was the minimum punishment they sought.

The police had a difficult time interrogating me. We had been having too much fun to get serious. During the whole time of my detention, I kept asking when they were going to bring me some pizza. I joked about life in Israeli jails. I told them that my name was Samson and I tore down those gates all by myself. They loved it. Every time I get arrested I try to break down as many barriers as possible between the police and myself. I joke, I engage them in serious conversation, I ask about their lives. I want to make peace with everyone and believe it can be done in the middle of direct action and public witness.

The first question was whether I was Amish. That resulted in a discussion of the Amish, Brethren, and Mennonites.
They said I was the first Amish terrorist they had ever arrested. We got into a big discussion of capital punishment. They
told me they were happy that Ayyash was murdered the other
day, because he was a terrorist and deserved to die. I agreed
that the bombings Ayyash supposedly committed were horrible, but that I didn't think he should have been killed.

I asked if Yigal Amir, the man who killed Prime Minister
Rabin, should be killed. They hedged. Those who support
capital punishment are not consistent, not objective. We are
much more likely to kill someone from an enemy group.
Note the disproportionately high rate of executions of
minorities in the United States. We had a significant discussion of the peace process and what could be done for peace.
They told me I am naive because I think peace is possible. I
think they are naive. It is they who do not see the things that
make for peace.

Eventually they got around to questioning me seriously.
The police told me that to pacify the soldiers, someone needed to take the rap for the gates being removed, and that I had
been the one chosen. I refused to answer any questions that
would implicate others or myself, and refused to sign anything in Hebrew. I wrote a statement for them about the positive event of removing the gates, how it was a responsible
act of empowerment for the Palestinians, a step toward
democracy and peace, and that I hoped Israelis would use
this event as a stepping-stone toward more freedom and reconciliation, rather than rebuild the gates.

I described the role of CPT in being a positive nonviolent
presence, and stated that we did not initiate the dismantling
of the gates. I tried to describe how we have been working to
reduce the tensions in Hebron. They told me that we had a
responsibility to inform the police of what was happening. I
told them they should thank us for our role in promoting
nonviolence and peace, and working to de-escalate clashes. I

told them about our defusing a tense situation on Sunday. They responded by asking me what authority we had to be working for peace. As Omri put it, "Otherwise we have anarchy." Really? Anarchy or total control by the state are the only two alternatives?

It seemed difficult for them, but they told me they would seek to have me deported and I would be held in jail. They put me in a cell by myself. I said I wanted to be in a cell with Palestinians, but they said they were afraid the Palestinians would kill me. So I was put in solitary confinement. Maybe I am a threat to the state of Israel as it now exists. But I am not a threat to the better Israel that could be.

Soon I was alone in a small cell where I would spend the next two days. I felt confident, powerful, and exhilarated. I looked forward to the exciting experiences that lay ahead. I could not sit still. I paced back and forth, singing and praying. I was grateful for all the good worship songs I know. And I kept adding new words as I sang.

I accepted this as a time of spiritual retreat. What better place is there to pray than in a jail cell? I just wanted to open my heart to God. As a part of this retreat, I decided to go on a complete fast, not eating or drinking anything until I was released. I realized that this could be seen as upping the ante for the police, but I tried to keep it low-key. I only talked about it when asked, and then my reply was that I was praying. When they asked more about why I wouldn't eat or drink I said it was because I was not free, that I would eat and drink as soon as they gave me my passport and told me I could leave.

Omri came by yesterday and asked me if this is a hunger strike. He told me that Nelson Mandela and Martin Luther King Jr. always drank while fasting. A lot of police showed a lot of concern for me. They kept asking if I was all right and if I wouldn't eat something. They even took me out of the cell to check my blood pressure.

I finally got calmed down enough to go to sleep and had

a good rest. I faintly heard the early morning Muslim call to prayer and even took a shower, my first real shower since I came to Hebron. What a luxury. But I was careful to only use a little water. Trying to be a responsible citizen of the earth includes not wasting Israeli jail water.

One of the first things I did yesterday morning was to destroy some prison property by taking down all the sexy pictures of women on the walls of the cell and throwing them in the trash. When Omri came by in the morning I told him I had committed another crime and that I would confess. He asked what I did. I told him I destroyed prison property. He asked if they were pretty. If they were pretty, it was a crime. I told him they were very pretty. He smiled and said it was a serious crime and that I would be charged with another offense.

I thought about my cell. I wished I could see all the brave people who have been in this cell over the years. It was built by the British in the 1930s as a means of maintaining control over the people here. Then the Jordanians took it over, and now the Israelis. How many people over the years have been in this cell because they wanted to be free, who dared to question the unjust order that was being imposed on them? I suspect the "cloud of witnesses" is great. I felt honored to be in their presence.

I also thought of the suffering of the Jews, of the early Christians, of those who suffered from the Crusades, of the Anabaptists, of Mordecaia Vanunu who is in an Israeli prison for revealing that Israel possesses nuclear weapons, and of the vast numbers of people who over the centuries have had the courage to stand for truth and justice. I was at peace. Soon the Palestinians will take over this facility. Will it be any different then? Will they also imprison people who will not bow down to oppression?

As I looked out of my cell I could see a lot of activity by the Israeli police. There are many of them, and they all carry automatic rifles and handguns. There are police and guns everywhere. *The* national symbol of Israel should be a gun. Guns are their source of security. Guns are their gods.

I am thinking not only about the atrocities of Israeli occupation. I also remember that this is the military that trained the security system for drug cartels and repressive military dictatorships in South America, and that has worked closely with the apartheid government in South Africa.[1] There is something very nasty at the core of this system.

Yesterday was a good day. I did a lot of singing and praying, a lot of reflection, and some catching up on sleep. The fasting went amazingly well. I was able to do some joking with the police when they stopped by my cell. I got fingerprinted in the afternoon. They joked that they had finally caught "Carlos the Jackal," a widely hunted person accused of various terrorist bombings.

Last evening for the first time I started feeling anger. They had been telling me that I might or might not be deported, that they wanted to deport me, but it was difficult for them to do so. All day I didn't know what was going on. I was told on Monday evening that I would be transferred to Jerusalem. I was told last evening that I would be deported today. They wouldn't tell me anything about a hearing, where the hearing would be, or when I might leave here. They denied me a phone call. One policeman slammed the door at me in disgust.

I don't want to be deported. I would hate to miss out on the last ten days of being in Hebron. I want to continue my work. I want to be with the people. But maybe being deported will help make our voice louder and strengthen what we are trying to do. I am content to leave it all in God's hands.

One of the advantages of being in jail is that one is stripped of much of one's power and control, and made vulnerable. I have to look to God. I can't do anything. But in that vulnerability there is a tremendous power.

---

[1] See Jane Hunter, *Israeli Foreign Policy: South Africa and Central America* (Cambridge, Mass.: South End Press, 1987).

A policeman came by this morning and told me everything was okay. I wondered what that meant. I am beginning to feel some hope that they will release me soon. I know they can't hold me for more than forty-eight hours without a hearing. I would like to be released. I want to get back to work. But, as God wills, as they say here. I am content.

At about 10:00 this morning the head policeman came to my cell and told me to come with him, that they were taking me directly to the airport and deporting me. For the first time I made a vigorous protest. I told him he couldn't do that because I had not been able to contact a lawyer, and that I first had to have a hearing before a judge. He told me that he would take me to our apartment to get my things, and then directly to the airport. I continued to protest.

It turned out he was joking and I fell for his joke. He took me to Omri's office and they informed me that if I signed a statement, they would release me. I didn't know what to do. Was signing any statement too much of a concession to their unjust system? My mind was not really clear. I was very weak. After a little discussion and some joking I agreed to write my own statement, which was acceptable to them. I also agreed to come back to the police station any time they call me or face a charge of $500. They gave me back my passport and I agreed to eat. I started by drinking very slowly.

I wanted to leave, but they said I couldn't because it was not safe for me to be out on Arab streets. They told me the Arabs would kill me if they saw me. I didn't take that as a joke. I think it came out of a genuine concern for me. They have such an intense fear of the Palestinians. Fear is a major factor in the problems here. How can we get beyond fear? People are so trapped and enslaved by their fear.

I ended up hitching a ride in a police van to Kiryat Arba and walked home from there. The police were very concerned about my safety. They also told me the Arabs would kill me. Actually, I did have some fear in that Israeli police van. What if the Palestinians attacked that van? I was glad to get out and be on the streets with Palestinians again!

I almost never made it home. I walked home by a back way behind the mosque/synagogue and was stopped at a military checkpoint. When I told them where I was going they told me I couldn't go there from here. I replied that if I couldn't go there from here, I would have to stay here. I don't think they got the humor. They kept telling me that it was impossible to go down into the market. I pointed out to them the street right in front of us that would take me where I wanted to go. They told me I couldn't go there because the Arabs would kill me.

I told them I live down there, and walk the streets all the time without fear. They thought I was crazy, but eventually they let me go. As I walked down the street I was greeted by friendly Palestinians. I felt quite safe. And exhilarated. What a joy to be back with these wonderful people.

There is another reason I almost didn't make it home. When I got down into the market people recognized me and mobbed me. I was greeted with hugs and kisses. They told me now I was a Palestinian. Many of them had worked at removing the gates and saw me being arrested. It was difficult to get home. Everyone wanted to greet me.

I don't know how to describe the tremendous joy I felt. The feelings of removing the gates, the sense of liberation, the arrest, the time in jail all came flooding over me. The best word I can use to describe my feelings is gratitude. Deep gratitude. Gratitude for the experiences of the past three days, gratitude for being allowed to have ten more days here. Everything seems like a gift.

This evening some of us went to visit Hisham, who was arrested when I was. He also was released today. I asked him what his time in jail (his first) meant for him. He said it only made him stronger. Do the Israelis not understand that? They are strengthening those they consider their enemies. Fear makes us do stupid things.

January 13, 1996, Saturday

I stayed on the street all afternoon, walking back and forth, talking to people. We decided in our meeting last evening to focus more on relating to Israelis today. There were lots of Israeli visitors and we did a lot of talking. We received some hostility, but not as much as on some previous Saturdays. Many of the local settlers wouldn't look at us or respond as we greeted them.

I had a very brief conversation with one of the local settlers. He actually shook my hand. I told him I wanted to talk with him. He replied, "No, you don't want to talk with me." I repeated that I did. Then his wife said, "You don't want to talk with him." The implication seemed to be that he was so mean and bad that I would not want to talk with him. I do hope to talk with him sometime.

One group of about six teenagers was quite hostile all afternoon. At one point they cursed me and one of them spat at me. I went up to him and calmly asked him why he had spit at me. He then kicked me in the stomach. I calmly asked him why he kicked me. He said it was because I loved Arabs. I said I did love Arabs, but that I also loved Jews. He didn't believe me. I told the teens that I have many Jewish friends. They cursed me and told me to go to hell. I told them it was rather serious to tell people to go to hell. They said God hates Arabs, and loves only Jews. This conversation lasted about five minutes. I wonder what it might mean in their lives to spew out such hate and be responded to with calmness and love.

Jeff carried his foam football around, throwing it to lots of people, including Israelis, Palestinians, and even a soldier or two. That seemed to help break down some barriers.

January 14, 1996, Sunday

This evening I read the collected news releases from the team here from June to September. That helped provide perspective on what we are doing. A clear pro-Palestinian bias comes through. CPT is standing with the Palestinians. I mean this as an objective observation, not as criticism. Given the situation here, the overwhelming oppression, the imbalance of power, the rigidity of the settlers and the military as a whole, and our commitment to social justice, what could CPT do differently?

Our work here is an experiment. Is it possible to be effective as international observers and get as involved as we have? Do observers need to be more neutral? Obviously we have succeeded in winning the trust of the Palestinians, but we have been much more than a solidarity group. We have spent many hours listening to soldiers and settlers, and work closely with the Israeli peace movement.

January 15, 1996, Monday

After our time of worship we noticed a lot of police activity in the big parking lot below the mosque/synagogue. There were many soldiers and police and more were coming in. They had horses, buses, and troop carriers. It was clear that something big was about to happen. We tried to find out, but no one seemed to know anything and the police weren't talking.

A Palestinian man told us he heard on the radio this morning that the military was removing six settler families from Hebron today. We wondered from which settlement and what our role might be. Would there be shooting? We decided to spread out. Cole and Jeff headed up toward Beit Hadassah. Cliff and I kept surveying the area around the park. Everything seemed normal in the market. Someone told Cliff that the six settler families were being removed from Kiryat Arba. Soon the military vehicles started heading out that way. Cliff and I followed.

The settler families were being removed because they were living in houses that, according to a recent Supreme Court ruling, had been illegally built on land confiscated from the Al-Jabri family. It was a landmark case. We had been considering moving in there ourselves, as an act of civil disobedience, to protest the illegal presence of settlers there. The military decided to move the settler families out so that the Border Police could move in, thus setting aside the Supreme Court decision.

I was not prepared for what I saw. Hundreds of police and soldiers stood around the buildings from which the families were being evicted. There were holes in the tile roofs where the soldiers had entered the locked buildings. Soldiers looked out of the windows. Soldiers and police were everywhere. Settlers were crying, screaming, and yelling. It looked like some of the settlers had been arrested.

I saw many small clashes with the police and soldiers. One young settler, carrying a big fancy decorated Torah scroll, repeatedly tried to break through police lines to get back into the settlement. There was a lot of pushing and shoving. Small groups of settlers would start yelling and screaming at the soldiers. It was all in Hebrew, but it sounded like curses to me. The police and soldiers were taking a lot of abuse. It was amazing how calm they remained. They would never have taken that from Palestinians.

After a while a bus pulled out with the settlers who were being removed. They looked like other people I have seen over the years being arrested for civil disobedience. They waved and shouted and seemed in a defiant mood. They drew cheers from the crowd of settlers. Soon the authorities brought in big moving vans to move out the settlers' possessions.

The main role I saw for myself was listening to the settlers. I wanted to feel and understand their pain. I was aware that they were living illegally on stolen land, that they were living lives of hate. But I wanted to understand. After all, these were human beings who were hurting.

What I heard was that they felt betrayed by the Israeli government which is seen as surrendering to the Arabs. They consider this to be a terrible sin against God for which Israel, or at least the present government, will be severely punished by God. When they heard that I was a peacemaker they told me they do not want peace. This is the beginning of war. The Israeli government, not the Arabs, is their real enemy, they said.

I was told that Baruch Goldstein was a saint, who acted on a clear revelation from God when he killed twenty-nine Muslims praying in the mosque. He was one of the most holy and righteous persons who ever lived. I was told that all this land, all the way to the Tigris and Euphrates rivers, belongs to the Jews, and that all Arabs will have to leave. God loves only Jews. All Muslims and Christians have to leave. The Arabs are an inferior people, like animals, and are hated by God.

At one point a group of about ten Palestinian women wanted to get through the street. They were escorted by about thirty soldiers while the settlers yelled and screamed curses at the women and the soldiers. What an awful, detestable scene. I felt both disgust and a sense of compassion for these people, so caught up in their fear and hate. Later they hit and shoved a Palestinian woman who was then escorted through the area by the soldiers.

After about three hours the police started putting all the settlers in military vans. A policeman grabbed me and was ready to put me in with the settlers. Apparently he thought I was a settler. I explained that I was an observer, not a settler, so he let me go and told me to leave the area. Now I am sorry I didn't get into the van with the settlers. It could have been quite a learning experience. It is probably best I didn't, however.

Later in the afternoon we saw about twenty Palestinian children playing "Palestinians and soldiers," a variation of cowboys and Indians. Some were pretending to throw stones at the soldiers. Those pretending to be soldiers would shoot at those who were pretending to throw stones. Then those pretending to be Palestinians would run away. They were having fun. They were also acting out what they have been experiencing. Both the Palestinian and the Israeli settler children are being deeply affected by the fear and hate so prevalent in this beautiful city.

January 16, 1996, Tuesday

After supper, Cole, Jeff, and I went for our evening patrol. When we got outside we heard automatic weapons fire from beyond the cemetery. We decided to investigate. When we asked what was happening, the soldiers only would say that this is war. It seemed a little crazy to me, but we decided to head for where the shooting was happening. It seemed like the right thing to do, but I was afraid. We took the long way around Tel Rumeida. We heard sporadic shooting. We concluded that it was coming from a Hamas neighborhood. When we got to the area everything was quiet.

Not long after we returned home we heard a loudspeaker announcing a curfew. We decided to investigate. I went downstairs and stuck my head out the door. A soldier saw me, aimed his M-16 at me, and charged. I quickly got my head back in the doorway and ran up the stairs as fast as I could. I could hear the soldier kicking the metal door downstairs. For the first time, I completely lost my courage. Cliff then went out on the street and talked with the soldiers. I felt like staying in, and didn't go out again this evening. I was afraid.

We soon learned from a neighbor that someone killed two soldiers between here and Jerusalem and that the whole West Bank is under a week's curfew. Great. I am now guessing that the shooting we heard this evening was Hamas celebrating the killing of those soldiers. How sad. When will it ever end? For each retaliation there needs to be a retaliation by the other side. As Martin Luther King Jr. put it, "An eye for an eye and a tooth for a tooth will leave everyone blind and toothless."

January 17, 1996, Wednesday

After a night's sleep I got my courage back and went out on the street at daybreak this morning. I wanted to know what was happening. Cliff went with me. We learned that the curfew ended at 5:00 this morning. That is interesting. We heard last night that it would last for a week. Is the presence of international election observers a factor?

January 18, 1996, Thursday

This evening Cliff and I went with a Palestinian friend to a meeting in the village of Yatta. It turned out to be a weekly gathering of the Islamic Dahwa movement. People come to meet, pray, and spend the night together. It seemed like a retreat center. The Dahwaists seem to be (to use Christian terminology) a pietistic, evangelical renewal movement. They believe the answer will be found in turning back to God, in living more faithfully the life God calls us to, and in having a deep renewal in our hearts.

They want to find God's peace and salvation in their own lives, establish love and community between Muslims, and deeply share their lives with each other. They claim to be apolitical. They seemed critical of other Islamic renewal movements like Hamas, because they are too political, too interested in using force to gain their goals. They want to depend only on God.

I have found the Palestinian people to be warm, open, and hospitable, but I have never experienced here in Hebron as much openness as this evening. Almost everyone greeted us with hugs and kisses. The handshakes were long and intense. Never in my time in Palestine have I experienced so much love and sense of community. We were totally accepted as Christians.

I told one of them about a group of Christians going to Mecca to discuss faith issues with the Prophet Muhammad. When Sunday came, Muhammad prepared the mosque for the Christians to have their meeting for worship. The man

said he knew the story. I wish more people knew the story.
I continue to be impressed with Islamic spirituality. All of
life is to be lived under the will of Allah. There is no separation between sacred and secular. I also appreciate the mod-
esty in dress. Women do not dress as sex objects. It is such a
relief not to have to be constantly struggling against objecti-
fying women who are dressed in suggestive ways. This
Palestinian, Muslim culture seems to me to be much closer to
what God wants for us than is Western culture. I do appreciate the freedom men and women have to relate to each
other as persons in Western culture. Can Christians and fem-
inists take the lead in helping us move toward a more healthy
relationship between men and women? The Muslims have
something to teach us.

It also is a blessing that drinking alcohol is prohibited by
Islam. Things would be a lot worse if alcohol were added to
the mix here in Hebron. That would only increase both the
violence and the oppression. Not once have I seen alcohol
here in Hebron. Why can't most Christians see how destructive alcohol is?

January 19, 1996, Friday

I spent much of the day walking around in the rain keeping a tab on how many Israelis were coming into town. I
watched a number of busloads of young Israelis coming into
the settlements. Our main concern today was trying to get as
much information as possible about what to expect on election day tomorrow. Not much is clear to us. Probably half of
the people here in Hebron will boycott the election. The general word is that Palestinians will not disrupt anything. The
main concern is what the settlers might do. I have never seen
so many soldiers here. One soldier told me he is expecting
trouble from the settlers.

Some people are saying that the settlers are upset about
the Palestinian elections happening on the Sabbath, but more
importantly because they see the elections as a step toward

legitimizing Palestinian control over the West Bank and Gaza. That is troubling to settlers who want the whole area to be exclusively Jewish, and so they may want to disrupt the voting to make their point. They see the election as a sin against God.

The conservative religious Jews have called for lots of people to come to Hebron to pray at Abraham's tomb tomorrow. We also heard that because of the importance of this event, Jews coming here are being given a special dispensation not to have to follow Sabbath rules tomorrow. That means they can drive on the Sabbath this week.

We also heard that Avri, our soldier friend, has been accused in the beatings of Palestinians and in beating a journalist friend of ours yesterday. The journalist is in the hospital with back injuries. We were told that when he was confronted by a journalist this morning about his behavior, Avri threatened to break his bones. Other journalists have been filing complaints. We contacted military leaders and made a complaint. They promised to investigate. My guess is that the pressure and frustration here is getting Avri down. I would like to talk with him before I leave.

This evening we had a meeting to prepare for tomorrow and to orient Jennifer Fisher and Roger Manley, who came today to be with us for a few days. Jennifer is spending two months in Israel and the West Bank studying peace efforts and will be with us for about a week. Roger is a photographer doing a museum story of life here. Carmen Pauls came back today. So for tomorrow we will have seven in our team.

In our meeting we tried to speculate on what might happen tomorrow during the election. The big question was what the settlers might do. We talked about worst case scenarios and about our fears. But I sensed peace in everyone. We knew we had to trust God and walk in openness and love. We talked about how this was going to be a new situation for all of us.

We then talked about our roles tomorrow as peacemakers. We reaffirmed that our primary role was to be a violence-deterring presence. We talked about being creative, throwing the foam football, blowing bubbles, and doing things to change the mood. We talked of the importance of always remaining calm, never running. We recognized that in a stressful situation, we can be role models for others. If we run, that will encourage others to run. If we are calm and rational, that will encourage others to remain calm. We agreed to work in pairs in order to keep track of each other and to support each other. We assigned people tasks.

We made one last patrol through the area before going to bed. Everything seemed quiet. It looked like there was a big meeting of settler leaders at the gift shop.

January 20, 1996, Saturday

Today was the big day many people were awaiting or fearing. The Palestinians finally were being given the opportunity to vote. Cliff and I went out for a walk at 6:00 this morning. Everything was quiet.

After breakfast we went to the park for a time of worship at 7:00. We wanted to start early this morning since the polls opened at 7:00. We started walking around. There were journalists and international election observers everywhere. That helped make it feel safe. They were especially gathered at the polling place in the school near the mosque/synagogue. The morning was quiet. There were not a lot of settlers on the street. They were probably having meetings and Sabbath prayers.

I saw Avri, our soldier friend, and decided to take the initiative and talk with him. I went up to him and told him I will be leaving Hebron tomorrow and that I was sorry I had caused him grief and that our relationship had broken down. That seemed to disarm him somewhat and he talked with me. For the past week he would not even look at me. He shared his frustrations with me, especially over the fact that I was involved in the illegal activity of removing the gates.

He said we are taking the Arab side. He referred to the good conversations we have had in the past. We ended up shaking hands and saying good-bye to each other.

I am thankful for that talk. I was able to connect with him again as a human being. Maybe because of this encounter he will not be as violent today. I have been wondering if maybe I should have confronted him with all the horrible things he has been accused of doing in the past few days. I wonder about that, but I think it was best that I didn't say anything more. Certainly he already knows how I feel about that, and may even know that we have made complaints about him.

There was a group of Japanese Buddhists praying and fasting for peace in the park by the mosque/synagogue all day. I felt moved by their chanting and drumming. We can use all the prayers for peace we can get. It added a different spirit to the atmosphere here. The Buddhists were quite a curiosity. Lots of Muslims gathered around them trying to understand. Many Jews also stopped by as they were coming out of the synagogue. The Buddhists brought the Muslims and Jews together. It was something new coming from outside this situation, a gift of grace. Today there were Buddhists, Muslims, Jews, and Christians all together in Hebron.

I got involved in a Muslim-Jewish-Christian dialogue. Some young Jewish guys about 18 years of age started taunting me, calling me a Nazi. I managed to break through that by asking them questions. They started answering my questions. That led to a big discussion of God's calling and promise to Abraham. The Israelis responded that the Arabs are children of Ishmael and don't count.

The Jews asked me why I was a Christian. I responded that it is because I believe that Jesus was the Messiah. That led to a big discussion, with the Muslims mostly agreeing with me. I tried to point out that God's call to Abraham did not mean that the Jews are special or better than others, but rather they have had a special role in sharing God's salvation

with the whole world, and that their current exclusive understanding of that chosenness is a rejection of that call and can
only lead to God's judgment on them. It was a wonderful
dialogue, done in a calm way to the beat of Buddhist drumming and chanting. Amazing.

I engaged in many little acts of peacemaking as I walked
up and down the street. I saw a Palestinian woman trying to
walk by a large group of Israelis on the street up by Beit
Hadassah. I walked close behind her to protect her until she
was past the Israelis. I doubt that she ever realized what I
had done.

I greeted many Israelis with "Shabbat Shalom." Many
responded appreciatively, and I got into conversations with
some of them. I was trying to set a mood by reaching out to
them. I also received a lot of hate. I kept getting cursed, spit
at, called a Nazi. I was jeered, ridiculed, and threatened. I
must have received at least 20 death threats today. Anat
Cohen and a man with her were particularly rude. Much of
the hatred came from children. I grabbed Jeff's foam football
and threw it to the young boy with whom I have had several good conversations, but who is still very hostile. He
caught it and threatened to keep it. I just stood there and
waited. Soon he threw it back to me and I threw it right back
to him. We tossed it back and forth. He couldn't resist the
temptation to play, even with someone he considers a Nazi.
Another small victory. The cycle of hate was temporarily
interrupted by a football. How simple. I also threw the football with one other group of hostile youth.

At one point I noticed a group of about eight Israeli
teenagers who were obviously looking for trouble. They were
harassing Palestinians, many of them older men. I started following them. That got them upset with me. Finally they came
and asked me why I was following them. They called me a
Nazi and Hamas. One of them had a handgun in his pocket.
I was feeling scared, but remained calm and open and friendly to them. Soon they could no longer keep up the hate.

Something human in them responded to me and they started to ask me questions. They wanted to know why I have a beard without a moustache. They asked me about the Amish and we had a big biblical discussion. Another little victory.

I spent a lot of time dealing with settler children who were being very rude to Palestinians. They were feeling very bold and free to try to create an incident, knowing they would be protected by the soldiers. Repeatedly I intervened, told the children to stop it, and stood between them and the Palestinians. At one point, a group of children began taunting me, cursing me, and threatening me. The TV cameras zoomed in on them. I allowed the scene to continue for a few minutes so that the world would be able to see the fear and hatred of these children. The children didn't realize that they were showing their worst side to the world.

I listened to a local settler who has been hostile to me and who told me recently that I wouldn't want to talk with him. He shared how one-sided he feels our team has been. I shared a concern about how full of hate the settler children seem to be. He dismissed that by saying they are simply being children. I think the problem is deeper than that. Children are not naturally hateful. They are reflecting the deep fear and hate that they see in their parents' hearts. Both with him and several other times today I noticed that when I greeted adults, the children closely watched their parents to see how they would react to me. I told him I will be leaving Hebron tomorrow and that I will be praying for Hebron. We shook hands and parted in peace.

I met Noam Arnon and said good-bye to him. I told him that the Bible tells us to pray for the peace of Jerusalem, and that I would be doing that in a deeper way than I ever have before. He didn't say much.

This afternoon I met Nick Rahal, a U.S. congressman from West Virginia who was here as an election observer. He was out in the streets talking to people and learning first-hand. We reported to him on our work here in Hebron. He seemed eager to learn. I also talked to quite a few reporters. I talked with an Israeli peace activist who was observing the scene. She lamented what she saw happening to the soul of Israel. She sees the whole scene of occupation as a tragedy for Judaism. *Ha eretz* (the land) has become the center for Judaism and is an idol. She shared that there is a deep spiritual emptiness in Israel, and orthodox, settler ideology is rapidly filling the vacuum.

By late afternoon I was worrying about what would happen when it got dark and the reporters and international observers had left. It seemed to me that tension was building. The settlers had been quite provocative all afternoon. Hundreds of them were marching through Palestinian neighborhoods, chanting and singing, waving the Israeli flag. And in such a defiant way. All this on the Palestinian election day! Add to that all the little provocations, the little insults to Palestinians, and the soldiers harassing and detaining Palestinians.

At about 4:30 Cliff and I were walking down Shuhada Street near Avraham Avinu when we saw a group of settler youth running into the market. We saw them jump on a young Palestinian. Soon a group of soldiers were there rubbing his face in the dirt and then dragging him across the street. A group of settler youth were following, trying to hit and grab him. It looked like the settler youth were trying to kill him. The soldiers were both protecting the boy's life and roughing him up.

Soon we saw a mass of settlers running. It looked serious to me. I walked after them and saw a group of settlers around a teenage settler girl sitting in the street. I saw blood on her. It looked like she might have been stabbed. The settlers were becoming hysterical. I then knew we were in the middle of a settler riot. People were running everywhere. It was clear to me that this was a situation for the police and soldiers to handle, not us. I decided to stay off to the side. I saw some shopkeepers quickly locking up their shops. They were being threatened by settlers, so I stood in front of them to protect them.

The settlers then started turning their wrath on me. I quickly moved over toward some soldiers where I thought I might be more safe. Soon, however, I was being attacked by the settlers. They were yelling and screaming at me. They started hitting me and grabbing and pulling at me. It felt like they wanted to kill me. I remained calm. Soon police grabbed me and put me into a police van. About twenty to thirty settlers were gathered around the van, yelling and screaming at me. I couldn't understand what they were saying, but had the impression that they were accusing me of stabbing the girl. The only words I could understand were Nazi and Hamas. I wondered if I would be charged with attempted murder.

I knew most of the police in the van from my time in jail. They refused to talk with me or tell me anything. I was caught in a never-never land. I had no choice but to be calm and wait. I sat in the van, watching the riot. I watched the settlers destroying Palestinian property, but the soldiers didn't try to stop them.

After about an hour the riot calmed down and the police drove me up to our street and warned me for my own safety not to return to the area of the riot. They also wanted to make sure that I really was leaving Hebron tomorrow.

My understanding now is that the police trusted me and so didn't believe anything the settlers said about me, They held me for my own protection, and out of fear that I would get back into the fray. They also probably felt frustrated with me because they had to deal with me in that situation.

I came up to the apartment and felt relieved to be home. I felt drained. I felt like I had given everything and had nothing more to give. But I was at peace.

The others gradually came back. None of them had gotten into any trouble. They saw settlers breaking the windows of a car which belonged to a Palestinian friend of ours, and soldiers arresting a Palestinian friend that the settlers had been harassing. We had a meeting to talk through our feelings and share what we had experienced during the day. That was helpful. It was quite a day for all of us.

January 21, 1996, Sunday

We called Noam Arnon this morning to ask about the girl who was stabbed yesterday. Noam told us she is doing well. As I reflect back on yesterday, I am not sure what I would have done differently. Because of my being active yesterday (and my whole time here) in intervening in conflicts and reaching out to settlers (and being in their faces), I acted as a lightning rod for the settlers' anger. That may have been good. It may have focused some of their anger on me, keeping it from being directed toward Palestinians.

As we walked down the street this morning, we saw soldiers dragging a young Palestinian out of the market. They held him a few minutes and then let him go. We were told that he had a PLO decal on his bike, and the soldiers found this offensive and punished him. The Palestinians gathered around us and asked us if this is what peace means. They were angry and cynical. I understood.

As we walked down to the park for our time of worship, I was filled with emotion. I felt the pain of the people here, and an incredible sense of joy for the privilege of being here. Our time of worship was for me a time of joy, thanksgiving, and praise to God. I appreciated picking up trash in the park one more time. The police and soldiers left lots of trash yesterday. Our work was cleaning up after them. We have done a lot of cleaning up after the soldiers, especially the pain and suffering they have left behind them. I also thought about not getting all the work done in the park that I hoped to do. I am leaving behind much unfinished work. But it is not my calling to do everything.

My five-week experiment in peace-making last year has whetted my appetite for more time in Hebron. I want to return to continue the work of listening, praying, observing, and acting. I want to learn more, and better understand God's work in liberating the oppressed. I long to see enemies reconciled.

January 28—March 21, 1997

January 28, 1997, Tuesday

I am back in Hebron after a year away and hope to stay until March 6. How great to be back in this amazing place.

Cliff Kindy and I came on the same plane, but since we had some fear of not being allowed into Israel because of our past arrests, we acted as if we didn't know each other until we got through security at the airport. Although it was dark, I recognized many of the sights along the way to Hebron. We walked up the stairs to our apartment and were greeted by Pete Byer and Terry Remple. We got caught up a bit on what is happening here and I soon went to bed.

It was good to see Dianne Roe this morning. At breakfast time our whole team was together. Five of us. A good group. We had a time of worship and then went in different directions. Terry and Pete left to do things in Jerusalem. Dianne, Cliff, and I went for a long walk up to Hebron University.

What a thrill to walk through the busy market. I was greeted by many people, many of them mentioning the opening of the gates last year. It was thrilling to see the people freely walking through the open arches.

I wondered how things would be different here now. Last May, Benjamin Netanyahu was elected the new prime minister of Israel, as the head of the conservative Likud Party. What difference will it make for life here? Just a few weeks ago the Israeli government signed the Hebron Accords and turned over 80 percent of Hebron to the Palestinian Authority. The other 20 percent of Hebron, including the old city and areas around the settlements, remain under Israeli control. It doesn't seem like much has changed in the Israeli-controlled area.

We visited with a Palestinian friend and talked about the future of CPT in Hebron. She encouraged us to focus on the problem of the settlers, helping make it possible for them either to leave or to live under Palestinian law. We were also encouraged to address abuses committed by the Palestinian Authority.

Cliff and I went on to Hebron University. I talked with students while Cliff met with a professor there. All of the students sounded critical of the recent Israeli withdrawal from 80 percent of Hebron, saying that what is needed is a comprehensive peace that deals with the injustices they experience every day.

After supper Cliff and I went on patrol around the city. We spent some time talking to soldiers, who all seemed very friendly. We met two TIPH (Temporary International Presence in Hebron) people from Norway. About thirty-five of them are here now, but there will soon be more than 100 of them. They are here as part of the Hebron Accord and their mandate is only to observe and to report to Israeli and Palestinian officials. They are not allowed to intervene. They come from Norway, Sweden, Denmark, Switzerland, Italy, and Turkey.

This is Ramadan, the Muslim month of fasting. While back home I decided to fast for the whole month, both for personal spiritual reasons and for solidarity with the people here. So I get to observe the last half of Ramadan here. I look forward to that. Fasting is important for me, and I want to identify as much as possible with the people here. I continue to feel the urgency of Christian/Muslim dialogue. My fasting is a prayer for my time here.

Someone told Cliff a story yesterday that was meant as a critique of Arafat. A messenger was sent by the king of Persia to Caliph Omar. He was told that the caliph could be found at the mosque. The messenger went to the mosque, but could find no one there but a man sleeping under a tree. He woke the sleeping man and asked him where he could find Caliph Omar. The man said, "I am Caliph Omar." "But how can you be Caliph Omar if you have no guards?" Caliph Omar replied that if one rules the people fairly, one can sleep in peace. Arafat had 150 bodyguards with him when he came to Hebron recently.

January 29, 1997, Wednesday

We went to the park by the mosque/synagogue this morning for worship. We focused on trusting God in the midst of despair. It meant a lot to me to be able to do some cleanup in the park again, as part of our worship.

We spent much of the afternoon in a team meeting. It was our first real meeting and it went well. I think this team will work well together. We spent time reporting our conversations with Palestinians over the past few days. All of us are hearing concerns about the possibility of an explosion between settlers and Palestinians. Things seem tense. Almost everyone seems critical of the peace process.

The rest of the meeting was the beginning of an evaluation of our work in Hebron, and assessing whether we should continue the project here. CPT's commitment has been to stay one month after redeployment in Hebron. There was a partial redeployment of Israeli soldiers here on January 17.

We thought of many reasons to continue our work here, including the issues of land confiscation, settlement expansion, home demolitions, and the control of Jerusalem. We agreed to focus more on structural violence. Much of our emphasis has been on dealing with visible street violence. We noted that we have built up a lot of credibility in Hebron, that issues are clearly defined here and illustrate what is happening in the rest of the West Bank.

We had a discussion of the settlers, a major reason for our being in Hebron. What should be our approach to the settlers here? Should we deal with them or ignore them? How can we help Palestinians deal with the settlers? How much should we reach out to the settlers? We talked about facilitating contact between Israeli peace groups and Palestinians in Hebron, following up on dialogue between descendants of pre-1929 Hebron Jews and Palestinians here, and relating more to religious Israelis, such as Rabbis for Human Rights.

We learned that on Monday a number of Jahalin bedouin families were forcefully removed from their homes, which were destroyed by Israeli bulldozers. On Tuesday another Palestinian home was demolished in Ramallah.

I struggled with a lot of anger today about the Israeli government demolishing Palestinian homes, confiscating more and more land, and ignoring both the humanity of the Palestinians and the agreements they have signed. I do not want to act out of anger and I want to love the oppressors. I know that is the only way that can lead to a better future. It is a deep spiritual struggle.

January 31, 1997, Friday

This afternoon Cliff and I walked around the area of the mosque/synagogue. This was Friday prayer time, and it is Ramadan. There were thousands of people praying on the street that leads up to the mosque. It was quite impressive to watch the mass of people leave at the end of the prayers. It was also dangerous. The soldiers seemed quite insensitive to the Muslims. They blocked the way. They rudely disrupted a camera crew that was interviewing a young Palestinian woman who had just come from the mosque. The Israelis drove an ambulance up through the crowd of worshipers, and then back down. The Muslims were serene, in a prayerful mood, and showed incredible patience with the intrusions into their holy time. I continue to be amazed at Palestinian patience and self-control. They have a lot to teach us about nonviolence.

The settlers discovered me this afternoon. I greeted three teenage boys with "Shabbot Shalom" and they responded in a very friendly way. Then one of them recognized me and started shaking his finger at me and telling me off in Hebrew. He seemed to be saying that they will get me. That didn't feel very good and brought up a lot of fears.

Cliff and I passed a group of about six teenage settlers. We said "Shabbat Shalom" and they responded in a friendly way, except for the last one, who kicked me in the stomach. It didn't hurt. I couldn't think of a better response than to just keep walking. One settler drove past me in a van and spat at me. He missed.

February 1, 1997, Saturday

It was a busy, intense Saturday. I spent most of the day walking the streets, talking to people. I had a talk with a settler I remember from last year. He again expressed concern that we are perceived by the settlers as being identified too much with the Arabs. He said we should not be living in an Arab neighborhood. He asked why we are not publicizing injustices committed by the Palestinian Authority.

I wanted to respond to him about that, but a group of settler teenagers came by and seemed to be telling him in Hebrew that he should not be talking to me. He didn't back down. In fact, he gave them quite a lecture. I wish I could have understood what he said. I then said that it was obvious that the youth were very angry with me, and that I wanted to listen to their concerns. He translated my comment, and the youth responded, saying that when a girl was stabbed last year, I tried to hide the knife. That surprised me. I told them I did not hide any knife.

A Palestinian journalist started taking pictures of the settlers gathered around me. A settler told him to stop taking their pictures on the Sabbath, but the Palestinian ignored them. Then a settler attacked the photographer and soon there were lots of other settlers there. The soldiers dispersed the crowd and the disturbance was soon over. But so was our conversation.

I headed back toward home and met some other settler youth. They were very hostile and one of them said, "Kill him." I feel like a marked man. Later some settler youth walked by me. They looked hostile. One of them turned around and kicked me in the leg. It hurt. I said "Shabbat Shalom" to them and they left. I wonder, is it lawful to kick people on the Sabbath?

A short time later another group of hostile settler youth walked up to me. I looked them right in the eyes and said, "Shabbot Shalom." They only spoke Hebrew to me, except for the curses which were in English. I told them I would be happy to listen to their concerns. More curses. As they left, I said, "God bless you."

The streets were packed this afternoon. I have never seen so many Palestinians or settlers on the street. A large number of Israelis have come here for the Sabbath. It was even hard to walk sometimes. It was also potentially a very dangerous situation. With all those people, one spark could have ignited a terrible tragedy.

I greeted a number of the settlers as I stood by a military checkpoint. Those from outside Hebron were friendly. I said "Shabbot Shalom" to one couple who turned out to be a Palestinian married to an American. They live in Saudi Arabia. I was embarrassed, but they took it as a joke. When the man learned that I am with CPT, he told me he keeps up with our work on the Internet. He knew all about us and what we are doing.

While standing at the checkpoint I was harassed by some young settlers. One came up to me and said, "You will die today." Others cursed me. Some just stood there and glared at me. They showed an incredible amount of hate.

As I thought about this dangerous situation and the hostile youth, I decided to share my concerns with two Israeli police who were watching the crowd. They agreed that it was a dangerous situation. I reported that I was kicked twice and given several death threats, and that the young people seemed to be going around trying to create an incident.

The police seemed eager for me to press charges. I told the police that I didn't want the youths arrested. I only wanted someone to exercise some discipline with them. I suggested someone should talk to their parents. I pointed out the offenders to the police, who ended up giving them a stern lecture.

I came to the apartment and found Cliff. We went over toward the mosque/synagogue and saw a car stopped at the checkpoint there. The car was full of people from Turkey and had diplomatic plates. When the Israeli soldiers learned that the people in the car were Muslims, the soldiers told them that since they were Muslims they could not proceed. They protested, the soldiers radioed to their commander, and the word came back that they could not pass. The people from Turkey said they wanted to go to pray, but were told they could not proceed by car. So they turned around.

The situation was sad, but also hilarious. The Turkish diplomats had a good sense of humor and we laughed and joked about it with them and the other international observers (TIPH) who were present. We suggested to the Turkish people that they should change their religion. We all laughed. It was so absurd.

Soon an Australian film crew in a car with yellow Israeli plates drove up and was immediately allowed through. One's religion affects one's civil rights here, even for diplomats.

Today leaves me with a lot of questions about how to relate to the settlers. Several times today I tried to reach out to them by saying, "I know you are angry with me and I am ready to listen to your concerns. What do you want to say to me?" That had some limited success. Am I a liability to the team because of the settlers' intense hate for me? I am not sure they are actually ready to kill me, but I do think they would beat me up if they had a chance. I am wrestling with feelings of fear.

February 2, 1997, Sunday

On the way to Jerusalem this morning we were stopped at the checkpoint south of Jerusalem. The Israeli soldiers made the four Palestinian women in the taxi get out because they didn't have a permit to go to Jerusalem. We left them standing there by the road. I was pretty upset by the injustice of the situation and that I had done nothing. I didn't want to interfere with the taxi and was unsure of what I could do. I now wish I would have just briefly let the soldiers know that I considered the situation to be unacceptable. So I, a privileged American Christian, went to Jerusalem to worship while my Muslim sisters were left standing by the road. Ninety-five percent of the Christians and Muslims on the West Bank are forbidden to worship in Jerusalem because they don't have a permit to go there.

It was good to be back and reconnect with people at St. George's Anglican Cathedral. I was touched by Naim Ateek's references to Jesus not being welcome in various towns. I am not welcome among the settlers in Hebron. During Naim's Arabic sermon I did a lot of soul searching concerning my feelings about the settlers and their hatred toward me, struggling with how to respond to them out of love.

During the discussion period there was a lot of talk about Hebron. They talked mostly about the need for a Christian presence in Hebron. We were asked whether we as Christians feel welcome in Hebron. We do feel welcomed by the Muslims in Hebron. Over and over, Palestinians ask us if we are Muslims, and when we tell them we are Christians they tell us we are welcome.

We then went with the church group to a restaurant in Jericho. Dianne and I rode with Beth and Jonathan Kuttab, and had a good talk about CPT. They emphasized the importance of a Christian presence in Hebron and our dealing with the settlers, especially our risking our lives in a nonviolent way. They also emphasized the importance of confronting racism and apartheid in all its forms, because racism is an affront to faith in the God of Abraham. They suggested that even if our focus were more on the larger West Bank, it still would be good to be in Hebron, since there are other groups working in Bethlehem and Jerusalem.

It was awe-inspiring to drive through the mountainous desert country between Jerusalem and Jericho. We saw a number of bedouin camps and drove by the Ma'ale Adumin settlement where the Jahalin bedouin homes were demolished recently.

February 3, 1997, Monday

This morning was a big day on Shuhada Street. As part of the Hebron Agreement, a part of the street was opened to some Palestinian public vehicles and taxis. There were film crews everywhere looking for a story. It turned out not to be much of a day here on our street. There was little Palestinian traffic.

The Palestinians got another half inch, but most of the Palestinians we talked to were cynical and said nothing has changed. The absurd thing is that there never has been a good reason for having the street closed. It was closed for Palestinian traffic three years ago to punish the Palestinians because the Israeli settler, Baruch Goldstein, killed twenty-nine Palestinians in the mosque. But the street remained open to settler traffic. I know it doesn't make any sense. As a friend put it, "The situation here transcends reality."

It must be a difficult day for the settlers here. They opposed the opening of the street to Palestinians, so this is another small defeat for them.

I saw Noam Arnon on the street and greeted him. We had a civil conversation. He said that CPT is one-sided. I asked him how he felt about CPT riding the number 18 bus in Jerusalem last year after it was bombed two Sundays in a row. CPT announced to Hamas and the Israelis that our team would ride the number 18 bus the following Sunday to protest the bombings and call Israelis not to give in to fear.

Noam said he didn't know about that. I brought up the subject of the rumors that I tried to conceal a knife a year ago. He said that he hadn't spread that rumor. I told him we want dialogue with the settlers here. He was noncommittal.

At noon we had a team meeting and made various decisions about our schedule for the next week. The main part of the meeting was sorting through the future of our project here. We agreed that we should continue the work in Hebron, dealing with issues around the settlers, but also expand to broader issues of systematic violence, including settlement expansion, land confiscation, home demolitions, and possibly issues concerning Jerusalem.

A Palestinian supporter came and talked with us about our future. He told us that by our actions we have put our concerns on the agenda of both the Israeli government and the Palestinian Authority. He said that opening the gate to Hebron University put the university on the agenda at a time when it was being ignored and even possibly slated for permanent closing. The Israeli government temporarily stopped most home demolitions after CPT people were arrested on the rooftop of a house that was about to be demolished. Opening the gates to the market put more Hebron issues on the agenda for the peace talks. He told us that Arafat at various times has called people in Hebron to check on issues that were raised by our actions.

As for what we should be doing, he had a number of suggestions. First, he said, he expects another massacre of Palestinians by settlers. He suggested that one way to try to prevent that is to make it widely known that a massacre is expected. The more it is expected the more difficult it will be for the settlers to explain it away as the act of some unstable, isolated individual, thus making it more difficult for the settlers to decide to go ahead with a massacre. He also had several specific suggestions involving our entering land that Palestinian farmers are forbidden to enter, and cultivating their land for them.

I was invited to a Muslim home this evening to break the Ramadan fast. After eating they took me to a small mosque and invited me to participate in the prayers. I explained that I am a Christian, not a Muslim. They said it doesn't matter, since there is only one God. They wanted me to pray with them. It felt right to me. So I joined them. I especially appreciated the kneeling with my face on the floor. What a powerful symbol for submission to God. It was a deep prayer time for me.

After prayers we went to Aref's home. The purpose of the visit seemed to be to convert me to Islam. Aref's approach was to explain that it is impossible that God would have allowed his Son to be killed, so Jesus could not be the Son of God. No father would willingly allow his son to be killed. A good father would be angry and kill the attacker. Since God is good and all-powerful, the Christian story about Jesus and his death cannot be true. He asked me how it would be possible for God to allow Jesus to die. I said it was very difficult to understand, but it was because of God's great love for us. I told Aref that even if he were to kill my son, I hoped that I would not kill him in return.

He said that Jesus said to turn the other cheek, but God's revelation through Mohammed was different. I told him that I have a deep respect for Islam, that there are many similarities between Islam and Christianity, but that the essential difference is the nonviolent redemptive love that we see in Jesus. I thanked him for helping point out the difference.

I am excited about this conversation. It is exactly the dialogue I want to have with Muslims. I am not interested in superficial differences. For me the central issue is the cross, the way of nonviolent, redemptive love, the atonement. This is the reason I am in Hebron, the reason why I am willing to risk my life here. It is because I believe that God's ultimate answer to evil and oppression is nonviolent love, the way of the cross. This is the reason why I am a Christian. The redemption myths of power and violence don't make any sense to me.

February 4, 1997, Tuesday

In our time of worship this morning Cliff focused on having the courage to cross over the line, to make ourselves vulnerable, to risk. That is the call of Jesus. Actually, I find it easier to take those risks here in Hebron than back home. Taking those steps usually is not something big and glamorous. It is small things like not ignoring racist or sexist remarks, like taking a stand, like being willing to lose some of our respectability and comfort. Every day each of us is faced with decisions of whether to say something that needs to be said, to take a small step of doing what is right, or to play it safe and be quiet.

Cliff and I discussed what we would do if we saw someone with a gun ready to commit a massacre. We talked about different scenarios and what actions would be appropriate. It sounded scary, and I had to ask myself if I would be willing to risk my life to save others. It feels a bit awesome. I hope I would be able to do that.

Actually, the most dangerous thing I do here is ride in taxis. There have been more Israelis killed in automobile accidents than Israelis killed in all of Israel's wars. Why do we think nothing of risking our lives in automobiles, but fear taking little steps of faithfulness?

Cliff and I went to visit Radi at his pottery shop, and learned that he is in prison. Israeli soldiers came to his home at 2:00 this morning and took him away. His friends said that no one knows where he is or why he was arrested. Why didn't they arrest him in the daytime?

Israelis say their first concern is security. These kinds of actions do not lead to security, but can only make Israel less secure. Several times in the past few days Cliff has confronted soldiers with their harsh actions and told them that they are acting as poor role models for the Palestinians. Do they want the Palestinian police to act that way toward Jews who may someday live under Palestinian authority?

This afternoon our whole team met with a Palestinian

friend and adviser, to get his advice regarding the future of CPT here. He expressed appreciation for CPT's work and our having been able to make a clear Christian witness in Hebron, something few could have done in this Muslim city. He pointed out that the "Christian" world has had more influence on the situation here than has the Muslim world. Sadly, much of that influence has been destructive.

Second, he pointed out that CPT has drawn the attention of the world to Palestine by exposing what is going on here. Someone has estimated that two million people receive CPT Internet reports. Through telling our stories we try to communicate not only what is happening here, but also the essence of nonviolent intervention and its basis in biblical faith. He thanked us for engaging the churches, both the Palestinian churches and the larger councils of churches. We were advised to continue our focus on the settlers here, and broader issues in the West Bank, including Jerusalem. He mentioned looking at the West Bank through the eyes of Hebron.

We got into a big discussion of whether we should expose the human rights abuses of the Palestinian Authority. He shared his own agony over that question. He said that we must recognize that the Palestinians are an oppressed people, not in control of their own resources and institutions, and are under tremendous pressure from Israel to be authoritarian and to not allow much freedom. He expressed concern that our actions not play into the hands of the Israelis, and suggested that it is the task of Palestinians to expose Palestinian human rights abuses. Besides, the whole world is already being exposed to what the Palestinians are doing wrong.

February 5, 1997, Wednesday

We learned that two Israeli helicopters crashed in Lebanon last evening. All seventy-three soldiers on board were killed. We have been talking to soldiers here this morning, sharing our sadness. Many of the soldiers here have friends who died in the crash. Some of them are from the same unit as the victims.

It is sad to learn of the death of anyone, especially a tragedy of this size. But that is not all I feel. Jesus said that those who live by the sword will die by the sword. How big a price are we willing to pay for security? But why pay any price for a security that cannot be bought by guns and soldiers? Jesus wept over the city of Jerusalem because its inhabitants did not know what makes for peace. When will we ever learn?

Around noon I was near the checkpoint below our apartment, and saw a jeep full of Israeli Border Police harassing Palestinians. I stood close to them and monitored everything they did. I was frustrated and was considering confronting them when one of them indicated he wanted to talk with me. He asked me where I came from and what I am doing here. I told them about our work here and asked them where they were from. I told them I was sorry about the helicopter crash.

Dialogue with our adversary will be greatly enhanced if we can acknowledge the pain and grief the "other" has experienced. We became human to each other. They shared their frustration that the Palestinians are so unwilling to cooperate and are so angry. I suggested that all occupied people everywhere are angry, and that the only answer to that is to end the occupation. They seemed to understand. I never did confront them with their unloving actions. I didn't need to. They knew I don't approve of their actions. I'm glad we connected.

The problem here is not that either the Israelis or the Palestinians are bad people. The problem is that relationships have been structured on the basis of powerful and powerless, them and us, which enables good people to do really bad things.

February 6, 1997, Thursday

We spent much of the day monitoring the soldiers around the checkpoint just below our apartment. For the past two days the soldiers have been stopping traffic, checking people's IDs, and generally harassing the Palestinians. The soldiers are acting in a most arrogant way, trying to act tough, speaking condescendingly to the Palestinians, and generally ordering people around. I even saw one soldier pretending to check IDs. He would take a Palestinian's ID, walk around to the other side of the jeep, not even look at the ID, and then turn around and return the ID.

We were a constant presence in the soldiers' midst, watching everything they were doing. I was writing or pretending to write in my notebook, making them aware that what they were doing was being recorded. Other team members were using our video camera. Was this helping to prevent violence? Did the soldiers act less aggressively because of our presence?

At 4:00 this afternoon Aref came and took our whole team to his house to break the fast. He used to live near here, but because of all the threats and violence from the settlers, he decided to move his family a little distance away. We had a wonderful evening. It turned out that he had invited a number of poor people from the old city to his home to share a meal. Muslims are encouraged to invite the poor into their homes during Ramadan. I learned that Aref and one of his brothers were in the Abraham Mosque when Baruch Goldstein killed twenty-nine Muslims as they were praying three years ago.

Another man, who was also wounded in the massacre, shared a statement he had written about the helicopter crash, seeing it as God's revenge on the Israelis for the massacre at the mosque. He pointed out that the crash occurred during the night of power, after an Imam in Al Aqsa Mosque in Jerusalem prayed that God would take revenge on the Israelis. There is a lot of discussion of this issue among the Palestinians.

I am uncomfortable with the concept of God being arbitrary, wrathful, or vengeful, and with our asking God to be vengeful. I am equally uncomfortable with denying God's judgment on injustice. There are consequences to our actions. The death of those soldiers is the result of many decisions Israel has made. They were on their way to do horrible things in southern Lebanon. If we could just conclude that vengeance is only for God to repay, that would be a significant step forward.

Our whole team decided to fast today, both in response to the Israeli call for a day of fasting, and to participate in Ramadan.

February 8, 1997, Saturday

Yesterday was the last day of Ramadan, so the next three days will be feast days. Fasting for the whole month has been good for me. The discipline, self-denial, prayer, and identification with the suffering of the people here have all come together for me in a deep way. The combination of prayer and action is true spirituality for me.

After our time of worship in the park, we met a group of United Church of Christ people who work in Turkey. We showed them around the settlements here and told them about the situation in Hebron. We then took them to a Palestinian home near Kiryat Arba. Our host talked to them about the problems Palestinians face living under occupation. In reference to the helicopter crash, he asked what people would be saying if those two helicopters had been from Syria or Iraq on their way to attack Israel. How much sympathy would there be for those soldiers? Would there be no criticism of the purpose of those flights?

We then went to see the Zalloom home which was demolished last year. This is where Dianne Roe and Bob Naiman were arrested for sitting on the roof before it was demolished. Actually four people were on the roof, but only two were arrested. I was overwhelmed with emotion and just stood there and cried. There was this big mass of concrete rubble, the concrete roof still intact, setting on the smashed walls. This was a home, a place where a family had lived, where children had played, a building in which the family had invested their life savings.

The Israelis said the family didn't have the proper permit. The home was demolished without a demolition order, and after then Prime Minister Perez had ordered a halt to all demolitions. The Israeli soldiers laughed and cheered as the bulldozer destroyed the Zalloom home. Members of the family stood with us as we tried to comprehend this monument to human cruelty. I asked our guide to tell the family that we are very sorry for what happened. That was a tender time for all of us.

Later, while Cliff and I were standing in front of the mosque/synagogue, a group of teenage settler girls walked by and asked us where we came from. We just started to answer when some local settler boys told them something and they immediately became hostile and walked away. I watched them across the street and decided to walk over to them and try to start a conversation. I asked if I could talk to them. They were quite hostile. I said I would like to know why they are angry with me. They said because I love the Arabs. I said I do love the Arabs, I love the Chinese, I love the Jews. One of them said, "So you love the whole world?" I said yes, there is one God who created us all.

Then one of them said I hid a knife that was used to stab a settler girl. I told them I didn't do that. They replied that is what they have been told and that they will believe Israelis, not me. I said they were free to believe whatever they wanted to believe.

They started criticizing the peace process, saying how Israel had given up so much to the Arabs and got nothing in return, how the Arabs want to take everything from Israel. The Arabs just want to kill the Israelis. At that point a young Palestinian entered the conversation, telling them the

Palestinians want to live in peace. "No, you want to kill us," they replied. He tried to reason with them, but their fears and prejudices were too great for them to hear him.

We came back and had a team meeting to discuss our direction. I did an exercise with the team, called "lies and secrets," a brainstorm on how to expose the lies about life here. For example, in the Civil Rights Movement in the United States, (1) the lie was that black people didn't want to vote, (2) the secret was that they were not allowed to vote, (3) the moral imperative was that all people should be allowed to vote, (4) and the alternative was to allow blacks to vote. To expose the lie, (5) blacks went en masse to register to vote, leaving the white power structure with the dilemma of (6) losing power if they permitted blacks to vote, and (7) having their lie exposed if they refused.

We then applied these seven categories to a number of lies about life here. These included ideas like "Palestinians are terrorists," "This land was given to the Jews by God," "Jews and Arabs can't live together in peace," and "Security comes from guns."

We discussed three concrete actions we might take to expose some of the lies here: to illegally rebuild a demolished house, to cultivate land near a settlement that Palestinian farmers are forbidden to enter, and to get a group of Jews, Muslims, and Christians to try to enter Jerusalem to pray, get turned back, and have prayers there at the military checkpoint. Often very simple actions can cut through very complicated issues and reveal the truth.

February 9, 1997, Sunday

Zougby brought a group of students from Notre Dame University for a tour. When they were ready to leave they said they wanted to drive up Shuhada Street where Palestinian traffic is prohibited. Zougby and the Palestinian driver wanted to push the boundaries a bit. We were not stopped at the first checkpoint, and got to Beit Hadassah where the soldiers were not sure they wanted to let us through. The two Palestinians in the van had put on our CPT hats. The soldiers didn't know what to do, but finally did pull back the spiked road block and we got to the next checkpoint where the soldiers also did not want to let us through. They were very suspicious of us and tried to question us. Zougby told the soldiers that they wouldn't want to make a scene in front of all these Americans. We then just started driving through and the soldiers didn't stop us.

The two Palestinians in the group refused to be paralyzed by fear or be intimidated by the Israeli soldiers. They took control of their lives and it was the soldiers who were left paralyzed and wondering how to take back control of the situation.

Before we said good-bye to the group, Cliff told a story about Zougby. Cliff was in a car with Zougby and a CPT delegation, driving at night. Zougby was in the front passenger seat. The car was stopped suddenly as two Israeli soldiers jumped out of the darkness, with guns pointed at the car. In English, Zougby said to the soldiers, "You may shoot." The soldiers immediately put down their guns and disappeared. The point of the story is that Zougby not only refused to be intimidated, but took the initiative, took control of the situation. If we can conquer our fears, we can be free to do what needs to be done and have more control of the situation than do those who have their fingers on the triggers.

This morning the Palestinian who hosted our tour group yesterday told Cliff that shortly after we left yesterday, a bullet hit the wall right beside him as he was standing by his house. He gave us the slug. It is a 9mm slug and was probably fired from an Uzi, the machine gun many of the settlers carry. His house is right by the Kiryat Arba settlement. The settlers probably didn't appreciate the presence of that group yesterday.

This evening Cliff and I visited a Palestinian family who asked us when we think President Clinton will get back their property in Israel for them that was stolen from them. He had to tell them that we didn't think Clinton would do that for them. They apparently had been wealthy, now have nothing, but still hold on to hope of someday returning to their home.

February 12, 1997, Wednesday

We learned of three important events that happened yesterday. The Israeli government finally released a large group of Palestinian women prisoners, they bulldozed a lot of Jahalin bedouin homes, and they bombed Lebanon. We see a pattern here. On the day they get positive news coverage for releasing prisoners, they remove the Jahalin bedouins and bomb Lebanon. They apparently do that, both to appease the Israeli right, and to have the cover of a positive news story.

There were more jets flying over Hebron again this morning. More bombing of Lebanon?

We took a taxi to Bethlehem this morning and met Carmen Pauls, who used to be on our team, but now works for the Mennonite Central Committee. She was delivering some clothes for the Jahalin who were evicted yesterday and invited us to go with her. First we went to a rocky hilltop near the Jerusalem garbage dump where around 200 bedouins were moved yesterday. The area is a big pile of rocks that was recently bulldozed, but not at all level. Large metal shipping containers were put on the rocks for the bedouins to use. Their goat herds wandered around with nothing to eat. Families were trying to make some kind of order out of the chaos. It was a sobering sight.

These bedouins had been evicted from their ancestral lands in southern Israel in 1950 by the Israeli Air Force, which wanted their land for its own purposes. Now they are being evicted again, because the Ma'ale Adumin settlement wants to expand.

We drove to the site of the demolitions. It was an overwhelming sight. Piles of rubble, which just one day ago had been bedouin homes, were scattered over the area. Carmen was here yesterday and said many Israelis had come to watch. That is really sick. The Israelis used African laborers to do the dirty work. Behind us were the fancy, splendid buildings of the settlers, and a huge array of unfinished new settler homes. The settlement of around 20,000 is rapidly expanding. Slowly, but surely, all the Arabs are being pushed out. The settlers hope to have this area annexed to Jerusalem. This raises the issue of European destruction of indigenous peoples. The comparison with the destruction of Native Americans is unavoidable.

We then went into Jerusalem and our team met with the staff of Sabeel, the Palestinian liberation theology center. We explored with Naim Ateek and the staff how we might work together more closely. They plan to come to Hebron to visit us soon.

We then went to West Jerusalem to meet Jeremy Milgrom and Arik Ascherman, the codirectors of Rabbis for Human Rights. Our team has done joint actions with them in the past, and we wanted to explore continued cooperation. We talked a lot about Masalam's land near a settlement by Yatta that the settlers are keeping him from farming. The whole CPT team was arrested there last year for trying to work on Masalam's land. We also talked about rebuilding demolished homes. Rabbis for Human Rights is considering rebuilding the home of a Palestinian family whose son was convicted of killing an Israeli and had their home demolished as punishment. I was deeply moved that they are even considering that. They also asked about building a tent of Abraham in Hebron for Purim, where Jews, Muslims, and Christians would be welcome. That sounds interesting.

February 13, 1997, Thursday

Cliff and I went to talk with journalists this morning and learned that five homes around Hebron were demolished yesterday. The demolitions were spread out over the area, the families don't know each other, and there was no warning. No support, therefore, could be organized. And it was all done under cover of the peace process. At one of the homes a woman was beaten by Israeli soldiers. She must have protested the destruction of her home. Israeli soldiers expect submission. The Israeli military also bulldozed farmland south of Hebron yesterday to prevent farmers from using their land.

So what is our role? I wish I could have been sitting on the roofs of those homes yesterday. I want to do something.

Yesterday they briefly opened the wholesale produce market down the street which has been closed since Goldstein did his abominable deed in the mosque. This used to be the largest wholesale produce market in the southern West Bank. It was supposed to have been reopened over a year ago. At about this time last year, our team, in conjunction with Israeli peace activists, did a symbolic opening of the market by setting up a little table and illegally selling tomatoes to call attention to the injustice of keeping the market closed.

The market now is symbolically open. The shop owners are there, but can't sell anything. There were lots of Palestinians gathered in front of the open shops when I got there around noon today. It looked like trouble was brewing. The settlers from the Avraham Avinu settlement just behind the market started to push the Palestinians out. The settlers feel the market area belongs to them, and they don't want the market at their front door.

According to what Israeli police told me, the soldiers considered it a dangerous situation and decided to clear the area. But the Palestinians resisted. There was a group of young boys around twelve years old in the front line of the Palestinians. They kept taunting and pushing the soldiers, but the soldiers slowly kept pushing them back. The soldiers were also pushing back settler youth. There were lots of journalists and cameras, so the soldiers were careful in what they did.

Slowly the Palestinians were pushed away and the settlers briefly reclaimed the area by the market. Their victory was short lived, however. After the crowd was dispersed, the settlers were removed and the place again belonged to the Palestinians. The settlers lost the battle. It must be difficult for the settlers to have to retreat another step. I expect there will be more clashes here.

In order to get a more balanced view, I tried to talk with settlers, but got cursed. I finally found a settler willing to talk. I listened. He explained to me that this whole area was given by God to Abraham, and how to deny that is to rebel against God. All the children of Ishmael must leave. All this property was stolen from the Jews. He criticized me for talking with Muslims and brought up the subject of the knife. I told him what happened. I don't know if he believed me. We parted in peace, even shaking hands.

It was a very dangerous situation this afternoon. There were hundreds of people pushing and shoving, tensions were high, the soldiers were scared, the settlers were indignant. All that was needed was a match. Even though I was a bit scared, it seemed good to be in the middle of it. I played the role of journalist, writing notes in my notebook. That seemed to give me extra freedom to be there and possibly some protection. I acted as an observer, seeing little opportunity for creative action to change the situation.

I saw officer Omri and a number of other Israeli police who had interrogated me last year. It was good to see them again and we had a good time joking together. They asked if I told the Amish in America about them. That interchange was quite human and I hope may be helpful for the future.

February 14, 1997, Friday

This afternoon I went for a fabulous ride through the mountains and valleys north of Bethlehem to Abu Dis for a demonstration near the Jerusalem garbage dump where the

Jahalin bedouin were moved. I arrived early, walked into the bedouin circle feeling a little uneasy about intruding, but soon found people to talk to. When I arrived I was the only non-Palestinian there. Others soon started arriving until there were 250-300 people there. I spent my time meeting many people, Jewish and Palestinian, people who have been putting their lives on the line for a long time. A number of them were people I have been wanting to meet.

Although the speeches were too long and no direction was given for what we should do, it was a most moving and inspiring time for me. At one point I just had to cry. I felt so deeply both the pain and oppression of the Jahalin, and also the power and beauty of Jews, Muslims, and Christians all coming together in common concern for a people who are being destroyed. My favorite sign was "Abraham was a bedouin." He was. Many strong statements were made about the racism of the Israeli government. As one Israeli put it, the only reason the bedouins were removed is that they are not Jewish.

At the end of the demonstration I asked everyone to pick up all the paper the demonstrators had scattered on the ground. I thought it rude to trash the Jahalin's desolate home and a desecration of God's creation. Soon lots of people were picking up their trash. Amazing. It all got cleaned up.

Terry came to the demonstration from Jerusalem. After the demonstration we were invited for a meal at MCC in Jerusalem along with some Palestinian Christian activists. I got a ride with some of the Palestinian Christians. Since the Palestinians were illegal in Jerusalem, we sneaked into the city by back streets and alleys. That was exciting. To get back the short distance to Bethlehem where they live, and to escape getting caught by Israeli soldiers, we went by a long route through Abu Dis and a narrow mountain road. Why do they need to live under such ridiculous restrictions? It is not a matter of security. Anyone can sneak a bomb into Jerusalem.

Cliff spent the afternoon visiting a recently demolished

home and a field that settlers destroyed the other day while being protected by Israeli soldiers. We also learned today that 700 Palestinian homes in the West Bank are subject to being demolished.

February 15, 1997, Saturday

After worship I walked around trying to assess the situation on the street this Sabbath. I watched settlers going back and forth to their prayers with their guns and fancy prayer robes. It is very hard not to be cynical, especially when they are cursing me and spitting at me as they did today. I saw more settlers with guns today than I have ever seen before. Others also noticed this. What does it mean? I was worried all day about what might happen.

There were a number of small incidents between Palestinian and settler boys. Both sides were looking for a fight. I saw settler boys throwing stones at the Palestinian boys. The soldiers detained a Palestinian boy and soon a crowd gathered around the soldiers demanding his release.

At about sunset we learned from TIPH that a Palestinian was wounded by a settler near the Kiryat Arba settlement. Cliff and I went out there and saw the young man being put on a stretcher and put into an ambulance. He looked severely wounded. We were told that four settlers stoned him and one of the settlers rammed the butt of his rifle into the man's face. The Palestinians were quite upset, yet they remained calm. Many were crying. We listened.

After supper we had a team meeting. We spent a lot of time talking about what we can do to stop home demolitions. Two people from the Palestinian Land Defense Committee came to our apartment this afternoon and talked with Dianne, Terry, and Cliff about what is happening. We decided to put out an alert to all our CPTnet readers to contact the Israeli and United States governments to demand a stop to home demolitions. We also plan to help facilitate Israeli peace groups getting involved with this issue.

February 16, 1997, Sunday

This morning Dianne, Terry, and I went to Jerusalem. I attended the Lutheran service, Dianne the Baptist, and Terry the Anglican. We are trying to relate to other churches here. It was difficult worshiping in a building built by the Crusaders, but I was deeply moved by parts of the service. The sermon was on Abraham sacrificing Isaac. Can we trust God so far as to let go of everything?

Cliff learned about soldiers raiding and ransacking a Palestinian home here in Hebron four days ago. The soldiers came at 5:00 in the morning, put the family in one room, tore up the place, and strip-searched the women. During Ramadan settlers started a fire in the kitchen of this house. Stones have been thrown at the house by settlers. The house is close to the Kiryat Arba settlement, and the settlers want the Palestinian family to leave the area.

We had a deep time of sharing and wrestling together in our team meeting this evening as we were seeking to find how to respond to recent home demolitions. We were told today that five more houses are scheduled to be demolished in Tarqumia tomorrow. We are dealing with something terribly evil. How can we expose, confront, and overcome that spirit? That is the task of nonviolent struggle. We feel that we have only barely begun to understand what that means. We feel the need to take new steps in nonviolence. But we don't know what those steps are.

Nonviolence is not a science. That is clear from living in the middle of this conflict and oppression. It is not something that can be calculated or quantified. It is an art. It involves being sensitive, open, and vulnerable. Yet nonviolence is more than art. It is prayer.

Dianne reported how, when she and others sat on the roof of the Zalloom house last year, it was a spontaneous act that was simply given. We then realized that most, if not all, of our actions have been gifts. We didn't plan the removing of the gates last year, the opening of the gate to Hebron

University, or other actions. Can we be open to be given new tasks now? Can we let go so that we can be led by God's Spirit? We are reaching out for something. It is important to not get caught up in impulsive actions, but to be open, creative, free, experimental, spontaneous, and patient.

We did come up with some ideas. We could carry signs on the street asking Israel to stop demolitions of Palestinian homes. We could begin a fast that would also take place in Israel and in Washington, D.C. We also thought of collecting rubble from demolished homes and depositing it at the Prime Minister's home. We have sent out an alert to get people around the world to call on Israel to stop. But there must be something more, something deeper.

We learned today that the Palestinian stoned and beaten by settlers yesterday has internal injuries. We were told that a settler was stopped yesterday from shooting Palestinians here in Hebron.

February 17, 1997, Monday

We continue wrestling and struggling and praying about what our response should be to the new wave of home demolitions. We are trying to think big. We are praying for a miracle. Cliff said we should be praying for the end of the occupation. Can we hope for a big miracle? Can we dare to do the impossible?

After our time of worship and team meeting this morning, I went to the Israeli police headquarters to make complaints about recent events. On the way I saw an officer whom Cliff and I had talked to various times last year. I shared our concerns about the soldiers recently ravaging a Palestinian home and forcing women to undress. He knew about it and would only say that it is being taken care of. I also mentioned the illegal construction at Avraham Avinu. It is important that the police know people are watching.

I then walked up to the new main police building to talk to officer Omri and report some of our concerns about recent events with him. That was a good conversation. We have a relationship of mutual respect. The police are in a new building, because the place where I was held last year has been turned over to the Palestinians.

When one of the police found out that I was on the scene Saturday where a Palestinian was injured by settlers, he wanted to question me. Since we had arrived there late, I could not be of any help. He said the police usually have no proof. He said the most important thing CPT could do is to carry cameras and help the police prosecute settlers by having pictures as proof. If settlers threaten us, he wants to prosecute them. Do we want to help prosecute people? Is that our role?

At that point one of the main officers I dealt with last year when I was in jail came in and was surprised to see me. He said he thought I wasn't allowed back into the country and seemed unhappy I was there. He was still upset about the damage to military property that occurred last year. I repeated that our main role was to prevent violence.

I reported the illegal construction and the demolition of Palestinian property at Avraham Avinu, and the danger of damaging an old mosque there. Omri seemed not to have known that there was a mosque there, and acted quite concerned. He agreed that there is danger of an imminent explosion. I told him that demolishing Palestinian homes is making the situation more serious. He didn't say much to that. I told him we may sit on top of houses scheduled to be demolished.

I then got into a conversation with another police officer who said that people like Ygal Amir and Baruch Goldstein were influenced by Moshe Levinger and other Hebron settlers. He said there is a fountain of hate here that many people are drinking from. I agreed that the fountain is big and many people are drinking from it. I said I fear for the future of Israel because of it, especially because of all the young settler children here who are drinking hate and how dangerous they may become. He replied, "So you see it too?" He is deeply concerned about the situation.

I mentioned that I met Moshe Levinger and hope to talk with him. He said I would be wasting my time. "They are crazy," he said. I don't agree. I will never give up hope for anyone. There is something of God in every person that we can appeal to. I want to keep trying, even when things seem hopeless.

Late this afternoon, Dianne and I went with a Palestinian who works for the Palestinian Authority, out to the village of Beit Anun, between the Israeli settlements of Harsina and Asfer. We went to see the Al Motur family home that was demolished February 12, one of five homes that were demolished in the Hebron area that day. The family has owned this land since Ottoman times.

This extended family had one of their homes demolished last year, and three more of their homes are scheduled for demolition *any* day now. It was sobering to stand on the big chunks of concrete that had been a home only days before. The Israeli bulldozers had been quite effective. In a few minutes a family's life savings and dreams were gone.

Why are these homes being demolished? The Israeli government says the only reason for demolishing these homes is that the family has no proper building permit. The government doesn't say that it is impossible for most Palestinians to get building permits. We were told that the Israelis have allowed construction of new homes only inside villages and towns. The reasons seem to be that the Israelis want to keep all Palestinian homes consolidated close together with large open, unpopulated areas between villages.

This makes it easier to control the Palestinians and leaves large open spaces for future settlement expansion. The Israelis also want to control most of the hilltops for security reasons. So the home demolitions are directed to scattered homes outside villages. In other words, we are seeing a policy of ethnic cleansing in order to create bantustans, surrounded by open area completely under Israeli control.

There were beautiful red flowers (lilies of the field?) growing around the devastated home. I felt a lot of sadness and anger, but the flowers reminded me that God, nature, or whatever one wants to call that Reality beyond human control, will have the final word. There is hope.

After viewing the demolition, we went to our friends' home for a wonderful meal and lots of good sharing. I spoke English with the young children who were delighted to practice speaking.

We then had coffee at his brother's house. We had a lot of fun joking about my beard, getting a second wife, and their knowing Arafat. Since they are well connected with Arafat and the Palestinian Authority, I shared with them my thoughts about the weakness of a structure that is organized from the top down as compared to the strength of a democratic movement where power comes from the bottom up. I also talked about building a nonviolent resistance movement that can win the support of the international community, and that such a movement is something Israel will not easily overcome.

When we came home we were stopped by a soldier when we tried to come down our alley. He said the street was closed. I said it didn't look closed to me. He was quite surprised to learn that we live here. He was concerned for our safety. I am concerned for his safety. It is not safe to be walking around carrying a gun.

February 18, 1997, Tuesday

Some journalists showed us video footage of three or four settlers at Avraham Avinu taking down their pants yesterday and mooning the journalists who were watching them. These are orthodox, religious people?

We had a team meeting after supper in which we did some orientation with Mark Frey, who arrived late last evening to join the team. We also did more soul searching regarding home demolitions. Dianne and Cliff are feeling clear that we should call for a worldwide fast, not only to end home demolitions, but also to end the occupation

February 19, 1997, Wednesday

We had a meeting after supper in which Mark shared his "life story." At the end of our meeting we heard sirens, so we headed out into the street. There were soldiers in full combat gear running down our alley into the market. Jeeps full of soldiers were racing up the street. It looked like something terrible was happening. My stomach was full of butterflies. Should we be out in the middle of this? We walked down to the mosque/synagogue. There were soldiers everywhere. Some were crouched down under the stalls in the market. They were ready for combat. There were lots of soldiers around the mosque and more coming in on troop carriers. Then they started unloading stretchers. They were also thinking about bodies.

We learned this was a training exercise. It was all a game. But not a very funny game. Getting ready to kill people is not a game. It affects our innermost being and has ominous concrete social results. We saw a big show of force, but I was reminded that there is another power, the power of love and truth, that no army can conquer.

We are in a serious struggle with evil powers. We see the concrete manifestations of those powers all around us. What would it mean to defeat those powers? Cliff reminded me that when a dragon dies it can cause a horrendous amount of destruction as its tail and body thrash about. But then I remembered that the Soviet Union and apartheid in South Africa were brought down with almost no thrashing of the dragon. How can that happen here?

We heard this evening that the Israeli military removed more Jahalin bedouins from around the Ma'ale Adumin settlement today. Seventeen families. About 70-100 people. And the jets we heard over Hebron today apparently bombed Lebanon again.

February 22, 1997, Saturday

Cliff and I did some patrolling together this morning. There were lots of soldiers and they seemed concerned about violence today. They are not allowing Palestinian cars to park on Shuhada Street, although the street is very wide. A soldier said it was for security reasons, because a lot of settlers will be on the street today. But they allow settler parking where the street is narrow. I have never seen the soldiers stopping settler cars, checking their IDs, or searching them, even though the main threat of violence today comes from the settlers.

I met a group of Christian Zionists and had a talk with them about issues here in Hebron. They support complete Israeli control over "the whole land of Israel." They didn't know how to respond to examples of the oppression they saw here, the anti-Christian attitude of the settlers, the existence of the Palestinian church and the oppression that Christian Palestinians are experiencing, and the question of why Jews are supposed to have dominance over Palestinian Christians. They seemed perplexed by the saying of Jesus, that the real children of Abraham are those who do God's will, and the fact that many Palestinians have more Jewish ancestry than many Israelis do.

I also met a Palestinian Jew who was born here in Hebron, and has lived here all his life. He is probably 75 years old, so he would have been here during the 1929 massacre. He is obviously respected by the Palestinians. I watched him engaging in spirited conversation with a number of Palestinians. They call him Ibni Khalil (Son of Hebron).

We have been wrestling with our direction, but we have been floundering. Our meeting this evening began in chaos. I felt a deep disunity among us. We were going in circles. I was feeling pretty discouraged. Then, I don't know what it was, but something happened. All of a sudden things started coming together. The meeting ended with the team asking me to draft a short, simple statement, saying that some of us would begin a fast on March 1 for 700 hours (29 days), one hour for each of the 700 homes with demolition orders. We will call on people around the world to join the fast to stop the demolitions. Coming together so clearly felt like a miracle.

February 23, 1997, Sunday

Carmen Pauls stayed with us last night, so she took us all to Jerusalem this morning. With six Americans in the car, we went right through on the new Jewish road without even being checked. Because we don't look like Arabs, we are given the special privilege that Jews enjoy. That doesn't feel very comfortable to me.

The others went to St. George's, but I decided to go to the Baptist church. Alex Awad, the brother of Mubarak, the well-known Palestinian activist, preached. I had met his mother in Bluffton, Ohio, about five years ago. Alex's father was killed by the Israelis in 1948, leaving a family of young children. The mother taught the children to forgive rather than harbor bitterness in their hearts. We need more of that spirit in this troubled world.

February 24, 1997, Monday

This afternoon Dianne and Mark went to visit various Palestinian leaders to get responses to our planned fast. Everyone they talked to seems enthusiastic about what we are planning. We have been getting a positive response from most people, including Israelis. The people at St. George's yesterday were very supportive.

The last two days Zleekha Muhtasib has been going around with Dianne and others to help make contacts and interpret. It is amazing what she has accomplished. She has contacted a lot of important people for us and will help get the permits we need. She truly seems to be a gift of God to us at exactly the right time. I thanked her for all the wonderful work she has been doing. Her reply was that we do not need to thank people who are only doing their duty.

She is actually a fairly well-known person. She was in the Ibrahimi Mosque and witnessed the massacre there, and afterwards was repeatedly interviewed by the media. She was on *60 Minutes* last fall talking about redeployment and the future of Hebron. Her father was "disappeared" by the Israelis in 1967. She has been feisty in her fight for justice and peace.

She ate supper with us this evening, after which we accompanied her to her home, past the soldiers. She experiences a lot of harassment from soldiers, including death threats. After saying good-bye to her, one of the soldiers asked us why we would associate with trash like her.

February 25, 1997, Tuesday

Terry attended a demonstration in Bethlehem today, protesting the building of a new Israeli settlement at Mount Abu Ghneim (Har Homa). This is a very serious issue for all sides. For the Israelis it means completing the ring of Israeli settlements encircling East Jerusalem. For the Palestinians it means the isolation of East Jerusalem from the rest of the West Bank. This would severely limit the movement of Palestinians between the northern and southern parts of the West Bank, thus effectively cutting the West Bank in two. It also puts a squeeze on Bethlehem, Beit Sahur, and other Palestinian towns. It would mean the destruction of Christian holy sites and of a natural wildlife area.

This is a serious violation of the Oslo Accords which state, "Neither side shall institute or take any step that will change the status of West Bank and Gaza Strip pending the outcome of the permanent status negotiations" (Chapter 2, Article 3, Item 7). But then there is Military Order 1025, issued October 4, 1992, which declares, "All land transactions committed contrary to the law . . . to have been done as according to the law in force."

Today was the third anniversary of the mosque massacre. Things seemed tense.

Down in the market this evening we saw three soldiers forcing themselves into a doorway of a Palestinian home. We stood in the dark and watched them. They were not very happy to have us watch them and they quickly left.

February 26, 1997, Wednesday

I walked up to Beit Hadassah settlement and saw a big busload of soldiers and a German film crew. The soldiers were being filmed running through the Palestinian neighborhood. I interrupted the filming, confronted the crew and the producer, and asked them if Palestinian soldiers could run through Tel Aviv neighborhoods like that. I asked if they had permission to climb up on Palestinian homes. Are they going to show the military mistreating Palestinians? The film crew and the soldiers were pretty upset with me. The Palestinians who were watching were upset with the soldiers and film crew. I told them I was an international observer and refused to leave when asked.

The producer said their film would be completely objective. I told him it is impossible to be completely objective. We all have our biases and perspectives. A completely "objective" film about the Israeli military will not tell the truth about the military. If they would tell the truth, it would no longer be considered "objective."

We are living in a very dangerous time. Could our fast be an answer to the imminent explosion? If people see a ray of hope it is less likely that they will be violent. Violence is an act of desperation. Violence is the inevitable result of oppression. Gandhi said that doing nothing is worse than being violent. If we want violence to end, we must take nonviolent steps to oppose injustice and point to a new way. If the world would have supported the Intifada the way it supported the freedom struggle in South Africa, the Intifada might have been successful. Can we still mobilize world support for justice in Palestine? Can we get the United States to end its immoral support for Israeli aggression?

February 27, 1997, Thursday

This morning Mark and I went to the Prisoners Club to pick up the leaflets they printed for us for the fast. They are excited about what we are doing and are making most of the arrangements for us. We got the Palestinian police permit today, and approval and support from the mayor's office. It seems like a miracle. We are doing so little, yet the doors are opening for us.

I spent time in the market this afternoon passing out leaflets, inviting people to visit us as we fast in the tent near the Red Cross building. The common people in the market were exited about the fast. That is encouraging.

I have been thinking how incredible the idea of our fast is. Imagine, a Christian group, with the support of Muslims, organizing a month-long Christian activity on the streets of this all-Muslim city.

I had a good talk with someone this morning about the danger of becoming marginalized for speaking the truth too clearly. I said that my having given up that fear gives me a tremendous freedom to speak the truth and do what needs to be done. To follow Jesus is to take up the cross, to become marginalized. To fear marginalization is to become a Sadducee, to work in the system, to no longer be a follower of the radical Jesus.

February 28, 1997, Friday

This afternoon Cliff had a discussion with one of Arafat's aides. He asked a lot of questions about CPT and the fast. He wanted to know our perceptions of the situation here. Cliff reported some of our concerns about the Palestinian Authority.

Cliff and I went out for a patrol this evening and checked the site for our fast. There were a lot of Palestinians building a huge structure to be covered by tarps. The tent will be 60 feet long and 15 feet wide. That is a lot of space. I was expecting a little tent.

I really can't believe this. Everything is coming together, everything is being provided, and we are doing almost nothing to organize the fast. What have we done? We took about two weeks to pray, wrestled with each other, and try to be open to God's leading. We took the time to come to consensus. We did a lot of waiting for Gods direction. We have no idea of what we are getting ourselves into, of what God may do with this.

Harriet Lewis came this evening to spend a few days with us and be a part of our fast. She lives in a kibbutz with Amos Gvirtz, an Israeli pacifist. It will be good to have an Israeli on our team to broaden our perspective.

March 1, 1997, Saturday

This morning we all walked up to our big tent to begin our fast. We started with a time of worship there, in the midst of all the noise of traffic on the busy street.

Since I recently finished a month of fasting during Ramadan, I am not eager to do another fast. But this fast feels right. I am doing a Ramadan type fast, with nothing to eat or drink from dawn to sunset. Cliff and Dianne are on a liquid-only fast.

The day went very well, I think. We never had large crowds, which is good. It is better that the fast build slowly, rather than start big and taper off. We had a good press conference in the tent with many Palestinian journalists. The best part of the press conference was the opportunity for Palestinians who are losing their homes and land to have a public forum to communicate their desperate situation. A Palestinian told us: "If you demolish my home, you take everything I have. If you confiscate my land, you take everything I ever will have."

We spent much of the day talking to Palestinians who

stopped at the tent. I most appreciated those who expressed their hopelessness and despair, telling us that we are wasting our time, that our fast will do no good. But they hung around awhile, and then seemed to find some hope again.

A lot of Fatah people came to the tent. I sense Fatah wants to get all that they can out of this. They put up their posters today. I am somewhat uneasy with this, not wanting to be used. On the other hand, we cannot control any of this. We are doing our little fast. The rest is out of our hands.

Our tent is in the area of Hebron controlled by the Palestinian Authority, well away from the settlers and Israeli soldiers. I think that is good. If we were near the settlers they would be challenging us and some of the focus would shift to them. We don't need to worry about being hassled by Israeli soldiers here.

I learned that a few settlers this afternoon tried to walk over into the Palestinian-controlled area here in Hebron, and were stopped by Israeli soldiers. I can see them making a big issue of this. Why can't Jews freely go anywhere they want to go? Isn't restricting their movement in Hebron racism? Of course, Jews should be able to go anywhere. But Palestinians also should be free to go anywhere. Ninety-five percent of Palestinians on the West Bank are not free to go to Jerusalem.

Yes, Jews should be able to freely go anywhere in Hebron, but these settlers are not ordinary Jews. Their presence creates strife rather than reconciliation. They have not been good neighbors. At the same time, Harriet yesterday accompanied us throughout Hebron. She was warmly received everywhere. Jews can go anywhere in Hebron.

As we left to come back to our apartment this evening we heard various gunshots. Who was shooting? For the first time this evening I saw several Palestinians with guns. We are told there are lots of guns here. Some Palestinians are saying they are ready for war with Israel.

March 2, 1997, Sunday

Harriet heard on the radio this morning that the Israeli government announced it is suspending all home demolitions on the West Bank. We are skeptical. We certainly are not ready to end our fast. In fact, this evening we heard that a family in Beni Naim was ordered to immediately evacuate their house. That probably means demolition. Is it a coincidence that after one day of fasting, the Israelis announce that they will stop demolitions? I am sure we are being watched. We know Arafat has been informed of our fast. He will be going to Washington today and meeting with Clinton tomorrow. Will our fast have any effect on those talks?

There was a constant stream of people coming through the tent today. Many wanted to share their stories of suffering under Israeli occupation. We listened to a lot of pain and anguish. *Many* of them spent years in Israeli prisons, some arrested as young boys. They said their time in prison strengthened them.

Many people from outlying villages came to the tent and told of their family homes having been demolished. CPT had sat on the roof of one of them. One person's house had been filled with concrete by the Israelis. That makes one big solid rock, which effectively prevents rebuilding. Farmers came to us telling us that Israeli soldiers are preventing them from entering their land, which not only prevents them from earning a living and thus weakens the Palestinian economy, but also makes it easier for the Israelis to confiscate their land. Land unused for one year can become Israeli state land.

Someone came to the tent this morning and took me to meet an official in the Palestinian Authority who also is in the P.A. secret police and close to Arafat. He spent fifteen years in Israeli prisons. He knew a lot about CPT. He said he had witnessed our opening the gate to Hebron University.

After all the formalities and expressions of appreciation, we had a good discussion of democracy and nonviolence. I told him some of what I want to say to Arafat. I told him that an authoritarian, top-down organization is weak and fragile. Organizations that are democratic and organized from the grassroots up are much stronger and more difficult to destroy.

I talked about Gandhi and King, whom he said he had studied. I talked about how Eastern Europe could not have gotten rid of Soviet oppression through violence. They would have been smashed quickly by Soviet forces. But they did win through a stronger force, the power of nonviolence. I suggested that the Israelis have a lot more guns than do the Palestinians, but the Palestinians have truth and justice on their side. I also suggested that violence on the part of the Palestinians hurts the Palestinian image around the world.

He said he understood, but that there is one difference: The Americans and the Russians are civilized people. Nonviolence can work with civilized people, but not with uncivilized people like the Israelis. How many times have I heard in the past that nonviolence worked for Gandhi because the British were civilized, but the Russians are not civilized. Nonviolence will never work against Communists. It is hard to see the humanity of our enemies.

We talked with some Hamas people in the tent today. One of them showed us a picture of his "martyred" brother, killed in Jerusalem. That was sobering.

We learned that the shooting last night was celebrating the wedding of a Palestinian policeman.

Anne Montgomery came this evening to join our team again. She is a Catholic nun, a veteran of the peace movement, and of our team here. She came here from delivering medical supplies to Iraq, an action that is illegal in the United States and could result in twelve years in prison and a $1 million fine for this humanitarian gesture.

March 3, 1997, Monday

The Palestinian Legislative Council declared a general strike for today to protest Israel's plan to build a settlement on Mount Abu Ghneim. Arafat is meeting with Clinton today. The strike was about 100 percent effective in Hebron. Every shop in Hebron seemed to be closed, except for pharmacies. We were told that never during the Intifada was a strike so complete. This solidarity should send a message to Clinton and to Israel. Some people criticized the strike because it came from the top down, rather than from the grassroots. They are critical of the P.A. discouragement of grass roots organizations. In fact, no marches or demonstrations were allowed in Hebron by the P.A. today.

Although there were not a lot of people on the streets, we had a busy day in our tent. Lots of people came by to express solidarity.

We heard that there was a fast outside the White House during Arafat's visit there today.

A group from the Palestine People's Party (PPP) was with us for a while this afternoon. Mohammed Horani, a member of the Legislative Council, also came and sat with us a while. I talked to him about the need to encourage grassroots organizations, something Arafat has been discouraging, rather than have the P.A security apparatus organize the people. That led to an intense dialogue between the PPP and Fatah people. The PPP were pushing Horani for more democracy and an end to jailing opposition people. Our tent seems to be facilitating a lot of dialogue.

There has not been much Hamas presence. I hope we can include them more. Several Fatah people expressed criticism of Hamas, saying that Islam should be kept in the mosques. They said that when religion is combined with politics, both religion and politics are perverted. They said there is "Islamic Hamas, Jewish Hamas, and Christian Hamas," meaning fundamentalism.

I wanted to say that when good religion is combined with good politics, there is a great power for good, but also so much religion is bad religion, and most politics is bad politics. Combining bad religion and bad politics is a disaster.

We need more of the religion of love, compassion, and mercy in politics. It is also true that making religion irrelevant to politics impoverishes both religion and politics.

Today we saw that a number of Fatah people with us had handguns. In fact, we had one tense time this evening. Palestinian police stopped a speeding Fatah car, which ended in a big argument between the police and the Fatah people. The police seemed to feel that their authority was being challenged, and the Fatah people didn't want to be ordered around. One policeman was so frustrated that he briefly sat down beside us in the tent with his head in his hands. At one point a policeman reached for his gun, but someone grabbed his arm, and things calmed down. We are going to request that there be no guns in our tent.

It was wonderful having Harriet here with us in the tent again today. Much of the time she is involved in intense dialogue with Palestinians. Today a Palestinian expressed lots of frustration and anger concerning Israelis to her. He then said to her, "Why don't you Jews go back to Egypt where you came from?" Harriet calmly replied, "But I have never been in Egypt." She was able to listen to Palestinian anger. We need more of this. She especially got involved in talking with some Palestinians from near the Kiryat Arba settlement, whose land the settlers are trying to confiscate. Kiryat Arba has already taken most of their land.

What an exciting day. So many different people coming together. This is the real peace, as one Palestinian said today.

March 4, 1997, Tuesday

In our time of worship in the tent this morning Cliff read from Jonah, how the city of Nineveh fasted and repented. An outsider called for repentance, the repentance came as a grassroots movement, and finally the leaders of Nineveh also repented.

The fast has been going well. It is a form of prayer, a way of making ourselves weak and vulnerable. It demonstrates that our concern is deeper than words. Often I feel over-whelmed by the power of what is being given here.

A big entourage of Palestinian officials came to visit the tent this afternoon. This included the mayor of Hebron, two other mayors, the P.A. governor of the Hebron district, and three Legislative Council members. It was mostly formalities, but we appreciated their outpouring of support. The Palestine Authority seems to be taking this fast very serious-ly. When they asked what they could do for us, I told them to bring Netanyahu. We laughed.

A Hamas leader came and gave us his support. He said that since Hamas is illegal, it would be difficult for them to be here formally, but was sure they felt comfortable with what we are doing.

We heard more stories of oppression today. One person came and said that two weeks ago the Israelis destroyed 500 of his olive trees. A family came and said that they have three families living together in their home and are not allowed to do any building on their land.

Again Harriet was a great part of our team. She has a lot of courage. She spent time walking alone through the mar-ket. At one point Israeli soldiers would not let her pass into the Palestinian controlled area because she is Jewish. They told her she could go back and around through the market, which she did.

We spent the evening at the tent around a bonfire, with lots of people gathered around. We closed the time with singing "We Shall Overcome," a song from the U.S. Civil Rights Movement. This song is taught in some Palestinian schools.

It is difficult to accept that I have only one more day left here. I really do not want to leave in the middle of this fast.

March 5, 1997, Wednesday

I walked through the market, saying good-bye to many friends. I have developed relationships with many people. I even saw officer Omri and said good-bye to him.

We heard that there was to be a home demolition near Kiryat Arba this morning, so we decided to all go out there. We got a taxi and found the home of Atta and Rodeina Jaber in the Beqa'a valley on the other side of the Harsina settlement. They were given an order this morning to remove everything from their house within two hours. We got there and saw a very simple house built on rocky ground. Just below the house was the new Jewish bypass road that took much of their farmland.

The extended family was there, the women sitting on the ground crying, the men wandering around aimlessly. It was the most tragic situation I had ever encountered. I walked through the empty house of two primitive rooms that had been home for these people. Their meager possessions were scattered on the ground and rocks. It was more than I could bear. I stood there and sobbed for awhile. How could anyone be so crass, so perverted, so criminal as to demolish someone's home? I saw schoolchildren come home to see the Jaber belongings scattered on the ground. I will never forget the horror in their faces. What did they do to deserve this?

I helped the family carry their blankets and clothes to put on a pickup truck. I felt like an accomplice to a horrible crime, but it felt right to help bear their agony. The family seemed grateful for our presence. They told us ten more of their extended family have homes slated for demolition.

A lot of people gathered there, including one member of the Palestinian Legislative Council, the mayor of Hebron, and other prominent people, many of whom we had met in our tent. They suggested we all gather in the house when the soldiers came with their bulldozer. Our team had a quick meeting and decided one of us should risk arrest. It was decided it should be Cliff.

Soon the political leaders announced that they were going to a house in Yatta that they heard was to be demolished. We decided to send Terry and Harriet with them. After some time we decided that Dianne and I should get back to the tent to meet guests we were expecting.

A Dutch couple who supports Palestinian causes in Holland came to spend some time in the tent. Then two Methodist women from the U.S. came. Soon two groups totaling about fifteen people came from Israel. One group was with Arik Ascherman and Jeremy Milgrom from Rabbis for Human Rights. The other group of Israeli peace activists came with Amos Gvirtz. A Palestinian from House of Grace in Haifa was with them. An Israeli woman who had just spent two months in prison for being a conscientious objector and refusing to go into the Israeli military also came. It seemed ironic that Israel would punish someone who has high moral standards, and support those who destroy people's homes.

What a wonderful encounter that was in the tent. Palestinian Muslims, a Palestinian Christian, Israeli Jews, and we European and American Christians were sitting in a circle sharing our hopes for peace. Hamas and Fatah were there. We had Hamas and Israelis sharing together. We were all brought together in a spirit of friendship and mutual respect. This is a taste of the real peace we long for.

Dianne then went with most of the Israelis and the Methodists out to see the Jaber home that was to be demolished today. I stayed in the tent and visited with a constant stream of Palestinians. It was cold and raining. I thought of all those possessions out in the rain at the Jaber house. God have mercy on us.

Before long Terry came back. He had been arrested in Yatta and charged with insulting a soldier. As they were getting ready to demolish the house, he asked a soldier if this was the kind of thing his mother had taught him to do. He was brought to the police headquarters here in Hebron, questioned, and released.

Soon everyone else returned. The soldiers never did get around to demolishing the Jaber home. We are not sure whether the order to remove all their possessions was only harassment of the family, or whether it took so long to demolish the home in Yatta that they never got around to the Jaber house. Will it be demolished tomorrow?

Harriet told her story of what happened in Yatta. The mayor of Hebron, a member of the Legislative Council, the head of Fatah in Hebron, and other dignitaries from Hebron were in the house that was to be demolished, along with members of the family. Harriet and Terry were with them. The Israeli soldiers tried to get them to leave, threatened them, and after a long, tense time, the Palestinians did leave. But they first stood up to the Israeli soldiers. The soldiers were not able to do their dastardly deed without opposition and protest.

The bulldozer quickly demolished the house. It was soon all over for the soldiers, but the pain, the anguish, the horror, will remain in the lives of those Palestinians for a long time. On Sunday the Israeli government had said it was stopping home demolitions. The Palestinians were right; the government was lying.

Soon I had said good-bye to the other team members and was in a taxi with Harriet, Amos, and other Israelis, headed to Jerusalem. We then got in the van of the Palestinian Christian from Haifa. They took me to the airport in Tel Aviv where I am now waiting for my 1:40 a.m. flight.

That ride was a special healing experience for me. I needed to be with loving, caring, open, compassionate Israelis, since I am filled with a lot of anger toward Israelis. We had a wonderful time of sharing about Hebron, peace, communal living, faith, sustainability, etc. Everywhere on this earth God has people whose hearts are open to love. I need to remember that.

I especially respect Harriet who was part of our team the past six days. It was good to have an Israeli perspective. She challenged us in a number of ways, and showed courage and sensitivity to the Palestinians. It is one thing for me to come into Hebron as someone removed from the conflict, but she had to cross "enemy lines" and reach out to those who are supposed to be her enemies, and who are supposed to think of her as their enemy. Barriers were broken down. Relationships were established. Harriet said she is coming back on Saturday. I wish I could be there.

March 21, 1997, Friday

I am sitting in front of the White House in Washington, D.C., participating in another part of our fast. Rich Meyer of CPT has been here for the past week and will be here until the fast ends Easter Sunday morning. I came yesterday to spend two days fasting here, to join the spiritual struggle here in the U.S. capital where so many decisions are made that result in the death and suffering of so many people.

Bringing the fast to this center of power is an experiment. There is so much we do not understand about the spiritual nature of powers like racism, militarism, and other forms of oppression. We are unable to see or understand the meaning and consequences of even little acts on our part. What we can do is take small steps of witnessing to the powers, and trust that somehow these steps may be used of God in the larger cosmic struggle of good and evil.

I just returned from spending much of the day visiting congressional offices in the Senate and House of Representatives. To each person I spoke with, I showed a piece of tile floor from a demolished home in Hebron, and explained that just recently children had been playing on that floor. I talked about home demolitions, our fast, and the importance of changing U.S. policy toward Israel.

It was sobering to realize not only the ignorance of people who are helping make momentous decisions, but even more the general lack of desire to learn more and question prevailing assumptions. There seemed to be much more interest in defending current U.S. policy in the region than in asking any serious questions about that policy, even of someone who has experienced the situation firsthand.

The high point of my time here was talking to Ted Strickland, who is the representative from my home district in Ohio. He listened. He questioned me to learn more about the situation in Palestine. He expressed genuine concern for what is happening to the Israeli and Palestinian people. He wanted to know about CPT. How refreshing it was to find one person who displayed an open, searching, caring spirit. I also had a good talk with an aide of Rep. Nick Rahall, whom I met in Hebron last year.

Yesterday afternoon I went to the State Department to talk with a staff person in the office of Israel-Arab relations. I was part of a group of five CPT members, plus Daryl Byler of the Mennonite Central Committee's Washington office, who introduced us.

Rich Meyer talked about the reason for the fast. I gave a brief report of my time in Hebron and the beginning of the fast while putting pieces of demolished homes on the State Department official's desk. Jeff Heie showed a large picture of a house being demolished, which seemed to shock the State Department officer. Bob Naiman talked about being arrested on the roof of a house that was being demolished. Wendy Lehman told about Hebron residents asking, where is the peace? We reported that Cliff and Anne had just been arrested trying to chain themselves to the U.S. Consulate in West Jerusalem, seeking to get the attention of the U.S. State Department. I used the big map of the West Bank in the office to demonstrate how the Israelis are confiscating more and more of the West Bank, and how this looks like ethnic cleansing and the creation of Bantustans.

This resulted in an hour-long discussion with the official trying to explain the reasons for U.S. policy positions, while we repeatedly questioned the assumptions behind those positions. The State Department man tried to defend the recent U.S. veto of a United Nations resolution which criticizes the building of a new settlement on Mount Abu Ghneim. He explained that the U.S. wants to keep the UN out of the peace process. We argued that keeping the UN out of the process works to both nullify past UN resolutions on Palestine, and to keep those nations that are critical of Israeli policy out of the process. We told him how disappointed we were with the Clinton Administration expressing only mild disapproval over major Israeli violations of the peace process, while continuing to give them more money to commit those violations. We pointed out that this makes U.S. policy appear not only unbalanced toward the Israeli position, but even subservient to Israeli interests.

We questioned the notion that it is better not to strongly object to Israeli policies, because that only makes Israel more intransigent. In response to that idea, we pointed out that when the U.S. finally ended support for apartheid in South Africa, that apartheid system soon ended.

We also questioned the notion that the U.S. government needs to defer to the Israel lobby, arguing that this gives a false picture of American Jews, the majority of whom do not support Israeli violations of Palestinian human rights, and helps feed anti-Semitism by exaggerating the power of the Israel lobby and ignoring the fact that most American Jews are not as unreasonable as U.S. policy would indicate.

The State Department officer took notes on what we said and promised to send our concerns to his superiors. We parted on a friendly note.

Everywhere I went I saw monuments that glorify past wars and reaffirm the country's commitment to violence as a way of life. I don't see any evidence that we changed any policy, but what we did seems right. It was one more little witness, one more step on the way. We made our witness one more time. We will need to continue making our witness.

Because of many commitments
and needs at home, I was unable
to go to Hebron last year. Now, two
years since last being in Hebron, I
am being sent by my community
for another tour of duty in
Hebron.

January 29—March 8, 1999

January 29, 1999, Friday

I am now back in Hebron, having arrived here this evening. Michael Goode was here to welcome me, and soon I was settled in. Dianne Roe came down from the women's apartment upstairs. It was good to see her again. Most of the team is gone for a few days.

Michael and I were soon out on the street doing night patrol. It was exciting to walk the streets of Hebron again. Immediately I was in the thick of things. An Israeli soldier stopped us to chat. He told us that one of our team had called the soldiers Nazis. I told him I find it hard to believe that any of our team would do that, and if someone did, I would express my concerns to that person. I explained that many lies have been spread about our team. Soon another soldier came and told the first soldier that he was not to talk with us. So we continued our walk.

We saw a group of about ten Palestinian teenagers. Soon some soldiers came, had them stand against a wall, and then searched them. They spoke rudely to the boys and physically roughed up one of them. I walked over and stood close to the soldiers, watched them, and asked them to treat the Palestinians with respect. As I confronted the soldiers, I thought of Cliff Kindy, who taught me to be assertive with the soldiers.

January 30, 1999, Saturday

It was exciting to walk around the market, see the familiar sights, and meet old friends. I was impressed with how much restoration has been done here in the old city during the past two years. Many of the crumbling 800-year-old buildings have either been restored or are in the process of being restored. That is encouraging. Those old buildings and archways are beautiful and give a feel for what life must have been like here 2,000 years ago.

Today was Sabbath, so Michael and I spent time on the street this afternoon. I was impressed with how mellow everything was. I did receive some hostility from a few settler youth, but I was cursed or spat at only about three times.

This evening Rich Meyer came back from visiting families whose homes are in danger of being demolished. Osaid, a young Palestinian, was with him. He had been translating for Rich. CPT has received some money from the Pontifical Institute to pay for translators, which is very helpful in visiting families. After visiting awhile, Michael and I accompanied Osaid out of the Israeli-controlled area to where he felt more safe. We did a patrol around the city. Everything was quiet.

As we were walking by the checkpoint below Tel Rumeida there was a group of about eight Israeli soldiers standing there. One of them seemed to mock us by singing in a high pitched voice, "CPT, CPT." I couldn't resist responding to that, so in a pep rally-type chant said, "CPT, CPT. Yeah, yeah!" They all laughed. I think it worked to counter the mocking spirit by getting us all to laugh together.

Sara Reshly came back this evening from a break time at home in the United States.

January 31, 1999, Sunday

We all headed to Jerusalem this morning for worship. Some Palestinian women who had no permits to get into Jerusalem were in the taxi. Near the soldier checkpoint before the tunnel, we turned off the road and drove to the top of the steep hill to let the women out so they could walk down the hill to the road on the other side of the tunnel and checkpoint. We drove back down the hill, went through the checkpoint, and on the other side of the tunnel picked up the women.

How sad and ridiculous. The restrictions put on the Palestinians obviously have nothing to do with security. They only have to do with making life hard for the people whose land the Israelis occupy. This means extra time lost for the Palestinians, extra wear and tear on their vehicles, extra fuel burned. It is another wire in the invisible cage built around those who are oppressed. I wondered why we didn't walk with the women, but was told that it might feel uncomfortable to them.

We got back and soon Jamey Bouwmeester, Pierre Shantz, and Joanne (Jake) Kaufman came home after being away a few days. Now the whole team is here, all eight of us.

February 1, 1999, Monday

We went to the park across from the tomb of the patriarchs and matriarchs for morning worship. It was good to be gathered as a whole team and to worship again in the park, in the midst of all the strife here. I then picked up a little trash there. This is no longer a team activity, but I wanted to do it for myself.

We then came back to the apartment for a team meeting. I am quite impressed with this group. So much wisdom and energy. It appears the team is working well together. Most of the meeting concerned details and tasks. It appears that opposing home demolitions and intervening on the street here are the two priorities right now for the team.

Jake, Michael, and I went to Jerusalem this afternoon to attend a demonstration organized by the Israeli Committee against House Demolitions (ICAHD). Last week the Israeli military demolished a Palestinian home in the village of Issawiyeh, just outside of Jerusalem. People of the village protested the bulldozing of their home, and the Israeli soldiers shot and killed Zaki Ubaied, a young father in his early twenties. He was shot in the head and neck with three rubber-coated bullets.

Israeli peace activists organized this demonstration, which began with a vigil in front of the National Police Headquarters in Jerusalem. I eagerly joined the group of about a hundred people, mostly Israelis and some Palestinians. I was given a large picture of Zaki to hold. I felt deeply honored and moved to hold his picture.

I met a number of Israeli peace activists I have known from the past, including Amos and Harriet, and Arik Ascherman. It was good to see them again and catch up on what has been happening with them. I sensed a lot of Israelis are discouraged, but feel the need to keep on keeping on. God bless them.

After about an hour we got in cars and drove to Issawiyeh. We walked in a procession down into the village. Some Palestinian boys helped me hold the picture of Zaki. We went to the home of Zaki's family, went in and greeted his parents and wife. Then, huddled together in the large living room, the Palestinians shared their feelings of anger and oppression to the Israelis in the room. The Israelis listened. How important it is to just listen to the cries of the oppressed. I deeply respect these Israeli peace activists.

We were served dates and coffee, and then walked back up the hill where we were treated on the street to fruit juice by the Palestinians.

The whole event was too profound for words. Israelis going to the home of a Palestinian murdered by other Israelis to express their sorrow and ask forgiveness. Jews, Muslims, and Christians standing together, opposing oppression and seeking reconciliation. Here was a sign of God's kingdom. Here was a sign of hope, hope expressed in concrete deeds, a true sign of peace. Issawiyeh means the place of Jesus. Tradition says that Jesus stopped here. I sensed Jesus was there today.

This morning the team began a seven-day fast, a time of

personal searching for clarity and direction. It is exciting to think of what could come out of this fast.

February 2, 1999, Tuesday

This morning I watched a large group of young women dressed in military uniforms come to the steps leading up to the Jewish side of the synagogue/mosque. They listened to a lecture by a soldier there. It was disheartening to see these girls being trained for war, being trained to oppress, dominate, and control. I wish they were being trained in nonviolence, in dealing with conflicts in creative, loving, and redemptive ways. How different from what I experienced yesterday, with Israelis going to Palestinians in humility and repentance. What does it mean for a society to force everyone, men and women, to be soldiers until they are in their late 50s?

I watched an Israeli soldier trying to give a young Palestinian a hard time. The soldier was holding his pass, and seemed to be trying to coerce the Palestinian into doing something. The Palestinian seemed to be refusing, The soldier was becoming more and more adamant and more and more angry. The Palestinian then simply turned his back and calmly walked away without his identity card. The soldier yelled and ran after him. The Palestinian didn't go far before stopping.

The conversation continued, but the Palestinian had won a major victory, because he made the soldier come after him, thus gaining a major amount of power in the situation. The soldier was quite frustrated and angry. I wonder what he would have done if I had not been watching. Soon a TIPH observer came and stood there with his camera ready. The soldier soon gave the man his pass back and the Palestinian walked away. The soldier went back to his post and sat down, really frustrated.

This afternoon I told this story to two TIPH observers who said they often find that, because of their presence, the soldiers back down, while if the observers are not there, the Palestinian is more likely to be abused. I heard a story of TIPH people walking around a corner where Israeli soldiers had detained a Palestinian, who was being very meek and submissive, cowering before the soldiers. When the Palestinian saw the TIPH people, he immediately straightened up and started arguing with the soldiers.

For our week of fasting we are trying to have an evening "meal without food," a time for prayer, reflection, and sharing. I missed it last evening because of being in Issawiyeh. This evening there was a lot of searching and seeking around what our response should be to the closing of Palestinian foot traffic on Shuhada Street in front of the Beit Hadassah settlement. For the past three months no Palestinians have been allowed to walk past the settlement. This means that Palestinians must walk a long way around, down through the market, or up a steep hill and back down. This is a clear violation of the Hebron Agreement two years ago and an affront to the United States, which spent $2 million two years ago fixing up this street, on the promise that it would be opened.

Our team, in solidarity with the Palestinians, is refusing to walk where Palestinians may not walk. We are explaining to the soldiers that we cannot cooperate with racist policies.

February 3, 1999, Wednesday

Doug Pritchard and Bob Holmes arrived this evening. Bob is a part of the Catholic Worker movement. He will be with us for two weeks. Doug is CPT director for Canada and will be with us for four weeks. Both are from Toronto. There are nine people on the team now, not counting Rich who is traveling with his wife.

We all had supper without food this evening, a time of sharing together. Much of it ended up as an orientation for Bob and Doug. Some of the discussion centered around the issue of Shuhada Street being closed.

Michael and I then took Doug and Bob out on night patrol. What better way to get them oriented? They seemed quite surprised at all the soldiers everywhere. I guess I have sort of accepted it.

As we were walking around we got a phone call from a friend that there was tear gas somewhere south of the market. Michael and Bob went to where tear gas had been reported. Other team members also ended up there. It turned out that for the past three or four nights soldiers have been shooting tear gas into a Palestinian house in the Abu Sneineh neighborhood. Our team members saw windows broken by the tear gas canisters. There was a strong smell of tear gas in the house. This neighborhood is known as a strong Hamas area.

February 4, 1999, Thursday

Our time of worship this morning was a send-off for Sara and Pierre, who were going to Jerusalem to the Ministry of Justice to try to get back their passports which were taken from them when they were arrested about three weeks ago (Jan. 10).

Maybe I should tell that story here. Because of a settler van being shot at and three settler women being injured, the Israeli-controlled area of Hebron was put under curfew for a week. This was during Ramadan, and included the closing of the Ibrahimi Mosque. In response, a group of Palestinians, dressed in business suits, attempted a nonviolent march to the mosque to protest the collective punishment, challenge the curfew, and pray at the mosque. The leaders of the march were committed to nonviolence and insisted that no stones be thrown.

CPT agreed to have a presence at the demonstration to help prevent any violence from occurring. Sara and Pierre were in the front of the group, prepared to tell any soldiers that the march was nonviolent and to intervene if there was any trouble.

Suddenly, a group of Israeli soldiers came running down a side street and took up firing positions near the march. CPTers immediately jumped in front of the guns, shouting, "Don't shoot, don't shoot!" The soldiers did not shoot, but were quite frustrated with the CPTers and wanted to disperse the crowd. They threw four sound grenades at the demonstrators that exploded in the middle of the crowd. They are intended only to make a loud noise, but they injured four Palestinians.

Instead of leaving, the demonstrators regrouped. The soldiers stood in a line preventing the march from proceeding. CPTers stood between the soldiers and demonstrators. There were negotiations between the leaders of the march and military officers. Then one soldier began aggressively pushing back demonstrators. Things became tense. A few stones were thrown. The soldiers again took up firing positions and again CPTers stood in front of the guns, begging the soldiers not to shoot. One of our team put her hat over the end of an M-16 rifle, and another her hand over the end of a gun. CPTers were physically removed from the front line of the standoff.

One officer was furious. This was the second time CPT had directly interfered with soldiers carrying out orders. He screamed into Pierre's face, telling him to leave the area. Pierre explained that the demonstrators were nonviolent and that the officer should keep his soldiers under control. The officer slapped Pierre three times in the face. Pierre replied, "That's going in the report." The officer then went to Mark Frey, yelling for him to leave the area. Mark remained still for a bit, and then moved back.

After about twenty minutes the Israeli civilian police arrived. The angry officer pointed out Pierre and had him arrested. Sara stepped up and asked why they were arresting Pierre. They immediately arrested her. They briefly detained two other CPTers, but they were soon released.

The standoff continued. The Palestinian leaders worked

hard to keep things under control. One Druze soldier was quite helpful, telling his soldiers to back off a bit. Since he spoke Arabic, he also called on the Palestinians to remain calm. The protest leaders decided to pray there in the street, putting down cardboard on the street to kneel on for the prayers. They then announced that the demonstration was over.

CPTers decided to leave the area, not wanting to give any support or encouragement for people remaining in the area which could result in violence. The point of the march had been made. CPT had done what we were asked to do. Journalists reported that things remained calm afterward, even though many people remained in the area.

CPT did what we say we are here for. We got in the way. We helped make it possible for the powerless to act. The curfew was challenged. We prevented violence. The soldiers paid a price, in the form of negative media coverage around the world.

Why was this action so effective? First, CPT has had over three years of training and preparation for this event through our experience in Hebron. The team knew the situation and could quickly assess the dynamics of what was happening. They were prepared to make quick decisions. They had developed many relationships here which helped form the basis for trust on both sides. They did not know what would happen that day, but they had prepared. Daily prayer gave spiritual grounding for what happened that day. They also had done nonviolence training. Having one side clearly committed to nonviolence made CPT's role much less difficult. It is much more difficult to intervene in clashes when both sides are using violence.

Those involved in that action feel that their standing right in front of the guns made it much more difficult for the soldiers to shoot. Being very close to the soldiers helped, for the closeness made everything more personal. To use violence against another person, one must first depersonalize the enemy. Likewise, having Palestinians eyeball-to-eyeball with Israeli soldiers made it harder to throw stones at the soldiers.

The event created an incredible amount of media attention around the world, exposing the situation here in Hebron and what is happening in the occupation. All over the world, that is, except in the United States. The United States media does almost no reporting of these kinds of actions. The events related in this book received almost no coverage in the United States media, but many were widely covered in the rest of the world.

Sara and Pierre were taken to court in Jerusalem the next day, Pierre in handcuffs with shackles on his feet. The police wanted them deported or banned from Hebron. The judge let them go. Charges were dismissed. Sara and Pierre are back here, doing the same things they were doing before.

I heard this story back home before I returned here, and shared it with quite a few of my friends. Many responded by praising the CPTers for their courage. I don't see it that way. To be brave is to muster up a great deal of courage, to exert a tremendous human effort. That is not what happened. I don't think it was courage. I think they were simply responding to God's Spirit. They were simply responding out of love, just as any of us would respond immediately to anyone we love who is in danger. That is not courage. That is love. Love is always ready to respond, to be there for the ones we love.

The point is not to expect that we should accomplish superhuman feats, and then shrink back fearing we are not good enough. The point is to be open to God's Spirit, to love. That is our task: to be open, to be ready to respond, to not be centered on self. That is something we can all do.

So I will not praise them for being brave. I can only thank them for being ready to respond to God's Spirit, for having spiritually prepared themselves, for choosing to be in a situation that requires openness and love. But the praise belongs to God.

Now, back to today. We began our time of worship with

Dianne sharing that we are on holy ground. Places of conflict and struggle are holy ground. God is especially present in places of suffering and oppression.

We walked up Shuhada Street toward Beit Hadassah and started climbing the steps there. We wanted to follow the more difficult way Palestinians are forced to walk because the street has been closed to them for the past three months. We planned to have a time of worship at the top of the steps. As we started up the steps a soldier stopped us and told us that we can walk on the street since it is now open to Palestinians. A victory! Holy ground.

We decided to walk *on* the street, and proceeded a short distance to the place where CPT had prevented the soldiers from shooting. We wanted to have a time of prayer on that holy ground. We then said good-bye to Sara and Pierre and sent them on their way. Unfortunately, they were not able to get their passports as was promised.

Shortly after we got back to our apartment we received a phone call that Fayez and Hudda Jaber's house was being demolished. Five of us quickly got a taxi out to the Beqa'a valley, just east of Hebron. When we arrived, the house had already been demolished. The bulldozer and soldiers were gone. A group of women sat in front of the ruins and a group of men sat on top of the collapsed roof. We silently greeted people and sat with them in silence. There was nothing to say. The horror was too profound for words. Everyone was in mourning. It felt like a funeral. We were on holy ground.

Many thoughts went through my mind as we sat there in silence. How can people be so cruel as to demolish someone's home? Lots of feelings of anger and disgust welled up in me. I thought of all the pain the family was experiencing. Fayez was visibly having a hard time. What was he to do with all the feelings welling up inside him?

These demolitions have nothing to do with Israeli security. In fact, they make Israel less secure by building hatred for Israel. This is an insidious, calculated policy of breaking the

Palestinians' spirit and destroying their culture. It is a deep personal affront to destroy a person's home. It deliberately aims at creating deep emotional pain and scars. These are not isolated acts of extremism by disturbed individuals. This is official Israeli government policy, paid for by the United States. All this is illegal under international law and a direct violation of the Oslo peace agreements.

The family explained to us that they have documents for their land dating back to the Ottoman period, and from the British period. This was the fourth time this family has had a home demolished. It happened first in 1982, then in 1989, then 1996, and today. Ten other homes within view from here have been demolished, and twenty-two more homes in the area have demolition orders. This is ethnic cleansing. The settlements of Kiryat Arba and Givat Harsina on both sides want to expand.

The family vowed that they will not give up. They will rebuild. Their spirit clearly has not been broken. I picked up an olive branch, a symbol of peace and hope, which had been broken off a tree by the bulldozer. That bulldozer was trying to destroy peace, but it will not succeed. God will have the last word.

All day I sat on top of the rubble with the larger Jaber family and many friends who came by to share in the pain. What an honor to have shared the day with the family. Fayez's cousin, Atta Jaber, came and spent the afternoon with us. It was his house that I was at on my last day here two years ago (March 5, 1997), a house we expected to be demolished. It was not demolished that day, but fell to the bulldozer last August. People quickly rebuilt the Jaber house, and this second house was demolished in September last year—twenty-seven days after the first demolition. The family then moved into a tent for several months.

One ray of hope was a call from a Jewish rabbi, Arik Ascherman, who called today to express his sorrow and offer support to the Jaber family. He works with Rabbis for

Human Rights and the Israeli Campaign Against House Demolitions (ICAHD).

February 5, 1999, Friday

After worship this morning some of us went out to the Beqa'a valley to visit families whose homes are under demolition orders. First we stopped at the home of Asmi and Jawaher Jaber. Doug did an initial interview with the family, which is being paired with his Mennonite congregation back in Toronto.

A major thrust of CPT work here now is opposing home demolitions. In addition to being ready to do civil disobedience when home demolitions are occurring, we have started the Campaign for Secure Dwellings (CSD), a program to pair Palestinian families who have demolition orders on their homes with churches, synagogues, and mosques in North America. The congregations are committed to correspond with their families, pray for their families, and to put moral pressure on their governments and the Israeli government to stop home demolitions. We now have paired over 50 families with congregations.

A major part of our work here is visiting these families, writing up profiles of each family to send to congregations, and making follow-up visits, which takes a lot of time given Arabic hospitality.

This campaign is closely linked with the Israeli Campaign Against House Demolitions (ICAHD), which works both at building opposition in Israel to home demolitions, and relating to Palestinian families, including illegally helping Palestinian families rebuild their homes. This work was started by Harriet Lewis who spent a week with us during our fast two years ago. After she personally experienced a home demolition that week, she went back to Israel determined to work against this monstrous evil. I now see that CSD and ICAHD are results of our 700-hour fast two years ago.

We walked to Fayez and Hudda's house which was demolished yesterday. The family had already started clearing away rubble. They were digging out their belongings from under the rubble, putting them on top of the pile. It was not a pretty sight.

Our next visit was with Atta's parents and his larger family. In back of the house is a large cave which was hollowed out of the rock a long time ago, and had been the family's dwelling in the past. Down near Yatta, many Palestinian shepherds still live in these caves. CPTers have witnessed the bulldozing of some of these cave homes.

I saw where the Israelis bulldozed the orchards and gardens behind the Jaber house last September and then again a few weeks ago. Atta's brother Jaudi had put a lot of work into this orchard. I was told it was a work of art, sculptured terraces on the hillside. Now it is a piece of rough, bare bulldozed land. This is a first step for the nearby settlers to confiscate this land. The settlers have also bulldozed a road above the house.

Almost immediately after signing the recent Wye Agreement, Ariel Sharon, the Israeli Foreign Minister, publicly urged the settlers to seize every hilltop. The government's wishes are being carried out.

Atta walked me part of the way to Omar and Lamia Sultan's house. I saw the ruins of Atta's two demolished homes across the bypass road from his parents' home. Atta said he will not clear the rubble from his houses, but keep them as is for a museum. Atta pointed out two hilltops which have recently been confiscated and new roads built on them. I also saw the new gas station being built on top of the Jaber family vineyard.

I had several reasons for visiting the Sultan family. This was a follow up visit for CSD, checking how things are going for them. I brought them a letter and some pictures from their paired congregation, College Mennonite Church in Goshen, Indiana. Even though they have a demolition order on their house, the Sultans are doing construction around the house. I have to admire their determination and resistance.

Another reason for visiting was to have an Arabic/English lesson with their son, Be'heh. After visiting with his father, Omar, a feisty man whom I immediately liked, Be'heh and I started our language session. I did some reading to him from my Arabic book, and he read to me from his English book. Mostly I helped him with his pronunciation and answered a lot of questions he had about what he read. Be'heh is in his last year of high school and wants to go to England to study. Will he ever have a chance?

It started raining and sleeting and I had some concerns about getting back to Hebron. I started to walk, hoping to hitch a ride to Hebron, but the family stopped me and insisted on driving me back to Hebron in their truck.

This evening the whole team went to Jerusalem for a Bible study which meets monthly at the home of Tom and Karen Getman. Tom is the World Vision director in Jerusalem. In addition to connecting with many evangelical workers in Palestine, we had a good Bible study. After the Bible study we stopped on the top of the Mount of Olives and looked over the city of Jerusalem. I recalled the prayer that Jesus prayed at this place. "O Jerusalem, O Jerusalem, if only you understood the way of peace." We need to pray for the peace of Jerusalem.

February 6, 1999, Saturday

After worship and a short team meeting this morning, we headed out to the Beqa'a valley to meet a group of Israelis who came to spend time with the two Palestinian families whose homes were demolished Thursday. They are from ICAHD and intend to help these families rebuild their homes. We met the group of about ten at Atta's parents' home. They were warmly received. They offered to help rebuild the terraces and replant the olive and fruit trees, but the family is fearful of what the Israeli response might be. We had tea together and then walked over to Fayez and Hudda's house that was demolished Thursday.

It was a powerful time. The Israelis came to apologize for what their country had done to this family and offer support in rebuilding. I felt overwhelmed with joy as I watched Palestinians and Israelis hugging and kissing each other beside the rubble. This is peace and it is possible. This is not the peace that lying government officials promise. This is real peace, the fruit of repentance and humility. The Israelis even brought a cake which we shared. There was also some joking around with Amos Gvirtz wearing Atta's kiffeyeh and Atta wearing Amos' hat. We were on holy ground.

The Israelis were visibly shaken by seeing the pile of rubble that only two days before was a home. They expressed a lot of anger and disgust at the Israeli government for this atrocity.

Our time this evening for our meal without food centered on brainstorming how we might support ICAHD in their campaign. We came up with a list of possible actions we could take. Actually, we have already sent out an urgent action alert, urging people to contact North American and Israeli officials to ask them to stop home demolitions.

February 7, 1999, Sunday

This evening at our meal without food we did more thinking about next steps in our campaign against home demolitions. Lots of good ideas were shared. It looks like we are going to suggest that churches do something around the theme "Tents for Lent" which would involve us having a tent here and asking churches in North America to set up tents to symbolize the lost homes of Palestinians.

We also got into a big discussion of whether to use words like apartheid, bantustans, and ethnic cleansing in our writings. Some feel that the words are too emotional and close minds, rather than facilitate communication. Others feel that these terms are accurate descriptions of what is occurring and that it is important to show the parallels between what is happening here and other historical events. There was agreement that we should not be making comparisons with the holocaust. Any reference to the holocaust can easily be misinterpreted.

When Cliff Kindy and Jeff Heie were arrested in the water truck incident three years ago, an Israeli soldier questioned Cliff why he was concerned about the situation here. Cliff explained that if he had been living in Nazi Germany he would have stood up for the Jews. For that, Jeff and Cliff were accused of calling the soldiers Nazis.

February 8, 1999, Monday

This morning we broke the fast which started last Monday. We had a half hour of silence, *and* then ate together. It was a joy to be eating together again, and to have this time together. We all feel good about the fast and agree that through it we have found a new sense of direction. We feel we are at the beginning of a new chapter of our work against home demolitions. It sounds exciting. We never know what to expect when we open ourselves to God's Spirit.

This morning five of us went to meet with "Major Rocky," who is the military liaison with international observers here in Hebron. We were meeting with him as a follow-up to Sara and Pierre being arrested. We didn't know what to expect. He had met with the team in the past and warned us that *we* have to follow the rules.

We met around the picnic table, behind a wire fence, in front of the police station by the synagogue/mosque. He had his M-16 and he had a bodyguard with an M-16. We were unarmed.

He began by repeating that if we are here we need to abide by the rules. We can observe and report, but not intervene. He said he has read our literature and understands that we believe in "getting in the way," but that if we do get in the way, we "might be" arrested. I had expected him to give us a hard time, maybe even threaten to expel the team. All he said was that if we didn't follow the rules, individually, there may be consequences, even not being able to come back into the country.

It seems that we have enough credibility and support here that it would be difficult for them to expel us. That is reassuring. We have had many arrests, but up to this point only Wendy Lehman and Bob Naiman have not been permitted to return to Israel.

"Major Rocky" is very articulate and likable. He speaks perfect English. He sounds quite liberal. We mostly listened. That was important, but we also asked important questions. Why are there double standards for Jews and Palestinians? Why is Shuhada Street closed to Palestinian cars? Why is Israel not abiding by the Wye and Oslo agreements or international law? Why is there collective punishment? His basic answer was security reasons. He kept referring to Arab terrorists, but didn't seem to be able to accept the reality of Israeli terrorism. He didn't want to discuss any issue in depth. His asking us to follow all the rules seemed rather ironic, since we would not even be here if Israel were following all their agreements and international law.

Here is a seemingly decent man who has accepted a worldview in which Israel is just, but threatened by enemies. He seems to be in denial about the injustices of the occupation. He told us how open, democratic, and fair the Israeli military is. We heard a classic example of the oppressor justifying the status quo, even seeing it as just. How do we break through these layers of protection? How do we help people see reality from other perspectives? I wish he could see what we are seeing.

February 9, 1999, Tuesday

Michael and I spent time walking the streets this morning. We stopped in the Ibrahimi Pottery Shop to talk with the people there. Radi Shabanah was there. He was in prison during my last time here. He told us that he was held for four months and never charged with anything, only accused of having thrown stones six years earlier during the Intafada. While he was in prison the military demolished his home. I was impressed with his attitude. I sensed no bitterness.

This afternoon Ahmed and Edna Sarbarnah came by and were very upset. Just yesterday they received a stop work order on their home. This is a first step to demolition. They are adding a room onto their house for their growing family. Ahmed was recently told by settlers that he could not prune his fruit trees. Edna is an Iraqi, Kurdish Jew who married a Palestinian. She is trying to raise her children in both cultures. They live in Beit Ummar. Abdel Hadi Hantash from the Land Defense Committee came and met with them and advised them on how to appeal in order to delay the process.

Abdel Hadi also reported to us that a shepherd near the Ma'on settlement south of Yatta was warned by Israeli soldiers not to take his 300 goats onto his land again or all 300 of them would be seized. The shepherd has deeds to his land, but the soldiers said it is state land.

February 12, 1999, Friday

This evening we did more brainstorming for our focus in the coming months. We hope to mobilize churches in North America to do something about home demolitions and land confiscation. The Chicago CPT office is putting together worship materials linking the suffering here to Lent. We seem to be pretty clear that we will put up a tent here similar to the ones Palestinian families are living in because their homes were demolished. We want to do some protest actions that will include civil disobedience. We want to rebuild homes, and we are planning to fast for Holy Week.

February 13, 1999, Saturday

We learned this morning that a group of people who have had their homes demolished tried to see Yasir Arafat last evening. They thought they had been promised that he would see them. They waited outside where he was staying until 1:00 this morning, but never did get to talk with him. They feel that Arafat has not shown enough concern about home demolitions.

After worship this morning we all went out to Fayez and Hudda Jaber's place for a day of clearing rubble. The Israelis promised to come today, pay for a tractor to help clear the rubble, and help work. The tractor turned out to be a big backhoe with a jackhammer, which easily turned the big slab of concrete to small pieces. It was sickening to see all the Jabers' work and money reduced to small chunks of concrete, but the work needed to be done. We salvaged some concrete blocks and helped clear away the rubble in preparation for rebuilding. When I was here last Thursday, the day of the demolition, Fayez was really hurting. Today, he seemed strong and determined to resist and rebuild, knowing full well that his home may soon be demolished again.

It was a day of deep emotions for me as we Christians, Muslims, and Jews worked side by side, resisting the powers of destruction. I knew we could be arrested for clearing away this rubble, as Cliff Kindy, Arik Ascherman, and two Palestinians were arrested less than two years ago at the Zalloom home near here. There was a mixture of sorrow and joy. Plum trees beside the rubble were starting to bloom. The daffodils were about to open. This was a day of hope. We were on holy ground.

Members of other families who have experienced demolitions of their homes joined us. One Palestinian came from north of Jerusalem. The coming together of Palestinian families helps them feel less isolated. Atta Jaber called this the beloved community of the refugees of "98," since they had all experienced demolitions in 1998.

We had a short meeting with Jeff Halper, the leader of ICAHD. That group wants to make a big push before the elections, to do as much as possible to stop the Israeli government and the settlers from creating new irreversible "facts on the ground." As part of their international campaign, they intend to help rebuild as many demolished homes as possible in the next two months. They have money. One Jewish person living in England just donated $25,000. They hope soon to do a three-day action, with a big press conference on a Thursday, and rebuilding as many homes as possible on Friday and Saturday. This will be aimed at a world audience, as well as at Israel.

They intend this to be a no-lose situation for Israeli peace groups. If they are permitted to rebuild, that will be a victory. If they are kept from rebuilding, they will camp out there as an act of resistance that will bring even more attention to the situation and if the military soon demolishes these houses again, that makes the military look bad.

The Red Cross provided a tent for the Jaber family to live in. We all met in the tent, visited, and had a big meal of maqlube, a traditional Palestinian dish. Jews, Muslims, and Christians sat together on the floor of the tent around two big platters of food. Each of us had a spoon and ate together from the platters. That is peace. We were on holy ground.

This evening four Palestinians from Beit Ummar stopped by. Two of them have had their homes demolished and are considering rebuilding, which is an awesome decision, because the consequences could be quite severe. In addition to going through the pain of having another home demolished, they run the risk of being beaten and spending time in prison. We will have Jeff Halper meet with them.

February 16, 1999, Tuesday

I led worship this morning and focused on repentance on this day before the beginning of Lent. I have been thinking a lot about Major Rocky and his ability to compartmentalize his life, to not see what he apparently does not want to see, to live in denial of the oppression he is helping to perpetuate.

When I see people doing things that I do not like, I try to

ask myself if I also do those things. Each of us is a lot like
Major Rocky. We each see a little bit of the truth, and maybe
even are willing to give our lives for that truth, but there is a
vast amount of truth that we do not see, and maybe do not
want to see. How can we be more open, so that we can also
see what we do not want to see?

I gave several examples. We see a lot of oppression here,
but this is one small, minor part of the whole system of domination and oppression. Think of the coming ecological devastation that will result from our unsustainable lifestyles. It
would be horrible if all Palestinians were removed from the
West Bank, and I want to oppose that. On the other hand,
the Palestinians could go somewhere else. But where will
Palestinians and Israelis go when the ecosystem collapses?
My other example was that the suffering caused by the state
of Israel is quite small compared with the suffering caused by
alcohol and tobacco. They cause millions of casualties each
year.

I told the story of a socialist speaking at a forum back in
Ohio, denouncing the global capitalist system while drinking
a can of Coca-Cola. In the question period someone asked
him about the inconsistency of denouncing corporations and
yet at the same time supporting them. He replied that how
we live our lives has nothing to do with the evils of the capitalist system.

How am I like Major Rocky? How am I in denial? How
am I not seeing what is right in front of me?

Anne Montgomery arrived around noon today.

February 17, 1999, Wednesday

This morning we went up to Al Adal Street to set up our
Tent for Lent, this being the first day of Lent. We set up the
tent at the same place our tent was two years ago. That
brought back lots of memories, including excitement about
all that tent meant and the possibilities that can come out of
this one. After we had the tent up, we had a time of worship

around a little fire, focusing on our theme of "a spark under the ashes," referring to the hopes that lie under all the unrealized dreams and frustrations of the Palestinian people. Doug and I stayed at the tent until 1:00 when others came back and relieved us. We cleaned up a lot of trash around the area and talked with curious people about the meaning of the tent, which symbolizes the tents which are given to Palestinian families after their homes are demolished.

This afternoon Doug and I went out to the Beqa'a valley to do CSD home visits. We went to Asmi and Jawaher Jaber's home, where we visited about two weeks ago. There are about twenty people living in their modest house, including their children.

Before 1975 their family lived in a cave shelter. In 1975 they got married and in 1982 built a two-room house for their family. They expanded this house in 1987, but didn't finish it. In 1996 they started to finish the house. They got a stop work order on November 5, 1998, and were told by the Israeli authorities that the area around their home belongs to the Israelis. The family has deeds dating back more than a hundred years.

Asmi said he told the Israelis that they are the new people here, that the land belongs to his family. He asked if he should live out in the wind and rain. The soldier said it meant nothing to him. The family has experienced continual harassment from the settlers, including having their car hit by two settler cars. Asmi suffered permanent injuries from that incident, and is unable to work.

We then went to the home of Abdel Jawad Al Rajabee and his brother Hammad Ramadan. They have thirty people living in three rooms and are building an addition to their house. They have received a stop work order on both the house and on a big cistern they are digging nearby to hold water for their farming. They said they will not stop building until the Israelis kill them. They also said that settlers have killed some of their grapes by poisoning the ground in the vineyard. They said they are willing to live in peace with the Israelis, but do not want this constant harassment.

Yesterday a bulldozer operator was arrested across the road for trying to dig a hole for a septic tank. The owner of the land had been given a stop work order, but felt the need to do something about the pool of raw sewage behind their house. Why would the Israelis prohibit a family from installing a septic tank behind their house? It seems rather clear that the Israelis intend to clear the whole area of Palestinians.

February 19, 1999, Friday

This morning at our team meeting I shared my concern about some team members drinking alcohol when in Jerusalem. I said that I would strongly oppose any drinking in our apartment, because if word got out in Hebron that we were serving alcohol here, it could discredit or even end our work here.

One of the arguments used was that we do many other things that are offensive to Muslims, such as men and women being together and women not covering their heads. It seems to me that this argument only raises more questions of what unexamined cultural baggage we bring with us and unintentionally impose on the culture here. To what extent can we respect cultures other than our own? In what ways are we being culturally imperialistic? What does cultural sensitivity mean?

The history of Western involvement in the rest of the world is not a good one. We have a long tradition of imposing our culture everywhere we go. It seems to me that when important issues are raised, we may need to defy cultural norms. But if we do so, we ought to have *very* good reasons for our actions. I can think of no good reason to violate the Muslim taboo on alcohol. I think of many good reasons not to do. Do we work here to stop one evil, yet help to spread another evil?

All Muslims here assume that Christians drink alcohol, we were told. Muslims do think Christians have low standards of morality. It seems reasonable to counter that image, rather than support it.

I also voiced concern about engaging in secretive actions instead of being open about everything we do. We lose freedom and spontaneity when we become secretive. Being secretive has led to paranoia and divisiveness in many peace groups. It extorts a heavy price. Part of the power of nonviolence is openness.

Our team meeting mainly centered around issues relating to the tent. The decision to put up the tent was rather hasty, and we did not think through a lot of the issues. For example, how much energy should we put into the tent and how does that affect all the other work we are doing? There seemed to be agreement that we should not sacrifice the other work we are doing.

This afternoon Dianne, Doug, and I went with Tariq, our translator, to visit with Abdel Wahab and Zuhuur Idrees and their family, who have been driven from their land and now live in an apartment here in Hebron. On April 11, 1996, the Israeli military demolished their home, along with five other homes along the Beni Naim road near the Kiryat Arba settlement, just east of Hebron.

They had never received a stop work order or demolition order. But that did not prevent the Israeli military from demolishing their home. Abdel Wahab inherited the property from his grandfather, who divided his land among Abdel Wahab and his seven brothers. They spent approximately $30,000 on the house, and are still in debt, with nothing but ruins to show for all their effort and sacrifice. They had applied for a building permit.

We met Abdel Wahab's brother, Abdel Jawad, who was visiting his brother. His house was demolished on the same day. He had much the same story to tell. He said that an Israeli military officer had promised him that he would not allow Abdel Jawad's house to be demolished. On the day of the demolition, this officer was the one giving the orders. The family felt betrayed.

We saw a video of the demolition of their homes, taken by our journalist friend Mazen Dana. After he had done some filming, the soldiers chased him away and threatened to kill him. Dianne, Wendy Lehman, and Anne Montgomery witnessed these demolitions and are in the video.

It was difficult for me to watch the video with all the family gathered around us. It showed the women wailing and screaming, the children's faces expressing shock and fear, the men protesting, and the Israeli soldiers laughing as the walls of the houses crumbled before the bulldozer. Words cannot describe the insidiousness of destroying a family's home before their very eyes. The Israeli bulldozer systematically demolished each side of the concrete houses and then collapsed the concrete roof. The operator seemed to be quite experienced at what he was doing.

I wondered what was going through the minds of the children as they watched the video of their home being demolished. They will be telling this story to their grandchildren. If there is ever to be peace, injustices like this one must be dealt with and resolved. I apologized several times to the family because it is my government that paid for the demolition of their home. Their response was to welcome and accept us.

I wondered what these actions are doing to the soul of Israel. What does it mean for Israeli soldiers to laugh at another's grief, grief that they created? It seems to me that anyone who loves Israel must fight for the soul of Israel and work to stop this outrage. Supporting the actions of the Israeli government is not patriotism. I am grateful for ICAHD and the other Israeli peace groups.

The family expressed that their faith is in God. They have not given up. In fact, they said that they are ready to rebuild if the Israeli peace groups want to help them. We will give this information to ICAHD and the Palestinian Land Defense Committee.

This evening I read a booklet, *Hebron: Past, Present, and Forever,* written by Noam Arnon and published by the settlers here in Hebron. It does a good job of presenting the settler perspective of how Abraham and Sarah settled here, how Hebron became the center of Jewish life, and how the settlers see Hebron as an essential part of the "land of Israel." The book presents both the history of Jews in Hebron and the settlers' vision for the future: a growing, expanding Jewish community.

I could not but appreciate the hope and vision expressed in this book. Why should Jews not be allowed to live here? Why should they not be allowed to share in and live out the history of this place?

The problem with the book is that there is no recognition that Palestinians are also part of the history of Hebron, that Arabs are also the children of Abraham. The book presents Arabs only as terrorists and obstacles to Jewish dreams. Running through the book is the fear that Arabs want to kill Jews. There seems to be no understanding of why hostility exists between Arabs and Jews, or any vision of how both sides can get beyond the 1929 massacre of Jews and the 1994 Goldstein massacre of Arabs.

The story of the Hebron settlers is a tragedy. It didn't need to be this way. The settlers could have come here and been a blessing to Hebron. They could have been humble, they could have developed relationships with the Palestinians, they could have contributed to the economic, cultural, and spiritual life of Hebron. That didn't happen, and everyone is poorer for it.

It is hard for me to see how Jews can live here in peace and security if they are intent on confiscating Palestinian land, demolishing the homes of their neighbors, and treating the Palestinians as second class. How can there be peace or security built on the gun, rather than on God's love for all people? Are settlers willing to stop portraying Arabs as terrorists and begin expressing hope for peaceful relationships with their neighbors?

Can Palestinians be partners in a vision of a joint future for Hebron, or do the settlers envision an all-Jewish city with all Arabs removed? What steps are the settlers willing to take toward peace?

February 21, 1999, Sunday

Doug and I went to meeting for worship this morning with the congregation at Bethlehem Bible College. We then went to Jerusalem, walked around the old city, and then went to MCC for a hymn sing. This was a farewell for Carmen Pauls, who is going to Iraq with MCC.

As we were walking home from the taxi we were stopped by soldiers here at our street. They wanted to talk. They seemed open minded. When they referred to the violence of the Palestinians, I reminded them that eight Palestinians are killed by Israelis for every one Israeli that is killed by Palestinians. They said they are here to make sure that not one Israeli is killed. We said our purpose here is to reduce the number on both sides to zero.

February 22, 1999, Monday

We had worship in the tent this morning with some discussion of silence. What silences us? Our doubts and fears? The powers we are up against? Instead of being silenced, we can regain our courage and strength in silence. As we sat in silence, Israeli military jets thundered over us. The jets and guns are the antithesis of the power known in silence.

I spent the afternoon at the tent. Abdel Hadi Hantash came by. I asked him why there have been no home demolitions in the past two weeks. He said it is because the Israelis are feeling a lot of pressure right now, both at home and internationally. As soon as things settle down a bit, they will resume. So we need to keep up our work.

I just learned that ICAHD holds a vigil every morning at two homes in Jerusalem that are threatened to be demolished any day now. We need to keep the pressure on the authorities. I read that these homes are owned by two young families with no resources to go elsewhere.

This afternoon Doug and Dianne went to visit the Waheed and Manaal Zalloom family, whose home was demolished two years ago. This is the house where Dianne Roe and Bob Naiman were arrested for sitting on the roof before the house was demolished, where Cliff and Arik Ascherman were arrested for clearing away rubble. I was at the scene of the rubble several times two years ago. Waheed told Dianne and Doug that he was concerned about his children and grandchildren, fearing that they will hate the Israelis and not believe that peace is possible. This is a man who has experienced many horrible things from both settlers and soldiers. He said, "God addresses all peoples in the Holy Books. God did not create racism. The Koran says we are to love all people."

February 23, 1999, Tuesday
We had a big discussion about our tent in our team meeting this afternoon. It seems that the tent is a significant symbol for people in North America. We heard that Goshen College is putting up 48 tents, one for each home demolished in the Hebron District in 1998. That is encouraging. People are also staying in a tent at Messiah College.

We are having trouble seeing the significance of the tent for Hebron, however. Somehow it is not pulling people together here as we had hoped. We considered that maybe we should not put up the tent every day since it is taking a lot of energy. Instead we could put the tent up for special events.

February 24, 1999, Wednesday
This morning Yousef stopped by and wanted help, so Doug and I went with him and spent the day with his fami-

ly. Yousef and Zuhoor Al-Atrash have had a close relationship with CPT for the past two years. They live just south of Hebron at Al Sendas Mountain, in a beautiful area of rolling hills, vineyards, and olive trees. The Al-Atrash family has deeds for their land dating back to the Ottoman period.

Their first home was demolished in 1988. After the historic handshake between Arafat and Rabin on the White House lawn, the Al-Atrash family had a new sense of hope and rebuilt their house in 1995. This home was demolished on March 3, 1998. Zuhoor was alone with her youngest children when about 30 soldiers and a bulldozer came to the house. She locked herself into the house, but the soldiers broke in, put a gun to her three-year-old son's head, forced her out, and demolished the house. Most of their belongings were buried in the rubble.

This is no ordinary family. They immediately started rebuilding again. On March 8, approximately 100 settlers and about 30 soldiers came to issue a threat. They promised that if the family continued to rebuild, they would blow up the backhoe they were using. After this many Israeli peace activists and others started visiting the family. Arik Ascherman offered a rabbinical blessing on the house in Arabic, Hebrew, and English: "That house will stand that is built on a foundation of righteousness." CPT started a round-the-clock presence with the family as they continued to rebuild.

On March 22, while Rich Meyer was temporarily gone, soldiers came and arrested the parents and two of their children. An Israeli journalist recorded the event. Both CNN and Israeli TV showed soldiers beating, kicking, and dragging the mother by her hair over rocky, thorny ground. The mother and daughter were released that evening, but the father and son were held for a week. The soldiers confiscated the concrete mixer as part of this event. Israeli peace activists soon bought them a new concrete mixer.

On June 11, 1998, the soldiers again came and bulldozed

the house. This was the family's third demolition. Since last June the family has been living in a Red Cross tent on top of the floor of their former house. They have wooden pallets on the floor, covered by rugs. This is home for the parents and their ten children. The tent is surrounded by concrete rubble, the remains of their previous homes. Ten of their neighbor families have demolition orders on their homes. They are considering rebuilding again. Their Israeli friends are ready to help.

I am impressed with the strength of the Al-Atrash family, their resistance against oppression, against racism, against dehumanization. Around the tent and rubble, symbols of destruction, they are building terraced gardens, planting fruit trees and grapevines. I saw the new rosebush their fifteen-year-old daughter, Wila, has planted. Her former rosebush was smashed by a bulldozer during the demolition and became the inspiration for CPT's "Roses, Not Rubble" campaign, a slogan for CPT in the past year in our Campaign for Secure Dwellings. A lot of love is being put into those gardens, gardens which could be bulldozed any day.

Our work with the Al-Atrash family today is not primarily social service, but rather a statement to the Israeli government that the family has international support, and a warning that the Israeli government will pay a political price if they come again to destroy this family's dreams. We believe this is better protection than for the family to store up guns.

I was privileged to eat two delicious meals with the family in their tent today. I wish every Israeli, every person who fears Arabs or Muslims, could spend a few hours in that tent with the Al-Atrash family. They are not a threat to anyone. But they are threatened.

February 25, 1999, Thursday
At our team meeting this morning we decided to put up our tent two days each week, and to try to have some kind of special focus for those days. We also talked about sleeping

in Atta and Rodeina's tent one night. We are hoping to do several actions during this time.

Abdel Hadi came and informed us that there were clashes today between settlers and farmers just north of Hebron. The settlers were trying to prevent the Palestinian farmers from working their land.

Outside of the Ma'on settlement south of Hebron, the settlers bulldozed a big area of Palestinian land and began putting mobile homes there. This is, of course, illegal, but it is supported by the government. The soldiers detained a reporter for Palestinian Radio and prevented him from getting to the site to cover the event. At another place, four people were arrested yesterday for trying to plant trees on their land.

This is interesting. Everything is calm here in Hebron. I don't see soldiers or settlers harassing Palestinians. But out in the rural areas there is a massive land grab taking place. I guess this does not produce the publicity that demolishing homes does. Is the absence of home demolitions in the past three weeks a result of the focused international attention? Do we need to shift our focus to land confiscation?

February 26, 1999, Friday

I spent the morning scouting around to prepare for our role in a demonstration by the Hebron Solidarity Committee at noon today, in the park across from the Ibrahimi Mosque, to remember Goldstein's massacre of twenty-nine Muslims, killed while praying in the mosque five years ago yesterday. There were lots of police there and they were obviously prepared. They had put up barricades around a small area where the demonstrators would gather. I wondered what the settlers' reactions would be. Would many be there? Could we expect confrontations between settlers and demonstrators? What would our role be? We had agreed that since the demonstrators were calling for the removal of the settlers here, this was a demonstration we should not participate in. It is not for our team to take positions on issues that

Palestinians and Israelis need to decide. We can take stands on justice issues, however, and we do.

As it turned out, our presence was not needed. But it was interesting. There were about fifteen Israeli demonstrators, who in speeches over a megaphone mourned the massacre and called for the removal of the "racist" settlers, saying that nothing had changed since Goldstein murdered the Palestinians. They said that the mind-set behind that massacre is still alive, causing a lot of hostility and allowing a small settler community to dictate terms of life in Hebron.

About five settlers, including Noam Arnon, David Wilder, and Anat Cohen, were right in front of the demonstrators, yelling and interrupting them, calling them Nazis, and so forth. One settler woman told the news media her opinion of the Goldstein massacre: "You have to understand that hundreds of Jews have been killed by Arab terrorists. Sometimes we have to act to defend ourselves."

There were plenty of media people there, and the settlers were able to capture a lot of press attention away from the demonstrators. The confrontation lasted about an hour, and then everyone left. It was largely an event for the media. The whole scene seemed unreal. Here were the Israeli left and right wings confronting each other in a sea of news media and police, with a crowd of Palestinians watching from the sidelines. It did not seem like a very productive encounter, yet I had to admire the courage of Hebron Solidarity people who put themselves on the line in a hostile situation. How could they have been more creative in their witness?

I was mainly concerned about what was happening around the fringes of the crowd, and so spent most of my time walking around the edge, trying to be aware of the whole scene and possible problems that might evolve. The other CPTers all had cameras and were mostly in the middle, acting as journalists.

During the hour wait for the demonstration to begin, I had the chance to talk with quite a few people, including

David Wilder and Noam Arnon. I saw David walking around and wondered if I could talk with him. After waiting awhile, I cautiously approached him, greeted him, and asked how he was doing. He responded in a very guarded way, yet showed some openness to talking. It wasn't long before we were talking about CPT. I mostly listened. David said that CPT is a very negative presence here, that we are greatly adding to the violence and aiding and protecting the terrorists. He started to tell the story of how one CPT person had taken and hid the knife used to stab a settler girl here. I told him I was the one he was talking about. I told him how I remembered the event. I did a lot of active listening, repeating back to him that I heard him saying we are a nuisance and a threat to the safety of the settlers here. I said I thought it important that we be talking with each other.

Then I saw Noam Arnon. I went up to him and told him I had read his book, that I appreciated it, and that I had written a response to it that I wanted to share with him. He accepted the envelope and began to pour out a lot of anger toward me, accusing CPT of protecting terrorists, and endangering the lives of settlers by preventing the soldiers from doing their duties. He seemed to be referring to the event six weeks ago, when CPTers prevented soldiers from shooting nonviolent demonstrators. He said that if we prevent the soldiers from stopping the terrorists, the blood of innocent Israelis will be on our hands. He said that he saw us as greatly increasing the problems here. He told me that I am a member of the Ku Klux Klan.

He also brought up the knife incident again, and I again told him my story and reminded him of the Torah injunction against bearing false witness. He said he would check again with the people who claim to have seen me hide the knife. After listening to him express a lot of anger, I said to him that I think it is important that we be talking and suggested that he and several other settlers meet with several of us to try to understand each other.

I then said that I thought he and I have a lot in common. I said, for example, the settlers here believe in dressing very modestly, and that I respect that and share the same concerns about not dressing in provocative ways. I said that it would be good if we could affirm what we have in common. He seemed to appreciate my affirming one of his beliefs.

There was a lot I would have liked to have said to him about the horrible things we see in the settlers here, but that would have been totally inappropriate. I mostly needed to listen. Only God can change their hearts. But we can communicate God's love to them. I hope I did that. We parted on a somewhat positive note. I suggested he read what I wrote and then I would like to listen to his comments. He was noncommittal. As we parted, I said, "God bless you."

It is sobering to think how Israelis are being indoctrinated into a narrow, destructive theology, a theology that deeply contradicts the Torah, the basis of Judaism. According to the Torah, God's covenant is not only with Jews. God's covenant with Noah (Gen. 9:8-17) is not only with all people, but also with all creation. According to the Torah, God also made a covenant with Ishmael, the father of the Arab nations (Gen. 21:8-20). It is important that we worship the God of the universe revealed in the Torah, and not a little tribal god created out of our fear.

The call to Abraham and Sarah in Genesis 12 was for them and their children to be a blessing to the whole world. The coming of Israelis here to the West Bank has not been a blessing to the people here. It has been a curse, a contradiction to God's call to Abraham and Sarah.

February 27, 1999, Saturday

This was a quiet Sabbath. I spent much of the day walking the streets. Everything seemed calm. The settlers were carrying lots of guns today—handguns, Uzis, and other automatic weapons. This is the most settler guns I have ever seen since I arrived here this time. I wonder why all the guns today?

I have been reading about the Universal Declaration of Human Rights, which was adopted fifty years ago by the United Nations General Assembly. The state of Israel was also founded fifty years ago. The world has not done very well at respecting those standards by which nations can be judged. Here are a few of the principles (articles) that seem relevant to Israel/Palestine.

1. All human beings are born free and equal in dignity and rights.

2. Everyone is entitled to all the rights and freedoms set forth in this Declaration, without distinction of any kind, such as race, color, sex, language, religion, political or other opinion, national or social origin, property, birth, or other status.

3. Everyone has the right to life, liberty, and security of person.

5. No one shall be subjected to torture, or to cruel, inhuman or degrading treatment or punishment.

7. All are equal before the law and are entitled without any discrimination to equal protection of the law.

9. No one shall be subjected to arbitrary arrest, detention, or exile.

11. Everyone charged with a penal offense has the right to be presumed innocent until proved guilty according to the law in a public trial.

12. No one shall be subjected to arbitrary interference with his privacy, family, home, or correspondence, nor to attacks upon his honor or reputation.

18. Everyone has the right to freedom of thought, conscience, and religion; this right includes the freedom to change his religion or belief.

It is difficult to read these principles while living here in Hebron. I think of home demolitions, land confiscation, administrative detentions, torture, expulsions, denial of freedom of travel, ID confiscation, a double standard of justice, things that happen here every day. Why does the world not begin to put sanctions on Israel? The Palestinians keep asking me why there is one standard for Iraq, and another for Israel. What can I say? I am well aware that many countries violate these rights, including the Palestinian Authority and my own country.

These principles ring true to biblical faith. They are concrete expressions of the biblical doctrines of creation and the command to love our neighbor. The apostle Peter in the book of Acts affirms, "I truly understand that God shows no partiality, but in every nation anyone who fears him and does what is right is acceptable to him" (Acts 10:34-35). We must affirm the dignity and worth of every creature, for all have been created by God. To violate any of the above articles is both a violation of God's creation, and a violation of the command to love our neighbor.

March 1, 1999, Monday

I was walking up Shuhada Street this afternoon and saw some settler girls at the end of our alley. It looked like some Palestinian high school girls were confronting them. By the time I got there the Palestinian girls were leaving. I then noticed that the settler girls were trying to put up a banner. This is the Jewish festival of Purim, and tonight the party begins. Their banner had something to do with Purim.

I watched as they climbed up on a Palestinian house to tie up their banner. The soldiers just watched. I wondered if Palestinian youth would be allowed to climb up on a settlement building to put up their banners. Soon other soldiers came and seemed to be questioning the girls. It sounded like the settler girls were cursing the soldiers. Soon a mean looking settler man drove up and entered the discussion. The soldiers backed down, the banner went up, and it was all over. If the soldiers had not backed down, I imagine there would have been a big confrontation.

This being the big night for celebrating Purim, we wondered what to expect and what we should be doing. Last year on this night some settlers went on a rampage up into the Abu Sneineh neighborhood. They smashed the windows of ten or twelve Palestinian cars. The team had heard what sounded like gunshots coming from the area and went to investigate. Soldiers had sealed off the area, would not let Palestinians pass, and were trying to remove the settlers from the area. Some Palestinian youth were throwing stones at the soldiers.

Our journalist friend, Na'el, came late, when the problem was nearly over. Since the other journalists were leaving the area, he also began to leave. Suddenly the soldiers started shooting at him. People yelled at the soldiers to stop shooting, that he was a journalist. Na'el was shot four times, once while he was lying on the ground. He had a very serious head wound, was hospitalized quite a while, but now is fine.

We wondered what to expect tonight. As it turned out, everything was quiet. There were loud parties at Beit Romano and Avaraham Avinu, but no problems on the street.

March 2, 1999, Tuesday

We found out this morning that the settlers were going to have a parade today. So Mark Frey, who returned yesterday, and I went up to the checkpoint below Tel Rumeida and waited for the parade to come down the hill. There were soldiers everywhere. They were preventing schoolchildren from going to their homes, because the parade was about to pass. This was reasonable. People in every country have to wait for parades to pass. And making the children wait was for their own safety. But given the unequal power relationship between Israelis and Palestinians, even this seemed another building block in the whole system of oppression. I was impressed with the gentle, mild way the children, most of them girls, resisted. They kept challenging the soldiers, asking why they could not go, pushing a little, laughing, making a joke of it. They sure did not accept the role of powerless victims.

Soon the parade of a little more than a hundred people came. I wondered why there were not more, since the settlers claim that 450 settlers live here. They even had a band on a trailer pulled by a tractor. People were dressed in outlandish outfits. Purim is a bit like Halloween, a time to dress up in costumes and be silly. That sounds like fun, but in this context it wasn't very funny. In the context of the power dynamics and hostile relationships, it seemed downright offensive.

Some settlers wore big fake bushy beards. We think they represented Baruch Goldstein. Some of the settlers were dressed as Arabs. One settler woman had a Muslim veil over her face. It felt like an old-fashioned American minstrel show, in which white people made fun of black people by putting on blackface and acting stupid. Settlers making fun of Muslims is not funny, especially on the street here. The settlers were conspicuously drinking wine from bottles as they paraded on the street. This seemed intended to offend Muslims.

My favorite costume was a settler wearing a red kaffiyeh and one of our CPT hats. I thought that was funny. But the message was that CPT supports the "terrorists." That message was not very funny. I wonder how he got that hat.

I tried to keep some distance from the parade to avoid any confrontations with settlers. I greeted some of the settlers I knew. Some of them greeted me back. Some refused to acknowledge my presence. A few called me Nazi. One settler riding on the tractor motioned for me to come to him, indicating he wanted to say something to me. I went to within about six feet of him. He kept asking me to come closer, but for some reason that felt uncomfortable to me. He then told me that the settlers were going to get rid of us soon, and that he was going to kill me. He then, with a sinister look on his face, slowly slid his hand across his throat, indicating that he was going to slit my throat. I said, "Shalom, God bless you."

The parade lasted about three hours, slowly making its way down Shuhada Street to the Gutnick Center in front of the tomb of the patriarchs and matriarchs. There were various tense moments as the soldiers blocked all streets while the parade passed by. Some of the soldiers seemed very scared as they faced large groups of watching Palestinians.

The parade ended in front of the Gutnik Center where a big crowd had gathered. There were both Palestinian and settler youth looking for trouble, but nothing major happened. There were lots of firecrackers and toy guns, which was unnerving. I saw no settler guns. In the Gutnik Center children were pointing toy guns out the windows at the Palestinians and chanting, "Baruch Goldstein, Baruch Goldstein." I kept trying to position myself where there seemed to be the most chance of trouble developing. I also tried to be near soldiers to make it less likely a settler would attack me.

I would not say the day ended peacefully. I know the settlers didn't help their relationship with the Palestinian community here today. Their sad relationship with the people here was only reinforced.

March 3, 1999, Wednesday

I spent much of today watching a big settler party in front of the Avraham Avino settlement. Settlers were again dressed up in costume. There were a lot of children there, and lots of soldiers and police to protect them. I watched the soldiers pushing Palestinian children away. The Palestinian children were curious about all the costumes and party decorations. But they were pushed away. The party was only for Jews. This is apartheid in action. Suppose they gave a party and everyone was invited.

On the way up the street this afternoon Noam Arnon came up to me and said he read my review of his book. I said I was eager to hear his reactions. He said that I completely missed the point of his book, which is that Jews have been a small persecuted minority for thousands of years, and are a small persecuted minority here in Hebron, whom the Arabs want to kill. He asked why CPT doesn't say anything about Arabs killing Jews. Why don't we tell the Arab leaders to publicly condemn the violence of their own people? I tried to tell him that we condemn all violence, but that didn't satisfy him.

I said that my question about his book was whether he can accept Arabs living here with Jews. I reminded him that many settlers here have said that all of Hebron belongs to Jews and all Arabs have to leave. He said he accepts Arabs here. I said I appreciated him saying that. I asked him how we could get beyond the 1929 and Goldstein massacres and all the fear, but he could only focus on Arabs supposedly wanting to kill Jews.

This afternoon a settler came up to me on the street and wanted to talk. He said we are siding with the Arabs because we oppose home demolitions and criticize Israel. He said that only homes of terrorists are being demolished. He said that Prime Minister Rabin has given almost everything to the Arabs: over 90 percent of the West Bank.

I responded that, in fact, less than 10 percent has been handed over. He then admitted that this was true. I am trying to understand this. The settlers do not see themselves in any way as occupiers, but as a persecuted minority. Although many more Palestinians are killed each year than are Jews, the settlers can only see that Jews are being killed. Although settlers are confiscating Palestinian land every day and rapidly expanding their settlements, the settlers see everything being taken away from them. It sounds delusional to me.

At our team meeting this morning we talked about how our actions and those of ICAHD have succeeded in putting the issue of home demolitions on the table for the negotiations between Palestinians, Israelis, and Americans. We heard that U.S. Secretary of State Madeline Albright gets more letters about home demolitions than about any other Middle East issue. This is a result of coordinating concrete actions on the ground here with building support in Israel and North America, and with calling out that support for actions. In our urgent action alerts, for example, we call on our supporters to contact government officials about whatever issue we are working on.

Now that home demolitions have temporarily stopped, we feel we need to focus more on land confiscation. How can we do that? A demolished home makes a shocking picture, but a confiscated field looks the same as before.

March 4, 1999, Thursday

This morning five of us went with Abdel Hadi Hantash of the Land Defense committee to some land north of Hebron, just outside the settlement of Karmei Tzur. This land overlooks a gorgeous valley with a big mountain on the other side. Much of the bare, rocky mountain is terraced with narrow fields following the contours of the mountain. The terraces, which required much labor over centuries, hold the precious topsoil and produce a living for the farmers there.

Settlers recently bulldozed a road around the settlement. The new road is 500 to 800 feet below the settlement's boundary. This act was intended to greatly increase the amount of land owned by the settlement around its perimeter. The settlers have started putting in electric poles for lights along the new road. This is a first step in confiscating the land.

We heard that the Palestinian farmers have been protesting this illegal intrusion onto their land, and that the Israeli military has promised them that today they could return to their land. We went there this morning to accompany the farmers. We were prepared to be arrested if that seemed appropriate. When we arrived, a group of about thirty Palestinians were arguing with military authorities about the poles not having been removed, and their not being allowed on their land today as promised. The soldiers said that they needed to get a ruling from the court, and that they could not give permission for the farmers to return to their land as had been promised.

This, we are told, is standard procedure. The settlers confiscate, or put a road around Palestinian land as a first step toward final confiscation. The land then becomes "disputed land" and is put into the hands of the courts. After this, owners are no longer allowed on their land, and need to go to an Israeli court and fight to get back their property. They have only a slim chance of winning. This is not how I understand justice. If thieves come and take over my home, I do not expect the police and the law to be on their side, while I have to jump through legal hoops to get my house back. But things are different under occupation.

While the argument was going on we realized that down the hill, a group of elderly Palestinian women and a few men had begun digging out and sawing off the poles. We went and joined them. Soon some soldiers in a jeep on the road above us discovered what we were doing. They fired a shot over our heads to warn us to leave. Pierre called out to the soldiers, asking if they planned to shoot into an unarmed crowd. We continued our action, ignoring the soldiers. The soldiers then started firing tear gas canisters at us. My eyes and lungs began to burn. We moved just a short distance away from the tear gas, but continued our action. The Palestinian women started rolling big rocks onto the settler road to stop Israeli vehicles from approaching us. Palestinians started sawing off the next pole.

One elderly Palestinian woman began gagging and screaming, and seemed to be having convulsions. We later learned that this was an act. It certainly was an appropriate and powerful protest against the revolting and disgusting nature of the situation and the contemptible actions of the Israelis. The soldiers were not sure how to deal with these women, who were the heroines of the day. Their action went beyond reclaiming the land. Theirs was a proclamation of faith in God, in a love and justice that transcends unjust laws.

The soldiers came and told us to leave the area. At first we ignored them. I asked why the farmers were being ordered to leave their land. I asked why they were trespassing on Palestinian land and told them that I will leave if the Palestinians ask me to leave. I asked why they were protecting the settlers who are trying to steal this land. One of the soldiers referred to the holocaust to justify what they were doing.

In a very tense moment one soldier angrily said "bullshit." I gave him my standard reply to this kind of language. I informed him that I am an organic farmer, that I highly value bullshit, and that I wish that he would not use that word in such a derogatory way. A little humor seemed in order.

Since the Palestinians decided to leave and wait until Sunday before further action in the fields, we decided to also leave. This was not the time to be arrested. We, along with about ten Palestinians, walked very slowly up the long road, as slowly as possible, with about ten soldiers nudging us on. They were somewhat impatient with us. We were walking a fine line between resistance and compliance. As we walked we asked the soldiers lots of serious questions about the morality and legality of what they were doing and about the occupation in general. They heard an earful.

The high point for me was when we started singing, "We Shall Overcome." I had just told them about my having worked in the Civil Rights Movement with Martin Luther King Jr. We sang "We shall live in peace, Jews and Arabs together," etc. It must have been difficult for the soldiers. We were trying to confront them with the ugliness of the situation, and at the same time share a vision of a peaceful and just future.

In contrast to most land confiscations, this one has become public. That can make a big difference. The action this morning, with the news media present, puts pressure on the Israelis to do what is right, or pay a political price in the form of negative publicity. As one Palestinian said to us, this situation is set up to give the soldiers the chance to either do what is right, or to prove that they are liars, since they had promised that the land would be returned. Our team has been wrestling with how to focus world attention on land confiscations. This may be a new opening for us.

After coming back to Hebron, I went to visit a Hamas leader here in Hebron. He is one of the Palestinians who camped out for over a year on the border with Lebanon, refusing to be expelled from Palestine. Eventually Israel backed down. It was a warm time of sharing. I shared a bit about my interest in Islam and asked him what he thought was the essence and heart of Islam. He talked about the importance of faith and a personal relationship with God. He said Islam opposes violence, and claimed that some of the terrorist groups are supported by the enemies of Islam to discredit Islam, or supported by people who do not adequately understand Islam. He said there is a worldwide conspiracy against Islam. I apologized to him for the way Christians have treated Muslims in the past and also in the present.

He wanted to know about CPT, so I shared in depth about who we are. I also shared my dream of there being Muslim Peacemaker Teams (MPT). That led to a discussion of jihad (holy war) being a spiritual struggle. I quoted from Ephesians 6, that we wrestle not against flesh and blood, but against principalities and powers of evil. He said he believes the same thing. I left feeling very close to this man. We have a lot in common. It seems really important for Christians to develop relationships with people like him.

I highly value these opportunities for dialogue with Muslims. Possibly my most exciting experience sharing with Muslims was when two Hebronites, who were trying to get me to convert to Islam, took me to Friday prayers at Al Aqsa Mosque in Jerusalem. It was a thrill to experience the power of a large mass of people from all over the world kneeling before God with our faces on the floor.

Apparently my friends talked with an imam there and asked for help in getting me to convert, because after the prayers, a robed imam took me by the arm, led me out of the mosque, across the large courtyard, down into the old city, up the Via Dolorosa, to a mosque past the Church of the Holy Sepulchre. There I met with a group of Muslim leaders and had an intense dialogue. They pressed me to become Muslim. I shared with them my respect for Islam and the reasons it would be difficult for me to become a Muslim. I talked about the meaning of the cross, the understanding of love seen in Jesus, and my understanding of grace. As we left, I was hugged and kissed by all the Muslim leaders. What a privilege and gift that time was.

I was responsible for our time of worship this morning and gave a reflection on some of my struggles here, and how I am realizing how Amish I am. I am still very excited about CPT, but I am left with a deep uneasy feeling. It is not enough to oppose injustice and work for peace. Our task is much bigger than that. We are wrestling with principalities and powers. I am seeing that we can work for peace and still be serving the powers of evil in other areas of our lives. We can work for peace and justice and at the same time promote the cultural values of capitalism. Even worse, capitalist, technological, or sexist values can permeate everything we do.

The Amish understand that we need to live in a counter-culture that stands as a genuine alternative to capitalist society. It is naive to think we can both work for justice and accept capitalist cultural values. I then talked about 1 Peter 2:1-12, which calls for a new community, a new people.

Does our work for social justice become one more influence in the acculturation of Mennonites and Brethren into mainstream American culture? I have seen how participation in the peace movements of the 1960s included a major step toward acculturation for many Brethren and Mennonite youth. This included rejecting most of the Anabaptist worldview and reducing it to only a concern for social justice. I now look back on the peace movement of the '60s as an important aid for people in the peace churches in swallowing a big chunk of American culture. Is CPT a similar force of acculturation of the peace churches?

Is CPT, with all its wonderful aspects, another means for us to buy into capitalist values? I could have used many examples (alcohol, immodest dress, jewelry) but chose computers. Technology is not neutral. All technology carries within it implications and demands for values, lifestyle, and relationships. Getting an automobile means we lose close relationships with our neighbors, but develop relationships with people ten or twenty miles away. There is a deep wisdom in the Amish rejection of automobiles.

Technology has great seductive powers. It is difficult for me to argue that CPT should not use computers. They are an aid in getting our message out to the world. But with computers comes the world of the computer and video games, including violent games. Video games have a destructive effect on relationships in the team. Individuals spend much time playing alone or with one other person, which hinders the development of communal relationships. Not once since I have been here have we played a game together as a team. Play centers on the computer and is individualistic.

I then said a few words about the need for a new community, a real alternative to capitalist culture. My vision for CPT is not another capitalist reform, but the beginning of a new social order. I hope we don't think too small. Our call is to participate in the creation of a new social order. To the extent to which we cling to, are influenced by, and worship (give our devotion to) the old order, we are not open to the in-breaking of a new order.

March 5, 1999, Friday
JoAnne Lingle arrived this morning. She hopes to be here for a month. This afternoon we all went out to visit the Al-

Atrash family to celebrate Yousef's 39th birthday. A lot of people came. The family sang songs Yousef had written, songs about living in a tent, facing the rain and cold, and determination to never give up. There was a lot of joy and love expressed. They shared about their pain and suffering in losing their home, and their determination to not give up. They made a clear statement against terrorism, saying they do not want to engage in violence. They said they are willing to continue to suffer, but they believe peace will come.

The family was disappointed that no Israelis came. They called several Jews on the telephone to reconnect on this important occasion. Their Jewish friends have stood with them in their pain, and they deeply treasure those relationships. This is the love of God at work. We are witnessing miracles here. We were on holy ground this afternoon.

March 6, 1999, Saturday

I saw a picture of the women at the demonstration on Thursday in this morning's *Jerusalem Post*. It was a great picture, but gave the opposite message of what actually happened. The caption said that "Palestinians had tried to cut down streetlights around the perimeter of the Karmei Tzur settlement." This is factually correct, but gives the impression that the settlers are victims of Palestinian aggression. The opposite is true. It is the settlers who bulldozed a road and set up electric poles on Palestinian property. It is the settlers who destroyed Palestinian property, and did not remove the poles as they were supposed to have done. But the Palestinians are portrayed as aggressors. Those who control the media twist the facts to make them say what they want them to say.

March 8, 1999, Monday

On this, my last day here, I spent time tying up loose ends, walking around the market saying good-bye to people. I love this city and the people here. I don't want to leave.

After our team meeting this morning they had their send-off for me. CPT tradition is for the person leaving to give his or her final advice and wisdom to the team, and for team members to share with the person leaving. I shared my deep appreciation for the opportunity to be part of the team, and my respect and admiration for each team member. There is a lot of love, vision, and commitment here.

Going to Hebron seems to be
becoming a habit. I am excited
about CPT, part of my heart is in
Hebron, and I continue to sense
this deep calling to work for social
justice and reconciliation. So, I am
going back for a fourth trip to
Hebron. This stay will be for
nine weeks.

December 16, 1999—February 15, 2000

December 16, 1999, Thursday

I arrived back in Hebron last evening and was greeted by Natasha Krahn, Jake Kaufman, and Reinhard Kober, a schoolteacher from Germany. Later I saw Pierre Shantz. After a bit of orientation, I went to bed, totally exhausted, but too excited to sleep well. After a long time of lying awake, I was happy to hear the call to prayer this morning. I was eager to get up and get started. This is Ramadan, the Muslim month of fasting, which began on December 9, so I quickly ate something and got ready for another day of fasting. I began fasting back home as part of my spiritual preparation for my time here. I look forward again to participating in Ramadan here.

After worship, we had a team meeting. There are five of us on the team, a good group I think. Much of the time was spent brainstorming about how to respond to the massive amount of land confiscation and expansion of settlements happening now, despite the new government of Ehud Barak and the restart of the so-called peace process. The team has been thinking about dumping or sending dirt to Israeli embassies around the world to protest the greedy land confiscation. We played with variations on that theme and with ideas around Palestinian irrigation pipes which are being destroyed by the Israelis. It sounds exciting.

I spent the rest of the morning walking around the market, greeting many people I remember and getting a sense of where things are. It was interesting to walk the streets again and see how things have changed. They seem quite calm. The settlers are not nearly as provocative as they have been, and the soldiers seem more relaxed and less aggressive. Our team's work on the streets has almost ended, with the lessening violence and the presence of the international observers from Europe (TIPH).

As of last October, Shuhada Street is partially open to Palestinian traffic. Finally, after more than five years. The wholesale produce market and the gas station are still closed. There is a lot of construction at the settlement here.

Now there are stop signs and traffic lights in the Palestinian controlled part of the city, which until the past year were prohibited everywhere in the West Bank by Israeli authorities. I learned that most bypass roads, which were intended only for Jewish use, are now open to everyone. The Israelis figured out it was stupid to maintain "Jewish only" roads, since any vehicle on such a road would be an obvious target.

This afternoon I went out to the Beqa'a valley to visit the Omar and Lamia Sultan family, partner family to my home

Omar and Lamia Sultan, with grandson.

community in Ohio. That was a happy reunion, but I learned that they are receiving a lot of harassment from settlers who want their land. Since the end of November, settlers have been marching around their house at night, lighting candles, singing, and having prayers there. The settlers painted stars of David on rocks and planted grapevines in the field to claim ownership. The settlers are demanding that the Israeli military demolish the Sultan house. The settlers tell the Sultans that they are thieves, that this land belongs to the Jews. The Sultans seemed frightened and weary.

One of the purposes of my visit was to ask them how CPT could offer support. It has been suggested that I move in with the Sultan family and be a continual presence in their home. I didn't sense the Sultans are ready for that.

After leaving the Sultans, I walked back through the Beqa'a valley, trying to absorb the reality of what is happening here. As I looked at the hilltops being bulldozed for settlement expansion and the demolished homes, I was filled with a deep sense of awe at the magnitude of the evil being perpetuated here. I had to cry as I walked past the rubble of Atta and Rodeina's two houses.

I then walked to Atta's parents' (Abdel Jawad and Amni Jaber) house. I could hardly believe what I saw. In the last year, the hilltop behind their house, which was once their beautiful, sculptured orchard, has been bulldozed. A new subdivision is being built there, an expansion of the Harsina settlement, on land confiscated from the Jaber family.

A huge—and I mean huge—rock wall has been built right behind their house, at least 30 feet high and 500 feet long. The top of this wall will be the edge of the new subdivision. I couldn't believe it. In another setting, the wall with its huge rocks could be considered beautiful. But in this context, it is incredibly ugly. Walls that symbolize arrogance, theft, separation, oppression, are ugly. That wall is a physical manifestation of a very evil spirit.

I was greeted warmly by the family. When I pointed to the

wall, they pointed up in the sky and referred to Allah. They, like the Sultans, said their hope is in God. Faith born out of suffering cannot easily be dismissed.

I then walked to the ruins of Fayez and Hudda Jaber's home, and talked with Fayez's mother and family. I was warmly welcomed.

As I walked through the Beqa'a toward home, I was filled with all kinds of feelings. Now I am really back in Hebron. I feel energized. I am excited about what God can accomplish here if we open ourselves to God's Spirit.

What is going on here? Back in the United Sates our media tell us that the new Barak government in Israel wants peace, is ready to settle with the Palestinians, is returning land to the Palestinians, but here we see the opposite. Actually, Barak is expanding the settlements much faster than did Netanyahu. It doesn't look good to me.

This evening Atta and Rodeina and their three children came by our apartment. It was a joy to see them again. They said they had heard that "the old man" had come back, and they wanted to see him. Then Zleekha came. She was so much help in setting up our fast three years ago. It was great to see her again. She was in Jordan when I was here last winter.

December 17, 1999, Friday

After worship we had another team meeting. We made a number of small decisions and reassigned team responsibilities. I am to be the liaison person with the mayor's office, and to work with visiting families that are partnered with congregations in North America.

This afternoon I went back out to the Sultans. They insisted I stay for breaking the fast. The whole family was there, plus some of the extended family. I was really hungry from fasting, and there was plenty of food. We did a lot of good sharing and laughing together. I felt accepted into the family. They insisted that I spend the night with them. That seemed right to me.

December 18, 1999, Saturday

I woke up this morning feeling great, but really tired. I drank some coffee and tea last evening to be polite, so I didn't get much sleep. But I used my waking time well. I accepted that I would not sleep, so spent the time praying. Especially, I prayed for the Sultan family, the Beqa'a valley, the Israelis, for all the principalities and powers at work here. I could feel what a spiritual battle we are involved in.

I spent some of the night thinking through scenarios of what could happen and how I might respond if settlers came during the night, or if the military came to demolish the house. That could be heavy. The idea of confronting the settlers alone at night sounds rather scary. I would need strength beyond my own self.

The family seemed to be sleeping in, but Omar poked his head in the room, so I got up, greeted him, and then headed back to town for our worship and team meeting. I feel a lot of barriers were broken down and it will now be possible for me to sleep at the Sultan's place any time I may be needed.

I walked on the bypass road through the beautiful Beqa'a valley toward Hebron. It was sobering to see the beautiful vineyards on each side, knowing that under the road there used to be gardens and vineyards, people's lives covered up by rock and asphalt. But I guess being able to drive automobiles fast is more important than people's lives.

December 20, 1999, Monday

This afternoon Natasha and I went to the Beqa'a to do home visits. First we went to Kamal and Suba Jaber's home. They warmly welcomed us. Their house is very close to a soldier camp, which they feel protects them from settler harassment. The family built a house about five years ago, and it was demolished about three years ago. The rubble is still there. I was impressed with the lack of bitterness they seem to feel toward Israelis in general. They said they believe that Israelis and Palestinians can live together in peace. At present, they said, the Israeli presence is like a sore throat. It is not likely to kill you, but it is a bother, and you always know it is there.

We then went to Ayoub and Fatima Jaber's home. On the way we walked past the ugly remains of their two demolished houses. In 1995, with 40 people living in their house, and thinking that peace was coming, they built two small houses for their children. The houses were demolished in 1996. They were given five minutes to carry out a few possessions. Their daughter-in-law was in the house at the time giving birth to a child. She was removed so the demolition could proceed.

The family has seen a lot of harassment over the years from the settlers. Their home is not far from the settlement of Harsina, which is expanding in their direction. The settlers have confiscated the land at the top of the hill beyond their home, and have built a road on their land right above their house. Often settlers park their cars above their house and watch them.

We had a great visit with Fatima, who is a very strong, assertive woman. She said that less than two weeks ago, three or four settlers came to the door. Fatima asked them what they wanted. They said they were just passing through. She said, this is not a road, and you are not passing through here. They left.

We walked down the road past Fayez and Hudda's demolished house, greeted some of his family, and went to see Asmi and Jawaher Jaber. Asmi was not home, but we visited with Jawaher and other family members. I remember several visits with them last winter. They seem to be doing fine. She said that Israelis were taking pictures in the area last week, and she expressed concern that the Israelis could be planning something.

I asked her about the farming situation in the valley. She said that since the large greenhouses were under demolition orders, they have been sold and will be dismantled as soon as the crops inside are harvested. I wonder what is wrong with providing a living for one's family with a greenhouse. I learned that the big cistern and the house addition that Abdel Jawad Al Rajabee and his brother Hammad Ramadan were building last winter (see February 17) have been demolished.

As we started walking from the Jaber home we came upon several Palestinian farmers who were digging a hole and attaching a plastic pipe to a water line in the ground, so they could obtain water to irrigate their crops. This valley is a rich farming area, but is dependent on irrigation. As I watched the Palestinians shovel dirt into the hole to cover the newly installed pipe, I couldn't resist lending a hand. Natasha also took a turn.

Three weeks ago some of the team members were out in the valley, and came upon an Israeli backhoe digging a trench to cut off Palestinian taps into the water line. Kathy Kern went down and sat in the trench, stopping the work for over an hour. She was then removed from the trench by Israeli soldiers. She and five team members were detained for several hours and then released.

Water is a major focus of much conflict in this valley, as it is elsewhere in this region. The Israelis severely limit the amount of water available to Palestinians, but plenty of water is available for swimming pools and lawns in the settlements. The Israelis have cut and destroyed many thousands of dollars worth of Palestinian irrigation pipes here over the past few years. The Palestinian farmers keep reconnecting to the water lines, because they feel they also have a right to the water which they need.

The farmers used to get their water from the city of Hebron, but that was cut off in the 1980s. Their water then came from the Israeli water company, Mekorot. That source of water has now also been terminated. The Israeli military has also been demolishing cisterns for holding rainwater, and filling wells with sand. The screws are being tightened on the people in the Beqa'a.

The settlers seem to have a clear goal of taking over the whole Beqa'a valley to expand the settlements of Kiryat Arba and Harsina. In addition to taking over some hilltops, there seems to be a clear policy of trying first to destroy the livelihood of the people here and then remove them. The tearing down of the greenhouses and denying needed water for the fields are good examples of the economic pressure being exerted

Our team is wrestling with how to respond to all of this. We are exploring the possibility of my moving out to the Beqa'a, or even having a second team living there. Before we would do this, we want to carefully check it out with various Palestinians whose opinions we trust. Our opening a campaign in the Beqa'a would have consequences for the people there and so must be done carefully. We made a list of people with whom we will consult.

December 21, 1999, Tuesday

This afternoon I went down the street and saw a group of about six Palestinian and six settler boys together in front of the Avraham Avino settlement. The center of their attention was a donkey that one of the Palestinian boys was riding. I stood at a distance and watched. I was amazed. All the interaction between the boys seemed to be positive. It was encouraging to watch them. God's grace coming through a donkey.

This evening I learned that about 250 settlers had surrounded the Sultan house today, threatening to demolish the house themselves. The settlers had informed the press of their action. One settler had tried to enter the house. That must have been terrifying for the family. I wish I had been there to be with the Sultans.

December 22, 1999, Wednesday

This is early in the morning and I am thinking I should go out to the Sultans today and stay out there. I feel ready to go, yet I have some concerns for my safety. Would those settlers know me? Would they single me out for attack? I feel ready to die. I don't feel afraid. But I am concerned.

I have been thinking about what I feel about police protection. I do not approve of police protection. I do not want to be protected by a gun. I am clear on that. I would rather die than be protected by a gun. But somehow this feels different. We need to think on both a moral and a political level.

On a moral level I am clear. But I also wonder if it would not be right to inform the police here and the American Consulate that there is concern for my safety. That would challenge the governments of Israel and the United States to properly fulfill their God-given function of protecting the innocent and restraining those who are evil (Rom. 13). That would challenge them to stop protecting the evil ones and punishing the innocent. It could actually be a means of calling the governments to repentance. Am I making sense, or am I rationalizing?

In our time of worship this morning we remembered the massacre of forty-five *las abejas* (the bees) two years ago today in Chiapas, Mexico, where CPT has a team. We talked about the effect that people dying in a nonviolent way can have on the world.

In our team meeting this morning we talked about my going out to the Sultans. I shared my fears and thoughts. There was agreement that we need more communication with the Sultans and that we should go out tomorrow with a translator.

This afternoon Jake, Reinhard, and I went with Abdel Hadi Hantash of the Land Defense Committee to look at settler expansion. First we drove south to the Palestinian town of Beni Naim and saw the small settlement of Pene Hever, which was started in 1984. They have built a lot of new buildings in the last year and confiscated quite a bit of land around the settlement.

We were at the top of a mountain and could see the Dead

Sea to the east and over into Jordan. What a breathtaking view. But it was also painful to see. Most of what we could see has been confiscated by the Israelis, some of it in the past few months. Practically everything from here to the Dead Sea is a closed military zone. Palestinian families are being pushed out and removed. It was also sad to see how dry it is (We are in a severe drought), and how eroded the soil has become. Eking out a living on this soil is not easy.

We then drove north of Hebron to see the settlement of Karmei Tzur, where we engaged in an action on March 4, 1999. Abdel Hadi said that the Palestinians were successful in getting their land back and the settlers are banned from expanding there for now. But Abdel Hadi showed us where the settlers had begun to build a new road through a Palestinian vineyard there a few months ago, but were stopped by the Israeli authorities. All the stone and gravel remain in the vineyard, however. We saw six mobile homes recently moved to the edge of the settlement.

We then drove to Beit Ummar to view Karme Tzur from the north. We saw a lot of new buildings and more mobile homes. Abdel Hadi told us, and we could see, that many of the houses in the settlements are empty. They do not need more buildings. The building and expansion are for political reasons, for continuing the gradual process of taking more and more of the land here. They are staking claims. They are stealing little by little.

On the way back to Hebron I was dropped off near the Sultan house, situated along the new bypass Route 60, about 200 feet up the hill east of the road. There was a group of about twenty-five settlers there, halfway between the road and the house, with some of them down along the road. They had put up two large banners between the road and the house. At least ten Israeli flags were planted across the road. On the wall of the empty house just north of here the settlers wrote, "Givat ben Kiryat," the name of their supposed new settlement.

This is really strategic. If they can confiscate this land at the north end of the valley, then they can start pushing south in addition to east and north, in their attempt to confiscate this whole valley. It looks like this will be an important battle.

I took a back way to the house so the settlers would not see me. I am not yet prepared for a confrontation with them. First I want to connect with the Sultan family. I was warmly greeted by the family and was asked to spend the night here.

I learned that the settlers have been here since yesterday, having stayed here all night. They came to the house during the night and harassed the family. They shouted in Hebrew, "Thieves, thieves." They threatened to cut all the trees. One settler tried to get into the house. He shoved Lamia. He was arrested by the police, but then accused the Sultans of hitting him. The police took Omar and his oldest son, Fahed, to the police station to make a report. The family showed me two fruit trees that were cut by the settlers, and a rock wall that was partially destroyed. The family got no sleep last night and they seem very afraid. They said they feel alone.

After greeting the family, I started observing the settlers. They are gathered in a group below the house. I recognize a number of settlers down there, some of them leaders *in the* settler community in Hebron. I see a number of nasty young settlers from Hebron, some of whom have in the past threatened to kill me. Omar told me that Baruch Marzel, a leader of the outlawed Kach terrorist group, has come up to the house a number of times. It looks like a serious situation to me.

Police stopped down by the road at about 4:30 and removed the settlers from the land here. The settlers moved across the road and set up camp there. They built a fire as it was turning dark.

Several neighbors came to spend the evening with the Sultan family. It was getting cold, so we built a fire on the concrete porch in front of the house. We are sitting around the fire, keeping warm. Here we are, sitting around a fire, and the settlers across the road are sitting around their fire. Why can't we all sit around the same fire? There are about twelve of us sitting around the fire here, talking together about the problems with the settlers. I am impressed that instead of hiding in the house, we are out in the open where the settlers can see us, giving the message that we are not afraid, that we will not be intimidated.

It is 10:00. Everything has been quiet. The settlers are still across the road and have set up a row of lanterns. There has been a constant military presence down on the road. The Sultans think the settlers will stay all night. I wonder if they will come up to the house tonight. How will I respond if they do? It sounds scary, but I am at peace. Omar said he is staying awake outside all night, just like last night. He looks weary. I wonder if I should stay up all night. I don't really want to. I am very tired.

It is 10:30. The family said I should go to bed. I offer to stay up all night, but they insist that I sleep. They will call me if there is trouble. I laid in bed and cried awhile. I was so filled with feelings of disgust for the ugliness of the settlers toward this family and toward Palestinians in general, but also filled with gratitude to God for the alternative of love and peace I sense here. I am at peace.

December 23, 1999, Thursday

It is 5:00 a.m. I had a good sleep. I am looking out the window and see two settlers across the road, keeping their fire burning. I see the fire burning on the porch outside the window here. Both sides kept faithful vigil during the night. I am not aware of any trouble last night.

I left at 7:30 this morning to get back to Hebron for worship and a team meeting. We talked more about my staying with the Sultan family. A lot of concern was expressed about my staying there alone. I said I was completely comfortable with it, that staying there is what I want to be doing.

We decided to call for an urgent action alert, calling on

all CPT supporters around the world to contact Israeli government agencies and their own governments to call attention to what is happening here at the Sultan home. We believe that the more attention given to the situation here, the safer the Sultans will be. Evil works best under cover, away from the light of public exposure. An important element in the struggle against evil is exposing that evil with all its lies and distortions. We made that decision dependent on checking with the Sultans one more time on whether this is what they want. We want to be very careful not to impose anything on them.

This afternoon Jake, Zleekha, and I came out to talk with the Sultans. We brought Zleekha along both to translate, and to help make sure we do not miss any subtle cultural clues. We want to be very careful. With Zleekha's help we again asked about my staying here and whether they want international attention. They expressed a lot of gratitude for my presence here. They said I am part of their family. I must stay here. Omar said I am his brother (He is sixty-five and I am sixty). They said they welcome international attention. We asked them how they feel about bringing Israeli Jews here to support them. They said they welcome everyone here. It seems we should go ahead.

I stayed here and Jake and Zleekha went back to Hebron. Later this evening Jake called to say that the call for urgent action had gone out to the world. I told this to the Sultan family. They seemed very pleased.

Omar showed us copies of their deeds from the Ottoman times, deeds which are registered in Istanbul. The Turks occupied this land for 500 years. He also showed us documents from the time of the British and Jordanian rule here.

Everyone here is deeply troubled by what is happening. It is a terrible strain on them. They are very afraid. They don't know what will happen to them. Will some of them be put in prison? Will some of them be killed? Will their home be demolished? At any time a bulldozer could come and destroy what they have here. What does it mean to live without security? One of the things it seems to mean for them is that they are drawing closer to each other and to God. For many people, adversity brings them closer to God. I am hearing repeated references to depending on God.

At about 4:00 this afternoon, a big bulldozer came up the road and stopped at the settler camp across the road. Was the bulldozer here to demolish the Sultan's house? Was it here to tear up their gardens and fruit trees? I was struck with an awful foreboding of evil. It turned out the bulldozer came to level the rocks and dirt across the road to make a nicer place for the settlers to camp. In ten minutes it was gone. What a relief.

I spent the evening sitting around the fire. The settlers had their fire. It was a peaceful time for me. A number of neighbors came. At about midnight I went to bed.

December 24, 1999, Friday

I got up early and came out and saw Wahib, who had stayed up all night. He looked tired. We sat and watched the settlers.

I was thinking about the settlers camping out here and how I have done the same thing. I remember camping out the whole weekend from Good Friday to Easter morning in front of the nuclear enrichment plant in Piketon, Ohio, and another time in front of the military recruitment center in Athens, Ohio, during our war against the people of Nicaragua in the 1980s. I can identify with the settlers down there. Maybe I should tell them that.

It is interesting that the settlers have taken up the tactics of nonviolent action. These settlers have picked up part of the strategy, but they have missed the deeper philosophy. They seem to have missed the commitment to truth and love, to being vulnerable, to opening themselves to reconciliation with the "enemy." I see them down there with their machine guns, using some nonviolent techniques.

I spent part of the morning playing ball with the four boys here. Omar (9), Sameh (7), Hethim (6), and Amed (3). They have been pretty shy, so I wanted to break through their fears. They couldn't resist the opportunity to play ball. At about 12:30 I noticed that a settler was removing the Israeli flags across the road. Could I be right? Were they packing up and leaving? I watched, and sure enough, it wasn't long before they were gone. They have left. What does this mean? Have they ended their vigil, or are they leaving just for Sabbath?

This afternoon Pierre and Reinhard came to check on me. They and the rest of the team will be in Bethlehem and Jerusalem for the next two days for Christmas. I am happy to skip the Christmas celebration. I want to be here. I am celebrating the incarnation here with the Sultans. I want to see the reality of God's love become flesh here.

This is a Friday in Ramadan, a special day for Muslims. The Sultans invited their whole family here to break the fast this evening. Most of them came, plus other extended family members. There must have been more than fifty people here. What wonderful, gracious people. I especially enjoyed watching the young children play games on the porch.

I am grateful the settlers left today. This gave the family a much-needed break. The family could relax and enjoy themselves. I am impressed that in spite of all the fear and anxiety here, the Sultans have not lost their sense of humor. There has been a fair amount of joking around. I even told them a few jokes. Laughing can release a lot of tension and help keep us from taking the situation or ourselves too seriously. I read two funny stories in my Arabic book to Omar. He got a good laugh.

December 25, 1999, Saturday

Merry Christmas. Since everything has been quiet here, I decided to do a few things at the apartment in Hebron and then go to the peace walk in Bethlehem today. I got a ride part way into Hebron from the Sultans, but the road past Kiryat Arba was closed because of Sabbath. So I walked the rest of the way with settlers going into Hebron for Shabbat services. I greeted quite a few of them with "Shabbat Shalom."

I got into a conversation with one young settler couple as we walked. They asked me what I think about Jews living in Hebron. I said Jews should be allowed to live anywhere. They said that was what they wanted to hear. They said they want peace, but the Arabs do not want peace. I said that is what I hear from both sides. They said the Arab terrorists keep killing Jews. When I said that Israelis kill eight times as many Palestinians as Palestinians kill Israelis, they said they want to kill a hundred Arabs for every Israeli killed.

My heart goes out to these settlers. They seem like a nice couple, but they are bound up in fear. I told them about my staying with the Sultan family and what has been happening here. I want settlers to know they are being observed. They smiled, as if they knew a lot about what is happening.

After spending a little time at the apartment, I went to Beit Sahur to be part of the eleventh annual Christmas day march for peace. There were about 3,000 people marching, plus many more watching from both sides of the street. This march is sponsored by the Palestinian Center for Rapprochement in Beit Sahur. The theme this year was reconciliation between Muslims and Christians. We marched from Shepherds' Field to the city hall in Beit Sahur, where we were served dates to represent peace and the breaking of the Ramadan fast. Beit Sahur is 85 percent Christian and 15 percent Muslim. We then marched to Manger Square in Bethlehem, where there was music (including "Jingle Bells") and Muslim and Christian speeches about reconciliation.

I had a talk along the way with one of the founders of the peace center. He said the main work of the center is bringing Israelis and Palestinians together in dialogue. He was also one of the leaders of the famous tax resistance in Beit Sahur during the Intafada. Some people think the occupation of the West Bank could have been ended if all Palestinians had joined in refusing to pay any Israeli taxes. He told the story of how people in Beit Sahur refused to pay their taxes. As a result, their property was confiscated. The Israelis had loaded up all the household possessions of one family and then told the family that they could have all their possessions back if they paid just one shekel of their taxes. The family refused.

I then headed back to Hebron and got a taxi out to the Beqa'a. I arrived at the Sultan home at around 8:00. As I was walking up the road I could see lots of police lights and a large crowd of between 150 and 200 settlers on the road below the Sultan house. I could hear them singing. A few settlers arrived here at around 3:00 this afternoon, and then about four hours later the big crowd came for a rally. I am real sorry I didn't stay here today.

It is 8:20. I can hear a speech being given by a settler, with lots of applause. Soldiers are walking on the old road just below the house. I am tempted to go down and introduce myself, but decide not to. It sounds like the settler speaking is reading a prayer. I hear more singing, more speeches. There are about twenty-five Palestinians gathered here in front of the house. There is a somber mood since people are expecting the worst. But everyone is calm.

It is 8:45. I see the settlers dancing and shouting on the road. They are holding torches. The flames light up the area. Now I see about twenty settlers running up the hill just north of the house here. No, there must be fifty of them running up the hill with their flaming torches. I see police between the settlers and us. I do not know what to expect. Anything could happen. Some of us move up the hill and get within thirty feet of the settlers. There must be 100 of them.

I go up to a policeman and introduced myself to him. I tell him I am an American and am here to observe what is happening. I think if the police know there is an American with the family here, we will be more safe, and the police will act more responsibly. There are a lot of police and soldiers here. The police light a flare. The settlers move up the hill above the house. They appear to be claiming the land.

Before long the settlers are swarming down the hill, shouting and cheering. I hear the sound of rocks thudding against rocks. They are demolishing the rock wall just seventy-five feet north of the house. There must be 100 settlers all tearing down the rock wall as fast as they can. This is crazy. We all feel helpless.

I think my only role is to observe. Only the police and soldiers can deal with this. I introduce myself to more police. I want as many of them as possible to know that an American is watching them. I ask the police why they are just watching as the settlers demolish the wall. The police say they are waiting for a bigger force to come. Are the police really helpless, or are they complicit in this crime, as in so many other cases when they just watch or actually protect settlers as they demolish Palestinian property? If Palestinians ran amok like this, destroying Jewish property, they would be shot.

It is 9:30. The settlers are moving down the hill. Now they are on the old road just below the house. A number of us move down to within twenty feet of them, on a walled terrace above them. They start jeering at us and waving Israeli flags. I see contempt in their eyes. The Palestinians remain nonviolent. They are showing the settlers that they are not afraid. The Palestinians are very self-disciplined. If they threw one rock now, it could trigger disaster.

There must be a hundred settlers on the road right below us, plus others down on the main road. Now someone is giving a speech on a bullhorn. The settlers cheer. The Sultans, some of whom speak Hebrew, tell me the speaker has just announced that the settlers will come back here on Tuesday to demolish the Sultan come, bring in mobile homes, and start construction of a new settlement. Oh, no. What do we do now?

It is 10:30. It seems that all the settlers are gone. It is quiet. At least twenty-five Palestinians are sitting around the fire. They are in a troubled, reflective mood. The conversation becomes animated, with many conversations going at once. Feelings are being released. This family is being terrorized. Thoughts flood over me about what it would be like to have everything in one's life so threatened in this way.

This crisis can be seen as an opportunity. I wonder, how can we turn the energy of this ugly, evil situation into something positive and beautiful? How can this conflict be the occasion for reconciliation to come between some Muslims, Jews, and Christians? How can this nasty situation be turned into something good?

We need to get to work. We are going on red alert—which means the team will focus all our energy on this situation and call for worldwide support and action. Actually, Pierre, who came at about 10:00, is already on the phone, calling Israelis, press, and other contacts. We are going on red alert. We have a lot of work to do before Tuesday. We keep checking with the Sultans. They say they are eager to have lots of people come here.

It is 12:30 now. All the neighbors have left. We are sitting around the fire in silence, in a very somber mood. We go to bed.

This has not been a merry Christmas. But I have been thinking of how the Word can become flesh.

December 26, 1999, Sunday

I slept fairly well, in spite of the jumble of feelings within me. There are no settlers across the road. I have been thinking that maybe the settlers' announcing that things will happen on Tuesday was a trick, that they may do their thing today or tomorrow before we get people here.

The situation looks serious to me. I fear the settlers are

angry about the current peace negotiations with Syria and the possibility that Israel may give up the Golan Heights, and could cause a lot of trouble because of that. For the settlers, one of the worst sins a Jew can commit is to give up to Gentiles one inch of land that God has given to Jews. On the way to Bethlehem yesterday I saw a settler encampment like the one here, on the right side of the bypass road just north of Beit Ummar. On Tuesday settlers, backed up by Israeli soldiers, cut down 200 Palestinian olive trees near Ramallah. I am afraid this could be just the beginning.

Pierre went into Hebron this morning and Reinhard came out here to be with us. We want to keep at least two team members here all the time now.

Throughout this quiet day, we sat in front of the house, holding vigil. We saw no settlers, but the mood is heavy. There are fifteen people living in this house. Where will they go? There are empty houses in the settlement of Harsina across the way, but the Palestinians cannot go there.

As I sit here, I pray. I struggle with how to confront the massive evil before us. How do we avoid getting caught up in a hating spirit? We want to overcome evil, but not be overcome by it. The theory is clear, but how do we put it into practice?

I got a call from Adam Keller who works with the Israeli peace group Gush Shalom (Peace Bloc). They are working to get Israelis to come here and stay with the Sultan family. Exciting! And the Sultan family is eager to host them. Yes, good can come out of this suffering.

Adam Keller told me that the Israeli peace group, Peace Now, has been lobbying the Israeli government on behalf of the Sultans, and has been told by the Israeli military that settlers will be allowed to demonstrate here, but not to destroy property. I am glad Israelis are working to confront the Israeli government, even though I don't trust what the government says. What would happen if hundreds of settlers came here, determined to destroy things? What would the soldiers do? I would guess the settlers would love to have some martyrs here. And the government wants no settler martyrs.

The situation here is very serious. That means it has great potential for tragedy, but an even greater possibility for good. I would like to believe that the possibilities for good are much greater than the possibilities for evil. There is a force in the universe that is bent toward the good. Truth and love are at the heart of reality. Ultimately, evil runs counter to reality. Its defeat is certain. Evil simply does not have the creative potential that good has. Evil is stupid. Yes, evil is crafty, but it is stupid. Evil lacks hope, vision, and creativity. When we give ourselves to evil we can no longer see clearly.

From the Gospel we learn that evil is arrogant. This arrogance leads to evil overstepping its own power. The powers of evil crucified Jesus, but they did not defeat him. Part of the hope of the resurrection is that evil is defeated by its own arrogance. I do not know what that means for us here, but I am expecting God's victory.

This evening we again held vigil around the fire until 10:30. We saw no settlers, but more neighbors came to sit around the fire. The mood was much lighter this evening.

December 27, 1999, Monday

We saw no settlers today. But lots of people have been coming, including human rights activists and internationals. Jeremy Cornforth, from the American Consulate in Jerusalem, came to check the situation. We told him the story of what has been happening here and how the settlers are trying to take this whole valley. Omar showed him around the property. I urged him to contact President Clinton and Secretary of State Albright to have them put pressure on the Israelis to stop this oppression. He said he would make a report of what is happening here, and would visit me in jail if I am arrested. I appreciated his visit and his attitude.

Will they come to demolish this house tomorrow? The

question hangs over us. We wait and pray. I am glad this is Ramadan. This is an important time to be fasting.

The team has agreed that I should be spending all my time here, with no team responsibilities. That sounds great to me. I do feel a bit guilty about having all the "fun" here while others are doing all the work, like sending out reports, contacting people, and all the odds and ends that are essential to keeping the team functioning.

Israeli police came this afternoon and took pictures of the damages done by the settlers. They asked Omar if he has a permit for this house. He said no. What does that mean?

Omar told me he heard that the Israelis are confiscating another 1,500 acres somewhere between here and Bethlehem. He also said that the peace talks between Israel and the Palestinians have ended. He seems pretty upset. Omar and I broke the fast together this evening, eating in silence. Both of us were feeling very grim.

This evening as we were sitting around the fire, four Jewish people came to spend the night here. Their coming created quite a stir. When a taxi dropped them off down by the road, they were seen by soldiers, who assumed they were settlers. By the time they got up to the house, soldiers were shining spotlights around the hills here. Soon four soldiers came up the driveway.

The Sultans talked with the commander who was Druze and spoke good Arabic. He said they were looking for settlers who came in a taxi. Our Jewish friends explained that they had just come to spend the night, and confronted the soldiers with the horrible things that have been happening here while the soldiers watched. The soldiers expressed frustration with the settlers.

Then a beautiful thing happened. The Sultans brought coffee for the soldiers, under whom they have suffered.

There have been a lot of soldiers just below the house and down on the main road this evening. The presence of Jews and Christians, Israelis, Canadians, and Americans here is putting a lot of pressure on the military to do what is right. It would be pretty embarrassing to them if the settlers harmed anyone here. Maybe all the messages from North America and Israel to the Israeli government are having an effect. We learned that the College Mennonite Church in Goshen, Indiana, which is partnered with the Sultans, sent about seventy-five faxes to Prime Minister Barak. That is encouraging. I wonder how many messages the Israeli government has received.

The four Jewish people from Gush Shalom who came this evening are very special people. Adam Keller painted anti-occupation slogans on at least 117 Israeli tanks when he was in the Israeli military. He spent some time in prison and then was discharged from the military for being psychologically unfit for the military. I believe he is. Adam's wife, Beata Zilversmidt, is a holocaust survivor from Holland. Ira Grupper, former head of New Jewish Agenda, had been beaten and arrested in the Civil Rights Movement in the United States. Avi Goldberg is a student from Canada, and a serious thinker.

What a wonderful time we had sitting around the fire, with Muslims, Jews, and Christians sharing together in Hebrew, Arabic, and English. Beate told the Palestinians that they were bringing the weapons of hope. I could sense the Sultans were extremely grateful for the Jewish presence here. Wow! The ugly actions of the settlers are bringing people together.

We went to bed at about 12:30. I lay in bed, happy and full of hope. Jews, Muslims, and Christians are all sleeping in this Muslim home.

December 28, 1999, Tuesday

I woke up this morning excited and eager for the gift of a new day. There was a lot of good informal sharing as we got up this morning. We started sharing our histories, our fears, our doubts, and our visions for a new society. We stretched to communicate across differences in culture and faith. We connected with each other on a personal level, which could be very important if we go through difficult, stressful times today and need to exhibit a lot of trust for each other.

We learned there was an article about the Sultans this morning in the Israeli newspaper, *Ha'aretz*, saying that the settlers have been threatening the family and damaging property. The Civil Administration was quoted saying that the house will not be demolished because the demolition order is too old, and that they will not demolish homes that have been occupied for over five years. That sounds like a new policy. The Israeli government also said they would stop new settlements. It is great to have them say that, and to have it on record.

We had a short team meeting here at the house. We then had a meeting of our team and the Gush Shalom people to decide how we will work together as a team. I was chosen as the coordinator for the action today. Natasha and the Israelis will do presswork. The Israelis will relate to settlers. Jake and I are prepared to be arrested, along with Gush Shalom people.

We think the house will not be demolished today. Our main concern now is with what the settlers might do on the land just north of the house. Will they come with a bulldozer and level land to bring in mobile homes? Will they demolish the empty house just north of here? Will they try to start their new settlement today? If so, how do we respond? Will we sit in front of the bulldozers? Someone suggested that the military will defend us, and the Sultan house against the settlers, but if the settlers move on the land here, then the main concern of the military will be to protect the settlers and let the Israeli government work out whether the new settlement remains or not.

It is 10:00. Two Israeli police come to the house, concerned that an Israeli car is parked here. The car belongs to some journalists who are here. The Gush Shalom people tell the police they are here in solidarity with the Palestinians who are being threatened by the settlers.

It is 11:15. Some soldiers come up to the steps. The Israelis go down to meet them. We are informed that this is a closed military zone and that we all are ordered to leave. We have a quick meeting. This is not what we expected. It is decided that three of the Gush Shalom people will risk arrest. Jake will pose as a reporter, but probably will not be arrested. I am to hide in the house so I can be here if everyone else is removed.

It is 11:50. A police car arrives across the road. The others feel I should go in the house now. This is the first time I have ever hidden from the police. If the police find me, I will say I live here. I watch out the window and observe the action just below me.

It is noon. I see Pierre arriving in a taxi with a group he has been meeting with. They stay down by the road. There are lots of journalists here now. And a lot of Palestinians.

It is 12:30. A blue van with the pastors and others from the Lutheran church in Jerusalem stops down by the road. They join the others down by the road. There are a lot of people in front of the house. Now there are police on the porch talking to the Israelis who are prepared to be arrested. I expect the arrests to happen now, but I see all the police go down from the house. I call Pierre, who says people have been given fifteen minutes to leave. But no one is leaving. I see various interviews taking place with both Israelis and Palestinians.

It is 1:00. Everyone is waiting. An Israeli bus arrives with about 30 Israeli Gush Shalom members who have come to stand in solidarity with the Sultan family. I am glad they came, as this puts added pressure on the police. They are standing down along the road, holding banners in Hebrew and Arabic.

The fifteen minutes have long past. We have put the Israeli government in a dilemma. Anything they do now can only help our situation. If they arrest us, that gives us publicity and makes the military look unjust. What is wrong with visiting persecuted Palestinians and standing in solidarity with them? But if the government backs down and doesn't arrest anyone, then we have won. Either way, we win. Creating dilemmas for oppressors is an important, nonviolent strategy.

It is 1:10. There are soldiers and police walking up the hill, so this may be the end.

Now the police are speaking to the people on the porch. The police and Fahed are having an animated discussion. I now see a clear division between those ready for arrest and the others. There is a discussion between Adam and Beate and the police. Are they under arrest? Now I see everyone walking around.

It is 1:30. I see some police leave. Many of the Gush Shalom people are walking up to the house. I am excited about what is happening. The Israelis being here sends a clear message to the Israeli government, to the settlers, and most important, to the Palestinians. Jews and Arabs can live together in peace. Our protests have much more power when we embody the alternatives we seek.

I am told that the police have decided to make no arrests, so I now have come down to the porch. I learn that when the police came up the hill an hour ago to arrest people, Fahed the oldest Sultan son, told them that these people are his guests, they are welcome here, and that it is against Palestinian tradition to make guests leave. The police backed down. A victory! Israelis can stand with Palestinians after all. And the Sultan family has been made visible to the world. They are not alone.

And I am free now. We joke about my being the only one detained today. I walk down to the road and start talking to the Israeli demonstrators there, thanking them for coming. A van full of Israeli activists arrives: Arik Ascherman, Jeff Halper, Amos, and Harriet. It was great to see them. There must be fifty Israelis here. Uri Avnery, a former Knesset member, is also here.

I see two settlers across the road from us. Arik gets into a big discussion with them. One is Baruch Marzel, a Kach leader, and a man who has given me a death threat. I'll let the Israelis talk with them. The settlers must be angry. This was not a good day for them. I learned that the Israeli government raided the settler pirate radio station today. What does this mean for us? Will the settlers be here tonight? By 5:00 everyone has gone.

I think the Sultan family is pleased with what happened here today. I wish my Arabic was better so that I could talk with them on a deeper level. I have some uneasiness with the fact that the Israelis sort of took over the property here today. They didn't do it in a bad way, but the fact is that this property became the staging area for their protest against settlements and land confiscation. I think that was okay, but I want us to be very careful and not to impose anything on the family.

It is 8:30 and I am going to bed. I have given all I can give today. People are sitting around the fire, but everything is quiet. There are no settlers.

December 29, 1999, Wednesday

This was a quiet morning. I spent some time playing with the boys, writing, and studying Arabic. Around noon, other team members came out from Hebron, along with Gary Brooks, who arrived last night to join the team, and "Sally," an international friend. As they were about to leave, two soldiers came up to the house and asked me what I was doing here. I said, visiting my friends. I ask them what they were doing here. They said they were just checking the situation. They then left.

Soon three soldiers came and told us this was a closed military zone and that we all had to leave. I said I live here. One soldier was terribly arrogant and rude. I asked him why

I can't live here. Fahed told them I have been living here for the past two weeks. The soldier told him to shut up. He asked to see my passport. I hesitated. He promised to give it back in five minutes, so I gave it to him. I warned him to be careful, because my picture is extremely ugly. I thought a little humor was needed. He soon gave back the passport and they left.

The rest of the team left, leaving Sally and me here. We decided I should immediately get out of sight. Sally had already gone upstairs. I went back to my room upstairs where I was hiding yesterday.

It is 1:00. I see two settler youth get out of a car and start walking up the field just north of here, carrying an Israeli flag. The soldiers turn them back, because, I suppose, this is a closed military zone. They go back across the road and put up their flag. Two more settlers appear. Several police cars come.

It is 1:30. I see two soldiers walking up to the house. I wait. Omar comes up and says the soldiers want to talk with me. I go down and greet them with shalom. They tell me this is a closed military zone and I must leave. I ask them why I have to leave. They don't give a good reason. I ask them for how long. They say only for an hour or two. I mistrust them. I say I will call my team and walk away. They leave.

I call Natasha again, who says to do as I think best. As I am talking, I see twenty-five settlers across the road. Now they are running up the hill just north of here. There are a lot of police and soldiers, but they are not trying to stop the settlers.

It is 2:00. A policeman is coming up the hill. The Sultans talk with him. I am called down. I greet the policeman. He is very friendly, but tells me I have to leave because there are problems here. He tells me I can come back in a few hours. I tell him I live here. He doesn't accept that. He says there were problems here yesterday. I say, we created no problems. I tell him that for the past month this family has been terrorized and the police have not stopped the settlers, that I have seen settlers destroying property as the police looked on. I say I am living here as an international observer because the family is threatened. He says that he has two problems right now and I am the first. I don't say any more, but I think that I certainly have not been the problem here.

Why do they want me to leave? Is it because they don't want an observer? Is it because they have told the settlers they can't be here? Is it because they are allowing the settlers to be here today to equalize things with yesterday, and they want this to be the last day of demonstrations? Or because settlers say that if CPT can be here, they can too?

I go into the house, call the others. I am ready to be arrested. This is probably a bluff, and they wouldn't arrest me anyway. I don't know what is best. Should I leave? I feel I should do whatever the Sultans say, even if that is the wrong decision. I tell them that. They decide I should go to a neighbor for an hour or two and then come back.

I say good-bye to Sally who has put on a Muslim head scarf to hide her identity. She looks like a true Muslim. We are sure they do not know she is here. She can observe.

Fahed said he will drive me in his car to the neighbors' house. As we start to leave I see thirty settlers up at the vacant house. Are they starting a new settlement there now? I feel helpless. We start driving down the road, but a soldier jeep follows us, so we can't stop at the neighbor's house. We go farther and the soldiers turn around. We wait about five minutes and then drive back to Mohammed Jaber's house, which is not far from the Sultan house. I am warmly welcomed. We sit on the porch and have a good view of what is happening at the Sultan house. I see more settlers walking up the road past here. There are lots of settlers in the field just beyond the Sultan house.

It is 2:45. The settlers are coming down the hill from the empty house. It looks like they are having a rally just on the other side of the Sultans' house. What are the Sultans feeling? More terror? More stress? I see settlers walking right in front of the house. I wish I could be there.

It is 4:00. The rally seems to be over, but I see a few settlers milling around between the old and new roads below the house. Now I see about five settlers going up the hill just beyond the Sultan house. It looks as if they are planting something there. They are coming down the hill now. It looks like soldiers ordered them to come back down.

It is 4:30. A Sultan boy, Omar, comes and tells me I can come back to the house now, since all the settlers are gone. I am not sure what to do. I have been invited to break the fast with the Jaber family, but would like to go back to the house. I decide to eat with the Jabers. I had a beautiful meal with the Jabers. At about 5:30 I walked back to the house. Everything was quiet. All the settlers were gone. I was warmly greeted by the Sultan family. They expressed over and over again how I am part of the family and they don't want me to leave. I feel wanted and accepted here.

Sally left before I returned, but I learned that when the settlers tried to bring two camper buses here this afternoon, the police had them removed immediately. That is encouraging.

I also learned that the Israeli military dismantled the memorial to Baruch Goldstein at Kiryat Arba today. That seems significant. Has the Barak government decided to crack down on the settlers? The settlers must really be upset.

We spent the evening sitting around the fire. The family is upset. They called the settler actions disgraceful, and expressed a lot of anger toward Israelis. I learned that Omar's brother was killed during Sharon's invasion of Lebanon in 1983. They talked of many different family members who have spent time in prison. They asked how they can forget the blood of their brothers.

I spoke about being in a spiritual struggle and how that calls for radical trust in God. We talked about trusting in God. Omar said we need pure hearts. He said Muslims need to experience repentance and changed hearts. That is what is most needed. They seemed excited about the deeper conversation. One of them said I will go to heaven ahead of the Muslims. I know I am no better than they are, but it was good to hear that instead of constantly being told by others that I am going to hell because I am not a Muslim.

I also had a good talk with them about the importance of honesty in our relationships with each other, and that if at any time it would be better for me to leave, I want them to say so. They had a hard time with that. But they understood when I said they did the right thing this afternoon in asking me to leave. I said, treat me as a brother, not as a guest.

I thought this might be a quiet day. Oh, well.

December 30, 1999, Thursday

There is supposed to be a demonstration here today, organized by Palestinian Authority people, to protest land confiscation. Pierre, Jake, and Gary are going to participate. Natasha is here with me. I learn that the land north of here is a closed military zone today. It looks like the soldiers will not allow any demonstration here today. The demonstration is to begin at 11:00. At 10:30 lots of police and soldiers arrive. There are a lot of press and local Palestinians below the house. At 11:00 I see about 100 demonstrators marching around the corner about a half mile up the road. Three military jeeps are blocking the road. It looks like a standoff.

There are a number of Palestinian women in the field north of here. Two soldiers come to them and tell them to move. The women argue with the soldiers, but eventually come to this side of the wall. It is good to see a lot of women out.

I learn that at noon the deputy mufti of Jerusalem led the marchers in prayers, after which the marchers simply ignored the soldiers and marched down the road. I learn that the marchers include one Knesset member, Abed Malik Dahamshe; a former Knesset member and veteran peace activist, Uri Avnery; local Palestinian dignitaries; and a group from Gush Shalom. As they walk up to the house Omar hugs and kisses each of them. They sit together by the house.

At this point an Israeli military commander came and promised everyone that the Sultan house would not be demolished. This is part of what we wanted to hear. And the Sultans are getting the attention they need.

By 1:00 it was all over and the demonstrators had left. About an hour later four settler boys appeared across the road holding a banner saying, "This is our state." At one point there were eight settler boys there. Quite a few Palestinian neighbors are here watching. By sunset everyone had left.

I spent the evening with Fahed and his wife, Bassama, and their four children. They live in part of the house here. We broke the fast together, shared pictures, and I horsed around with the children. Fahed shared stories and pictures of his and other family members' times in prison, pictures of Omar's brother killed in Lebanon in 1983, wedding pictures, and pictures of their children. When you get close to people it is difficult to understand how anyone would want to harm them.

I feel deeply blessed. I also am praising God for the victories I sense we have witnessed here. I see the Spirit of God at work here in such a vivid way.

December 31, 1999, Friday

It was a quiet night. This morning I hiked halfway into Hebron, going over the hill across the road from the Sultan house, on the roads bulldozed by the settlers on Sultan family land. I was able to participate in worship and a team meeting. Much of the team meeting was spent discussing our work with the Sultans, and future actions. Things may cool down at the Sultans, but we expect the settlers may be creating more problems over the next months.

We had many victories in the past days. The Sultan home

is not demolished and the settlers have not started a new settlement here. It will now be much more difficult for them to do either. The Sultans are not alone. They received a lot of international attention. Their situation is public. They should be safer now.

These actions, and all the messages sent to the Israeli government by people responding to our alert, have certainly caught the attention of the government and helped open space for it to crack down on settlers. We got the attention of the government and a positive response in the well-documented promise by the government to not demolish the Sultan home. We effectively raised the broader issues of land confiscation and home demolitions, and helping to keep these issues on the negotiating table.

This has been a time of bridge-building among Palestinians, the Israeli Peace Movement, and CPT. We didn't keep control of the action, but threw the ball to the Israelis who did a lot of good work. And we are building a good relationship with the Sultan family and the people of the Beqa'a.

So what did CPT do? We were here on the ground, having already developed lots of relationships with people in the Hebron area, and in Israel, plus our international network. A very small number of us had put our bodies on the line. Not much.

It is important that we praise God and celebrate our victories. Too often we just keep going, unaware of all that has been accomplished, and then get discouraged.

I got back to the Sultan home at 12:45, and there were two settler boys across the road, holding their banner and flag. A third arrived about ten minutes after I got here. There is a soldier jeep on the old road just below the house. The settlers are being watched. At about 1:15 a van stopped across the road and picked up the settler boys. They are gone.

Much of the settler action out here was done by youth.

That is excellent training for them. It enables the youth to own the settler struggle, and gives them invaluable experience on the front lines. Training a new generation in hate and ethnocentrism is not a very nice thought, however.

At about 3:00 this afternoon a journalist came and wanted to know what is happening here. She said both Israeli and Palestinian television reported this morning that the Sultan family was evacuated by the Israeli authorities until the validity of their deeds can be checked. I learned that when the Sultans went to the mosque today, people asked them about being removed from their home. But they are all still here. What is going on? This information was supposed to have come from the Israeli government. Who was able to put this disinformation into the media?

I learned that the settler camp along the road, just north of Beit Ummar, was removed yesterday, and that TV news showed the settlers being treated quite roughly by the soldiers. I also learned that the settlers demonstrating at the demolition of the Goldstein memorial on Wednesday were also treated very roughly.

I will be the only CPTer here until tomorrow afternoon. Then we want at least two of us here in case the settlers come back after Sabbath. We will play it by ear after that.

In talking with the family this evening I asked what is needed. One of them said, we need broken hearts before God. I asked how we come to have broken hearts. He said, by completely depending on God.

January 2, 2000, Sunday

This was a quiet day, a day for reflecting. As I sit watching all the traffic on the new bypass road below us which cut this fertile valley in half and caused so much loss and pain, I realize that this is not much different from communities, farms, and hillsides all over the world that have been sacrificed in worship of the automobile. I wonder how can we oppose more bypass roads and still insist on using them?

I am thinking about hypocrisy. Are we CPTers self-righteous hypocrites who want to impose our morality on the settlers, but are unwilling to change our ways of living that destroy the lives of other people? We object to the settlers destroying others lives for their own selfish purposes, but we are willing to use electricity, cars, and airplanes in spite of all the devastation they cause, and the unspeakable ecological devastation they are creating for the future. What is the difference between the settlers and me? I guess I can argue that I am not motivated by hate, but that hardly sounds convincing. If you kill me, what difference does it make to me if you do it out of hate or selfishness?

The point is not to be immobilized by guilt, but to become liberated from our self-righteousness and our oppressive lifestyles.

January 3, 2000, Monday

I went into Hebron this morning for worship and a team meeting. Because things are quiet at the Sultans now, it was agreed that I should slowly move back to Hebron.

January 8, 2000, Saturday

Yesterday the three-day feast after Ramadan began. I spent today on the streets in Hebron because of the combination of Jewish Sabbath and the Muslim feast, a potential for trouble. Both sides ignored each other, however. This is different from past years when both sides were more confrontational.

I got into a discussion with a young settler who identified himself as a supporter of Meir Kahane, the former leader of the Jewish far right and founder of Kach. He said there can never be peace between Jews and Arabs, because Arabs are stupid and dirty, and they are all terrorists. This land is only for Jews: all Arabs must leave. He then told me how terrible Christians are. He said Jesus went off the deep end, distorted Scripture, dabbled in the occult, and became so bad the rabbis had to sentence him to death. Mary was scum, Jesus was scum, and his disciples were even worse.

There is nothing good about Christianity, he claimed. At least Muslims worship the same God as do Jews. Christians worship Mary as part of the trinity. He said Jews are allowed to go into mosques, but not into church buildings. I tried to be a good listener and apologized to him for all the horrible things that so-called Christians have done to Jews.

January 11, 2000, Tuesday

This afternoon I went out to the Beqa'a and had a good visit with the Sultans. No settlers have been there. Omar told me that the area around their house is a closed military zone, and will be in force until the legal issues of land ownership are settled in court. I don't think that will affect our visiting there.

January 12, 2000, Wednesday

Reinhard and I went to Sabeel today for a discussion of Palestinian Christianity. We learned that many of the Palestinians here now are direct descendants of the early Christians. This was illustrated by the story of a Palestinian Christian being asked by an American when she became a Christian. She replied that her great, great, great, . . . grandmother babysat for Jesus when he was little.

There are approximately 130,000 Palestinian Christians in Israel and 50,000 in the West Bank and Gaza. Christians are 2 percent of the total population. There are 3,000-5,000 Messianic Jews in Israel, and some Jews who have become Catholics. And, of course, some Christians have become Muslim and Jewish. There are possibly three-quarters of a million Russians in Israel, maybe 40 percent of whom are Christians. I have heard that there are a number of Russian Christians living in Kiryat Arba, and that they have created quite a stir by wanting to put up a church building there.

Part of the time was spent talking about the hope of

Palestinian Christians. Of course, their hope is affected by the reality of the occupation. I heard a desire for unity, a hope that some of the Palestinian diaspora will return, a hope that Christians will help influence the course of events in coming years, and hope of building good relationships with Muslims. I sensed vitality.

We heard a ringing critique of the Oslo peace process, which may be good to summarize here. The Oslo accord brought a ray of hope, but there isn't much of that hope left among Palestinians. The Oslo process was described not as a search for a real peace, but as an attempt to buy off the Palestinian independence movement, to have the Palestinian Authority do Israel's dirty work by setting up an apartheid system. Oslo took the slogans of the Palestinians and turned them upside down, making them work against the Palestinian people. For example, now the Palestinian Authority is treated as the only legitimate voice of the Palestinian people. The people themselves now have no official voice. Anyone who rejects the peace process is seen as being against peace.

In the Oslo agreement, the Palestinians recognized the reality of Israel, but Israel has not recognized the Palestinians. Israel recognized Arafat and the PA, but not the Palestinian people. The PA is expected to control and speak for the Palestinian people.

In the Oslo agreement Israel did not recognize that something is terribly wrong with occupation, a wrong that needs to be corrected. Still today, all relationships with Israel are on Israel's terms. Israel has opted for the solution of subcontracting certain responsibilities and symbols of sovereignty to the PA without giving the PA any real authority, and with Israel calling all the shots. The Palestinian Christians told us that there is less working together of Israelis and Palestinians today than before Oslo. The concerns of people on both sides have been handed over to the authorities on both sides, creating a malaise among grassroots organizations.

What does this mean for CPT? They said it was either a stroke of genius or divine guidance that led CPT to Hebron, because in Hebron all the issues of occupation are still clear. We are here, on the ground, in the middle of the oppression, simply pointing to the reality of what is happening now. We are not in front of TV cameras or talking to politicians, but are simply being a presence here. I heard a clear message that our work is to expose and unmask the sham of the peace process, point to the realities of oppression, racism, apartheid, and to help bring Israelis and Palestinians together. We need to make clear that this is not a Jewish/Muslim/Christian problem, but a problem of injustice.

I also heard them say that the main arena of struggle needs to be in the United States. I am feeling that we need to do something to bring Jews, Muslims, and Christians together in North America around the issues of Palestine.

January 14, 2000, Friday

This evening we went to a friend's house to watch videos. We saw a video of the "tomato action" last November. In the Oslo agreement, in the Hebron accord, in the Wye agreement, and the Sharm El-Sheik agreement, Israel promised each time to open the wholesale produce market here in Hebron, which is still not open. In late November the team tried to sell tomatoes there to call attention to Israel's refusal to live up to her agreements. The team was quickly arrested, held for ninety minutes, and released. It got lots of media attention. The team did a similar action there about three years ago.

We also saw the BBC video, *In God's Bunker*, which is about the Hebron settlers. In the video, the settlers are quite honest about their readiness to kill Arabs and their wish to remove all of them from the area. There was footage of children expressing hate for Arabs and the desire to kill them. We saw how the children are being indoctrinated into this hate in their schools. There was even a scene of settler children singing songs about killing Arabs. I recognized many of the children. Some of them, older now, were out at the Sultans. There were scenes of street violence, including settlers shooting Palestinians. It reminded me of how different things are here now, and the original purpose for CPT coming to Hebron. Now there is little overt violence between settlers and Palestinians on the streets.

I have been thinking about the settlers and their goal of expanding and taking everything here. That was their stated goal twenty years ago, but how close are they to accomplishing it? They have been confiscating more and more land, expanding their settlements at great cost to the Palestinians, but the possibility of removing all the Palestinians from Hebron is extremely remote. The Palestinians are also digging in. They are doing a huge amount of building in the areas they control, and their population is expanding rapidly. The settlers can only be a small minority in the Hebron area. The peace process, as flawed and corrupt as it is, will at least consolidate and legitimate Palestinian control over a fraction of the land and most of the urban areas in the West Bank. It would take a major war to reverse that. The settlers are also getting hemmed in by the so-called peace process.

January 17, 2000, Monday

Last evening Rusty Dinkins-Curling, Jamey Bouwmeester, and Dianne Roe came to join the team. That was a great reunion. I took Rusty on night patrol, orienting him to the city and telling stories of past events here.

In our team meeting this morning I proposed that in our Lenten action materials we request our network to contact U.S. government officials, asking them to make sure that any peace agreement includes compensation for Palestinians whose homes have been demolished. Since any peace agreement probably will include compensation to any settlers who have to relocate, it seems reasonable that Palestinians who have lost their homes also be compensated. We also recommended that this compensation be taken from any compensation given to the Israelis.

I then took a group of seven Japanese students on a tour of Hebron, ending here at our apartment. They are studying models of conflict resolution and will be working in Palestine on a project of conflict resolution sponsored by the Japanese government. They asked excellent questions, especially about whether dialogue and confidence-building measures between Palestinians and Israelis are actually counterproductive, serving to perpetuate and smooth over the deep conflicts that exist here, thus making it more difficult to deal with those difficult issues. Polite "dialogue" can also make it easier for those in power to continue their oppression. I agreed with their concerns, but explained that it is very important that we bring people together around the struggle for justice at the grass roots, in a deep way around something that is real. I used the example of bringing Israelis to the Sultan home, and how that can be the beginning of a new future.

January 19, 2000, Wednesday

Osaid, one of our translators, and his brother Waleed came to our apartment this afternoon. Waleed just got out of prison for being part of Islamic Jihad. He was in for six years. We talked about the meaning of suffering, that our suffering is not in vain. He said he agreed with that. Is talking about the suffering of the Palestinians a way of talking about the cross with Muslims? Avi Goldberg also came. This is amazing. Here was an Islamic Jihad person just released from prison, relating with a Jew. Wow! This is one little result of bringing people together at the Sultans.

January 21, 2000, Friday

Today we celebrated the Jewish festival of Tu Bishvat (Tree Planting Day) with more than 150 Israeli peace activists in the Palestinian village of Tiwane. This village is near Yatta, about ten miles south of Hebron, very close to the Israeli settlement of Ma'on. We went there to plant 100 olive trees which Israeli peace groups were bringing to the village as an act of peace and solidarity.

Last year settlers from Ma'on started a small satellite settlement on land owned by Palestinian farmers in the area. In November, in a highly publicized event, the Israeli government removed the Ma'on settlers from this land. The settlers protested, and argued that if they were not allowed on the Palestinian land, then, to be fair, neither should the Palestinian owners be allowed on their own land.

The Israeli government apparently agreed with the settlers, and on November 16, 1999, in an action not widely covered in the press, removed twenty families (300 people) from caves on their land. About two years ago the Israeli military bulldozed the entrances the Palestinians had built to these caves. The land taken from these people last year (now a military firing range) is part of a huge area of thousands of acres declared a closed military zone in the past year by the new Barak government.

The tree-planting action was organized by B'tselem, an Israeli human rights group, and supported by various other Israeli peace groups, like Gush Shalom, Bat Shalom (Daughters of Peace), and Rabbis for Human Rights. The action was an attempt to show that some Israelis care about what is happening to these farmers. Planting trees (olive trees are symbols of peace) also is a statement affirming Palestinian ownership of the land. The action was meant to create public awareness in Israel of the injustices here, and help pressure the Israeli government to reverse its recent actions. As one B'tselem activist put it, "We want to send a message to the Israeli government that the injustice being done here is not the way to make peace."

Rusty, Reinhard, and I went early with some Palestinian activists to the area. When we got close to Tiwane, we saw a lot of soldiers on the road ahead, so we got out of our taxi and walked around the hill over steep, rocky terrain, and came into the village from the back.

We were warmly greeted by the people there, Palestinians who live like bedouins. These are simple folk, subsistence farmers and shepherds, whose main source of income is selling cheese and yogurt made from sheep milk. They used to graze their herds on the rocky mountains in the area, and kept their sheep in caves during the winter nights. Now they are staying in nearby villages, keep their sheep in outside pens with no protection, and no food except for what they buy. Three homes in this village were demolished some years ago. Two years ago much of their wheat crop was burned by settlers. They have suffered a lot.

We never did plant any trees. The three buses of Israelis from Tel Aviv and Jerusalem were stopped by Israeli soldiers near the Ma'on settlement and told they could not proceed. Tense negotiations followed between the soldiers and peace activists. When two settler buses came, it became difficult for the soldiers to argue that the settlers could proceed, but not the Israeli peace activists. After an hour, the activists were allowed to proceed, but they were forbidden to bring any trees with them, and warned they could not leave the village to go on the farmland. The trees, I am told, will be smuggled into the village at another time. Why are olive trees considered dangerous?

When the buses finally arrived at the village, there was a big commotion as the 200 villagers gathered to see these strange-looking outsiders who were invading their small village, along with lots of press.

After speeches by Israelis and Palestinians, we were all invited into the homes of the village for tea, bread, and sheep yogurt. These stone huts are the simplest homes I have ever been in, but the hospitality was warm and gracious. They shared what little they have. Although the soldiers temporarily stopped 100 trees from entering the village, they could not squelch the message those trees were intended to bring. Jews, Muslims, and Christians broke bread together in hopes for a just peace.

January 27, 2000, Thursday

We went to Jerusalem for a meeting for worship and discussion at Sabeel at noon. This is an important connection with Palestinian Christian activists. After this we met with Arik Ascherman at the office of Rabbis for Human Rights to discuss our Buckets of Soil idea.

In our struggling to find ways to counter the continuing confiscation of Palestinian land, our team came up with the idea of Buckets of Soil. Jesus said that if someone demands your cloak, give that person your underwear as well, thus shaming that person with your nakedness. Someone on our team suggested that if the settlers want more land, let's give them more land. Out of this came the idea of taking buckets of soil to one of the expanding settlements here, and encouraging our worldwide network of contacts to send packets of soil to Israeli embassies with the message to stop land confiscation. We wanted to share this idea with Arik and hear his reaction. Arik said he liked our proposal and that Jesus' teaching has its roots in Judaism. He indicated he will help organize Israeli participation.

By the time we were ready to leave at 4:00 p.m., it was snowing hard. I was concerned about this all day because it was predicted that a major snowstorm would be hitting the area. It did, which is unusual for this region. As we were driving south out of Jerusalem, the road was getting more and more snow covered, and at one point, near Bethlehem, we had to get out and push our taxi. Soon our driver said he didn't think he could get to Hebron, and that he was going back to Jerusalem. We decided to get out and start walking toward Hebron, hoping for a ride in the night.

We started hitchhiking. A number of settler cars stopped, but were going to nearby settlements. I thought riding with settlers might be quite interesting. In this case, we would be dependent on them, creating a new dynamic. When settler cars stopped, I used the Hebrew word (Hevron) in asking if they were going to Hebron.

Soon a pickup truck used to transport workers picked us up. We sat in the back with two young Palestinians. It was snowing really hard. Some vehicles were stranded by the side of the road. Before long, traffic was not moving at all. We were stuck, but we were having fun. Our common plight had brought us all together. Palestinians, soldiers, settlers, and North American activists were all stranded, brought together by a snowstorm. Our differences no longer seemed important. Something bigger than us, and out of our control, had brought us together. We fight over things we want to control, but here was something none of us could control.

People who otherwise might be enemies now were acting as friends. Settlers, soldiers, and Palestinians were helping push each other's cars, each identifying with the others, all because of an act of nature. At this "checkpoint" we were all equal.

After sitting there for about two hours, I suggested that we start walking the ten miles toward home. As we started walking up the long hill, we understood why traffic was not moving. For over a mile, cars and trucks were jammed together on the slick road. No one could move. Some places it was even difficult for us to squeeze between the cars and trucks. At the top of the hill the road was free, and we soon got a ride into Hebron.

January 28, 2000, Friday

Today was a quiet day in Hebron, except for the many snowball fights in which I eagerly participated. I must admit I started quite a few of them. What a wonderful way to break rigid attitudes and patterned responses, and connect with people in a new way. I started one battle with about a dozen young Palestinians, all of them against me. Excitement and commonality filled the air. The Israeli soldiers were especially friendly and some of them even participated in the snowball fights.

The snow brought us together, but unfortunately, the snow melts quickly here. The oppression of the occupation continues. The problems here are too deep to be covered over by snow. We were, however, again given a glimpse of what can be.

This morning I walked by the mosque here on our street and was stopped by several people inside who insisted that I come in. They took me up to the front to some people huddled around a small heater. I greeted them and after a short conversation, they invited me to join them for Friday prayer. I accepted. For a long time I have wanted to join our neighbors in prayer. It was a real gift. The prayer time was a meaningful time for me.

This afternoon several teammates and I got into a conversation with a Palestinian who made racist remarks about blacks and Jews. We confronted him with what he said, saying we hear the exact same words said about Palestinians. That was difficult for him to hear. Maybe this will help move our friendship to a deeper level.

January 29, 2000, Saturday

In our team meeting this morning we worked out plans for our Buckets of Soil action. We planned it for Friday, February 11, at the entrance to Harsina by Atta's parents' place. We thought that the big wall behind their house, the expanding Harsina settlement, the new gas station, and Atta's two demolished houses there would make an ideal setting for our action. We worked out the scenario and divided up roles that need to be filled before and during the action. I am to be the overall coordinator. I immediately got to work and wrote up our plans and sent them to Arik Ascherman.

February 1, 2000, Tuesday

This afternoon I decided to go to the mosque for afternoon prayer. I felt I have an open invitation to go there. As soon as the prayer time was over, I was surrounded by about thirty Muslims questioning me whether I was a Muslim and why I had prayed with them. It was a wonderful time sitting together on the floor, doing some deep sharing. I felt a lot of love from everyone. I saw some wide eyes and puzzled looks on faces this afternoon when they realized that a Christian had prayed with them. When I told them I would not come back if anyone was uncomfortable with me being there, they all insisted I was always welcome there. This feels wonderful to me. This is stretching their consciousness, helping them see Christians in a new way.

A shop owner stopped me and wanted to know why I was in the mosque. That led to him urging me to become Muslim. He told me Islam is the only good religion. Another young man then entered the conversation who was more strident. He began saying that this land is only for Muslims, that all Jews and Christians must leave. Where have I heard that before? I told him that this land is for everyone, and told him the story of how the Crusaders removed all the Jews from Jerusalem, but when Saladin conquered and returned Jerusalem to Muslim rule, he invited the Jews to return to Jerusalem. The young man said he didn't believe that. I suggested he check it out. Is one of our roles here to counter the racism of the Palestinians?

Pierre was out on the street before supper and reported that everyone in the neighborhood is talking about my praying in the mosque. What am I doing? This could affect the team's relationship with our neighbors. Jamey said he thought this will strengthen our relationship with the people here. I think it is positive. I feel I should start going to the mosque somewhat regularly. I wish I could also pray with the settlers here.

These experiences also are deepening and confirming my

Christian faith for me. I am a Christian. I am not at the same place these Muslims are. I am simply opening my heart to God and to them, and making myself vulnerable to them.

February 3, 2000, Thursday

I saw soldiers checking Palestinians' identity cards down by the market this morning. One soldier was being rather rude to the Palestinians, so I asked him to treat everyone with respect. He said he was just doing his job. I said, "No, your job is not to be rude." He then said that he could tell I am from America, and that I have no right to tell him what to do in his country. I said, "No, this is not your country. This is occupied territory. I was invited here by the inhabitants, but you were not."

February 8, 2000, Tuesday

I spent the day distributing an Arabic version of our invitation to the Buckets of Soil action on Friday. It refers to Jesus saying that if someone who has power over you asks you to do some thing you should not have to do, sometimes as a form of resistance you can do more than you are ordered to do, to show that person the wrongness of what is happening and to offer alternative possibilities.

This morning I took a copy to a Palestinian friend. His response was, "This idea is really crazy, but I like it."

This afternoon I went out to the Beqa'a to distribute leaflets. I started at the southern end of the east side of the valley and walked the two miles north to the Sultan family, and then walked back south on the west side of the bypass road, talking with people and giving them leaflets as I went. I had a fantastic time meeting people I knew and others I had not met before. At many places I stopped and talked awhile. People seemed to react very positively after reading the invitation to join our action.

February 9, 2000, Wednesday

I realize how unbelievable this scene is. I am going door to door in this all-Muslim neighborhood, passing out tracts inviting them to a Christian action, explicitly based on the teachings of Jesus, and referring to Jesus, and I am so warmly received. It sounds impossible. And on Friday, in front of an ugly monstrous wall, Jews, Muslims, and Christians will come together again.

How is this possible? It is, of course, a miracle. I doubt our work could continue without all the prayer which undergirds it. Actually, all love and coming together of people is a miracle, something we cannot create or force. We can only open our lives to accept the miracles that are daily offered, or we can stubbornly resist and close ourselves to grace. The power of evil seeks to divide us, but the power of God brings us together in spite of the walls that divide us.

It is also true that, in a common struggle for justice, when we make ourselves vulnerable and authentic to each other, we find a deep unity between us. In a struggle for justice we are not arguing about abstractions that divide us, but are drawn together by the truth and love we are seeking.

February 10, 2000, Thursday

We were "invaded" by the CPT delegation this evening, ten of them. They had arrived in Bethlehem on Saturday evening and have been getting an orientation to the conflict here by meeting with both Palestinians and Israelis. They will be spending the next five days with us here in Hebron. One of CPT's ways of relating to conflict situations is to send short-term delegations of people who talk to people on both sides of the conflict, and then return home more aware and more able to work at the problems from their homes in North America, where many of the world's problems have roots. In fact, in the beginning of CPT, before we had long-term presence in areas of conflict, short-term delegations were the primary way of engaging with conflicts.

I led a nonviolence training this evening in preparation for our action tomorrow. This included role-play and wrestling with how we might respond to various things that could happen. I hope it helped us be prepared to creatively enter the action together.

February 11, 2000, Friday

After worship this morning we headed out to the Bcqa'a. We got there early. Soon about twenty soldiers and police appeared on the road right above the gas station that is being built on Jaber land. I knew they were there to "welcome" us. I immediately headed toward them and greeted them, shaking hands with a lot of them and using my few words of Hebrew greetings. I wanted to help set a positive tone in our relationship with them today. They informed me that this was a closed military zone, that we would not be allowed on the road, but could do our action on Atta's parents' land. I explained to them about CPT, and since they were gathering information about us, they listened carefully.

Soon more people began arriving, including about thirty Israelis and some Christian friends. We had a large banner in Arabic and English, which read, "Land Confiscation Is Not Peace." There were probably seventy-five of us.

The police allowed us to walk part way up the bulldozer-scarred hillside above the thirty-foot-high ugly wall behind Atta's parents' home, on the land that had been their beautiful, sculptured orchard. Now it is only bare rocks. I do not know how to describe the ugliness of this moonscape, which is being prepared for a new subdivision for the rapidly expanding Harsina settlement.

Abdel Hadi Hantash, speaking for the Palestine Land Defense Committee, reminded us that all this confiscation and building is illegal under international law and a violation of the Oslo agreement which Israel signed.

Abdel Jawad, Atta's father, walked up the hill carrying a large olive limb, loudly preaching to the soldiers about their having stolen his land and destroyed his trees. He held up the dead roots of a grapevine that had been bulldozed. This elderly man stood up to the soldiers and shared from the bottom of his heart. A lot of pain came out. His wife, Amni, also poured out a lot of pain, screaming at the soldiers.

We were soon stopped by a line of police when we tried to walk farther up the hill toward the settlement with our buckets of soil. That line then became the place for our action. We then, one by one, starting dumping our buckets of soil, each person making some kind of personal statement: Palestinians, Israelis, and internationals in Hebrew, Arabic, and English. We said to the settlers and to the Israeli government, "Here, you are so greedy that you take the land of these simple farmers, we will give you more. It was a powerful time. There was hardly a dry eye anywhere. I even saw tears in the eyes of the Israeli police standing between the settlement and us.

Arik Ascherman referred to the story of Naboth's vineyard, in which the rich King Ahab and Queen Jezebel wanted the small vineyard of the simple peasant, Naboth (1 Kings 21). Because Naboth had the courage to stand up to a powerful king and queen, he was killed and his vineyard confiscated.

Harriet Lewis spoke of her admiration for her Palestinian friends. "No matter how many times the bulldozers come," she said, "each time the Palestinians again wonder how it could happen. They can't believe that something that evil could happen. They never lose hope."

Rusty reminded us that the land was given by God to provide fruit, and not as a tool of domination.

There were a few settlers present, but they caused no trouble, except to call us Nazis. David Wilder circulated among us, filming everything and everyone. When he focused the camera on me, I smiled and said, "Shalom." He never said a word at our action. Some of our group saw him on the street here in Hebron this morning and he asked them,

Jews, Muslims, and Christians preparing to empty buckets of soil in front of Israeli police.

"Where is your dirt, or are you the dirt?"

After the action we were invited to the Jaber home for tea. We sat in a circle under a tree, enjoying the beautiful, warm day. Israeli police came and reminded the Israeli peace activists that this was a closed military zone and that they needed to leave. Atta took tea to the police, but they declined the offer. Apparently the police were concerned about the safety of the Israelis, especially Arik Ascherman, who is especially hated by the settlers. There was no hint that they wanted us CPT'ers to leave. The Israelis eventually did leave, but they took their time about it.

Arik Ascherman gave me a dollar for my trip home. There is a Jewish tradition of giving a person a gift or message to carry on a trip for someone at the other end, thus ensuring God's blessing on the trip, because an important task needs to be performed. I am to give the dollar to a needy cause or person when I arrive home. Avi Goldberg also gave me three shekels.

February 14, 2000, Monday

I went out to the Beqa'a to say good-bye to the Sultans. I noticed they had planted about a dozen roses around the house: a sign of hope. Lamia wanted to do something for my wife, Peggy, in gratitude for sharing me with them, so she gave me a pair of her slippers for me to bring back home. That was special for me.

When I left, I broke down and cried. Omar also cried. The love I have felt from the Sultans and so many other Palestinians, the way I have been accepted here, the awesomeness of having so directly confronted the powers of evil here at the Sultans, the powerful way I experienced the working of God in this place, the victory we witnessed here over the powers of evil; all those feelings were so beautiful, so overwhelming, that I could not contain it all. I cried a long way walking down the road through the vineyards. I sang the song I sang every day here called "Lord, listen to your children praying" by Ken Medema. It ends with the plea: "Send us love, send us power, send us grace."

I have been working hard at preparing this journal for publication, but feel one more trip is necessary to give a broader perspective, especially since Hebron is now a war zone.

December 13, 2000-January 31, 2001

December 13, 2000, Wednesday

I am now on a plane heading back to Hebron. What I will experience there promises to be very different from my previous trips. This time I am headed into the middle of a war. There has been a major uprising throughout the West Bank and Gaza. The current uprising was sparked by Ariel Sharon, former Israeli defense minister, invading Al Aqsa Mosque in Jerusalem on September 28, accompanied by around 1,000 Israeli soldiers and police. The Muslims saw this show of force as a provocation, and as a clear threat to their control of Haram Al Sharif, the place Jews refer to as the Temple Mount. It is no secret that many right wing Israelis intend to demolish Al Aqsa Mosque and rebuild the Jewish Temple there. It would be difficult to find a more emotional issue than this in the Middle East.

The action by Sharon ignited a mass of pent-up frustration, fueled with the failed promises of the Oslo Agreement, and the continuing injustices and humiliations of the occupation. With the collapse of the Oslo process this year, it has appeared to the Palestinians that Israel had no intention of ending the occupation. While the first uprising (Intifada) in the 1980s was largely nonviolent, this time some Palestinians are using guns in addition to street demonstrations. Inspired by Hezballah's victory in driving the Israeli military out of southern Lebanon this past June, some Palestinians are now waging a guerilla war against Israeli occupation. The Israeli military is responding with tanks and helicopter gunships.

On September 29, the day after Sharon went to Al Aqsa

Mosque, eight people, seven Palestinians and one Israeli, were killed in the protests that erupted. As of November 27, 303 people had been killed: 256 Palestinians and 35 Israelis, a ratio of seven to one. Over 15,000 have been injured.

Ramadan began two weeks ago, so fasting has been a wonderful time of spiritual preparation. I feel spiritually prepared and eager to get back to work in Hebron. Various people have urged me to not make this trip, saying that it is too dangerous, that they feared for my safety. I appreciate their concern, but it is important that we peacemakers not stop now. We in CPT have been saying that we need to be prepared to risk our lives for peace, that we need to take the same risks that soldiers take.

I also feel compelled to go back because my friends in Hebron are being shot at and subjected to horrible conditions. I want to stand with them, to be vulnerable with them. I care deeply for Israel and Palestine. I want Jews and Palestinians to flourish in God's love. Somehow I want to stand in the middle of the confusion and violence, and point to another reality.

I recognize that there is a danger. I accept that I might be killed. That is okay. I am sixty-one years old, have lived a good life, have experienced love. I don't have that many years left anyway. If someone is sent to war, it should only be people over fifty or sixty. It should not be the young who die.

Actually, for a Christian, being ready to die should not be an issue. In baptism we say we are giving up everything and dying to self. All of life is to be lived in submission to God's will. So, the only question is what God wants me to do. If nonviolence is real, if my faith is real, then it is at the most dangerous times that we need to act. We need the faith that leads us into the heart of evil situations, both to expose the evil and plant a seed of new life and hope. This is not to argue for stupidity, for irresponsibility, for seeking martyrdom, but to be open to respond in love in any situation.

December 15, 2000, Friday

I went to Hebron early this morning after spending the night in Jerusalem. Our taxi was stopped by soldiers at Beit Ummar and ordered to turn around. We went back about a mile and took a side road to near Hebron, just north of the Beqa'a. There soldiers had dumped a big load of dirt, blocking the road. We got out of the taxi, walked across the mound of dirt, where a number of taxis were waiting to take people into Hebron. I was told that some days it takes as many as four taxis to travel between Jerusalem and Hebron.

It was eerie walking through the empty, closed market, with not a person on the streets. There was a curfew again today in Hebron, the seventy-sixth day of the curfew. I saw a lot of rocks and the charred remains of fires on the streets. I thought of my friends as I walked past their closed shops.

Soon I was at our apartment and met Jamey Bouwmeester, Natasaha Krahn, Bob Holmes, Gary Brooks, Rick Carter, Anita Fast, and Kathy Kern. I got there right after worship, and was invited to go with Natasaha out to Atta's parents' house in the Beqa'a Valley and move in with them. The family has been under regular attack from settlers. The team is suggesting that I stay there. That sounds good to me.

We arrived a little before noon and were warmly greeted by the Jaber family. The family consists of Atta's parents, Abdel Jawad and Amni; Atta's unmarried sister, Kokab; Atta's brother Jowdi and his wife, Nihaad; and their five children: Hebah (14), Rubah (13), Abed (11), Shuroq (8), and Kokab (3). Abed is the only boy. They are farmers who raise grapes and vegetables to sell.

I am simply to be a presence here in the Beqa'a. I already know a lot of the people of the Beqa'a. The Sultan family lives just a mile north from here. For a long time the team has wanted more of a presence in the Beqa'a. I am here to help the team take another step in that direction. My only clear assignment is to make three phone calls in case there is any trouble here. First, I am to call Jeff Halper who is the head of ICAHD in Jerusalem. He will call Israeli security people and the Israeli press. I am to call a Palestinian journalist friend who will notify other Palestinian journalists. And I am to call the team in Hebron.

We had just begun visiting when we heard the sounds of rocks thudding on the roof of the house. For about fifteen minutes settlers were throwing rocks from above the big, ugly wall about twenty-five feet behind their house. The family was screaming in terror. What was about to happen next? We made our three phone calls. Soon soldiers drove up to the house and everything became quiet. CPT is learning that the military responds much more quickly to calls from internationals and Israelis than from Palestinians.

Since the beginning of November, settlers have been almost daily harassing the Jaber family, throwing rocks, vandalizing the property, breaking windows, destroying their garden. About six weeks ago the settlers destroyed about $500 worth of plastic irrigation pipes. The Jabers are now afraid to plant anything in that field.

The Jaber family has a long history of suffering at the hands of the Israelis. In 1975, the oldest son, Rajeh, was working for a settler and was severely injured in an accident caused by the carelessness of the settler. Both of his legs were broken. There was neither an apology from the employer nor any compensation. Although the Jabers have been here on this land for over 400 years, and have deeds to their land, they have already lost most of it, and what they have left is far from secure. In 1986, three acres of their land was confiscated for a road to Kiryat Arba. On June 6, 1989, settlers sprayed herbicide on their grapes, killing 400 mature vines. In 1995 the bypass road was built through the Jabers' land. In addition to losing a lot of land, they also had 1,200 heads of cauliflower, valued at $1,400, covered with rocks. Israeli authorities offered them $66 for the lost produce and land. The family refused the insult. Six acres of their orchard were bulldozed and confiscated in 1999. They started building an addition to the house, but received a stop work order and are afraid to build. We all cramp together in a small space.

This family was never rich, but they had a decent income from their land, selling fruits and vegetables. Now that they have lost much of their land, they are struggling to survive. They are partly living on donated food from other countries, doing some hired labor, and doing without. One example of the suffering inflicted on them by the Israelis is their not being able to afford to go to a dentist. Many of the family are suffering daily toothaches, their teeth are rotting, but they simply endure it.

There have been many settler rallies and demonstrations on the road in front of the Jaber house. It sounds like a repeat of the situation with the Sultans last year. A week ago

The author with the Jaber family in front of the Jaber home, with settler wall in back of the house.

two settler women were shot and killed by someone in a car passing their car on the road about a mile from here. That has greatly increased the tension here. Soon after the shooting, settlers took over the new house that Israeli peace activists have built for Atta and Rodeina, their third house.

Last Saturday, about forty settlers came out of Atta and Rodeina's house and went on a rampage, stoning Palestinian homes here, destroying Palestinian property, and shooting thirteen-year-old Monsur Jaber in the abdomen and left hand. Some Israeli peace activists came and went to the soldiers guarding the settlers in Atta and Rodeina's house and asked the soldiers why they were allowing these armed settlers who had just shot a boy to stay in a house that didn't belong to them. A soldier replied, "What do you want? He was just an Arab boy." Last Sunday the settlers were removed from the house. Soldiers are now living in it.

At about 3:15 this afternoon, Neta Golan, along with two women from Germany and Australia, came to the Jaber house in response to our calls this afternoon. All three come from Jewish backgrounds, with the German woman being a Christian. Neta is an Israeli activist who is giving all her time to working for an end to the occupation. She has been coming to Hebron in the past months to work with CPT, including sleeping in Palestinian homes that were being shelled by the Israeli military. I was impressed with how warmly this Israeli Jew was received by this Muslim family.

We experienced a spiritual victory last year at the Sultans, but that evil spirit is now manifesting itself in an even more powerful way. However, I can already see the beginning of the victory over those evil powers. Tonight, Jews and Christians will sleep in this Muslim home. I shared with Neta my vision that we need to end the occupation. She said that she and others have been thinking the same thing, and are starting to organize to end the occupation. Already appeals have gone out, inviting people from around the world to come here to give international protection to the Palestinian people. Meanwhile I learned that four more people were killed yesterday.

December 16, 2000, Saturday

We got up about 4:15 this morning and had breakfast, and then everyone went back to bed. Because of the Ramadan fast, we will not eat or drink again until after sunset. After daylight, Natasha and Neta left. Neta wanted to go to the village of Harres, near Nablus, for the funeral of a Palestinian friend of hers who was shot in the chest by Israeli soldiers. She has been spending a lot of time in Harres, being with the people there who are under daily attack from settlers. This fall she organized Israelis to harvest the olives there, because Palestinians were prevented by settlers from going to their land.

We saw her friend's funeral procession on TV this evening. Funeral processions of Palestinians killed by Israelis are a big thing here, and are given extensive coverage on TV, showing the bodies being carried through the streets. These scenes are shown over and over, in addition to scenes of clashes with Israelis, and some of the more famous scenes of Palestinians dying in the streets.

I spent the day working with the Jaber family harvesting turnips to sell. When we finished this afternoon I walked up to the Sultans. That was a joyful reunion. They seem to be doing well. This past September settlers had a short presence on the old road just below their house, but other than that, there have been no problems from settlers.

December 17, 2000, Sunday

Several times during the night I heard loud booms and rapid automatic weapons firing. I am told the loud booms are cannon fire from tanks stationed in and around Hebron. The fire each time lasted a few minutes. I was reminded this is a war zone. I felt helpless lying here. What can I do to stop the guns? Maybe my work is not to stop the guns.

December 18, 2000, Monday

We harvested turnips again today, which I enjoyed very much. But I had to wonder what I am doing here. I thought I came here to do important work. But I am washing turnips.

When I got to the CPT apartment last Friday, I learned some were going to a march, starting in Bethlehem and attempting to march through the checkpoint into Jerusalem for Friday prayers. I really wanted to be part of that march, but it seemed I should come here. Yesterday I learned that the march had been canceled. I am glad I came here. I need to remember that I am to follow God's leading, not my own desires. I don't understand what I am doing washing turnips, but it seems right. I don't need to see the purpose now.

December 21, 2000, Thursday

The whole team from Hebron came out this morning to visit me. That was helpful for me. We had a team meeting in which we talked about many of the practical details of my being here. I got to see Pierre Shantz and Anne Montgomery, who have been staying in Beit Jala.

I learned a little about what the team is doing in Hebron. There have been daily clashes between stone-throwing youth and soldiers who retaliate with massive force. Many of the nights are interrupted by intense gunfire, including cannon fire from tanks located around the city. Sometimes the shooting is from neighboring rooftops. A few times during intense gunfire, the team has hidden in the kitchen, where they are protected by two thick stone walls.

The team has often been out on the streets observing clashes. They have not found a way to intervene in these clashes, but have had a presence, hoping that people knowing they are being watched will have some effect on their actions. A few times team members have been caught in the middle of clashes, ducking behind cars as the shooting began. Once a Palestinian acquaintance was shot in the back of the head, after clashes appeared to be over and team members were heading home.

The team ignores curfews and has not been prevented by soldiers from walking the streets, which is ironic. We foreigners and Israeli settlers are allowed on the streets, but the people of Hebron are not. The people of Hebron are under house arrest, their homes having become prisons. Some of the schools are closed, some having been taken over by soldiers. There are two tanks in one schoolyard.

The Israeli-controlled part of Hebron is under curfew most days, with occasional short times when shops are allowed to open and people are able to get food. The team has brought food to some families who have been unable to leave their homes. One time the team distributed food that soldiers would not allow to be distributed by Palestinian municipal employees. Another time when soldiers were not allowing Red Cross and municipal workers to distribute food, team members talked the soldiers into allowing the distribution to continue.

Team members have often intervened when soldiers have stopped Palestinians on the street during curfew. Some of these incidents have included students returning home from school after curfew was reimposed, or people wanting to visit relatives in the hospital.

The team has called military commanders to request that they stop shelling a neighborhood, allow families to get food, or discontinue an oppressive policy. They also call Israeli friends who then call military commanders to make the same requests. This has seemed to have some effect.

On October 2, Anita Fast and Andrew Getman visited a family near the CPT apartment. Israeli soldiers had occupied one of their bedrooms in order to shoot at Palestinian demonstrators on the street below. The five children, all under twelve, were terrified. When the soldiers asked Anita and Andrew to leave, Anita said, "This is a private home." "Not any more," the soldier yelled. Having documented the situation, and not wanting to cause the family any more trouble, the CPTers left.

Team members have been visiting areas of the city hardest hit by shelling the previous night, listening to people's stories about enduring a night of having their house hit by bullets, seeing the tattered clothes hanging in closets where they were shredded by bullets coming into the closets, and hearing stories of people being killed and wounded in their homes. These neighborhoods are shelled after someone in the neighborhood fires at soldiers.

Palestinians believe sometimes this firing is done by Israeli soldiers, or comes from people who do not live in the neighborhood. Team members have been invited to spend nights sleeping in these homes, sharing the fear and terror the families experience. We have the sense that the main reason we are invited into these homes is that the people want the world to hear their stories. We are trying to tell these stories.

The settlers in Hebron are not under curfew, and now have more freedom to harass their Palestinian neighbors. They have been spray-painting anti-Arab graffiti on Palestinian walls, including writing on the mosque on our street that the Prophet Mohammed was a pig. Palestinian families living next to the settlements receive constant harassment, vandalism, and sexual comments from the settlers, and also from soldiers. Often soldiers watch as settlers harass Palestinians or destroy their property.

This is also a difficult time for the settlers. They are being shot at by Palestinians, and their future is quite uncertain. I am told that if the peace negotiations succeed, the settlers here will probably be removed. I would like to talk to the settlers here again.

It is hard not to be cynical about the peace process and the Barak government. Things have clearly deteriorated here during the last year. The economy is worse, Palestinians and Israelis are more alienated from each other, there are increased signs of apartheid, and the settlements keep expanding at a rapid rate. Barak has still not implemented the agreements made by the Netanyahu government.

Much has been destroyed during Barak's tenure, including the peace momentum, the Israeli national desire for peace, and the good will of the Palestinian people. I wish I could see one sign that the Israeli government wants peace. Of course, they want stability and calm, but do they want real peace, God's peace, the peace that comes with justice? I hear Palestinians saying that they now do not want any peace without justice. The goal of establishing peace through separating Jews and Arabs, of giving Palestinians small enclaves surrounded by Israeli military, with limited self-rule, has failed. Now a new search for peace must resume, a peace based on justice, mutual respect, and shared power.

December 22, 2000, Friday

I spent part of the morning watching Israelis building up the already huge wall behind the Jaber house, and filling in dirt behind the wall. The wall must be 30 feet high and 500 feet long. It was difficult to watch. I had to struggle with a lot of anger. Peace talks are going on right now in Washington, D.C. Here, the Israelis are expanding the settlements in violation of both international law and the Oslo agreements, and with apparent United States support.

I went up to the workers and asked them if they had permission from the owners of this land to be building this wall here. They replied that all this land belongs to the Jews. I asked them if this is shalom. No reply.

Eleven-year-old Abed taught me to plow with a donkey today. As we were plowing the garden, above us a big bulldozer and backhoe were piling up huge rocks on the wall above us. Those bulldozers have a lot of power. They are moving a lot of dirt. I am thinking of the Man who rode into Jerusalem on a donkey to point to another power, another kingdom, and another way to live. That power does not build walls, it tears them down.

December 23, 2000, Saturday

For the first time since I got here, I went into Hebron to share worship with the team. Two people were killed in Hebron yesterday, and there was a lot of shooting during the night. During shooting at night, there is little the team can do except lay low and pray. To go outside would be suicide. We want to do what needs to be done, but there is no point in taking unnecessary risks. Peacemakers do not need to have a ready answer to every problem. No one else does. We simply understand that violence does not solve problems, and instead work at ways of preventing violence and realistic ways of resolving conflicts.

The city was under curfew again today, so everything was closed. The only people on the streets were settlers. I greeted a few of them with "Shabbat shalom," including Anat Cohen, who cursed me.

I am spending much of my time trying to pray. But I don't

The Jaber house, the wall, and the expanding settlement above the wall. To the right is a new gas station built on Jaber land. In the foreground is the bypass road built through the Jaber land.

know how to pray. I am trying to open my heart to God, to express to God the pain and despair I sense here. I try to lift up the people here to God, to cry out to God for peace, but I feel very weak and inadequate to pray. I am grateful that I do not need to pray alone, for the Spirit of God groans and prays for me. I trust God can hear what I cannot express. It is a deep challenge for me, to cry out to God in ways beyond what I am able to express.

I do not see prayer as magic. I do not believe that if I say the right words, pray in the right way, or go through the proper motions, then automatically what I want to happen will happen. I have no power to manipulate God. On the other hand, I believe our prayer does have effect, first on us, then on others, and on God. There is power in prayer. But prayer is not simple or easy. Jesus said some powers of evil cannot be cast out without much prayer and fasting. We are facing massive, well-organized evil powers. To overcome those powers, people need to unite in prayer and action.

December 25, 2000, Monday

There is a large cave right behind the house here in which the Jaber family lived before they built the house. The cave is now their kitchen and pantry. It rained all night and a lot of water leaked into the cave. The Jabers said this has never happened before. I have been concerned about the safety of the huge wall behind the house which is built with large rocks and filled with soil behind it. The wall is built over the rock out of which the cave was chiseled. That there are now cracks in the cave makes me even more concerned. With enough rain, I am afraid the whole wall could come crashing down on the house.

I went into Hebron this morning to go to Jerusalem with Pierre. We talked with some soldiers on the way to the taxi. Yesterday Pierre came across soldiers refusing to allow an elderly woman to leave the Israeli controlled area because of curfew.

Pierre talked to the woman who said she wanted to visit one of her children in the hospital. Pierre asked the soldiers why they wouldn't let her go. They said it was orders. Pierre said, no it is not orders, you have a lot of discretion and you are just being mean. The soldiers became rude, so Pierre said, "You treat the people here like dirt. You would not want Palestinians to treat Jews like that." Pierre was threatened with arrest, but then the soldiers let the woman go, and Pierre left the scene.

One of the soldiers we talked to this morning was in charge during Pierre's confrontation yesterday. We had a good talk about what the soldiers are doing here, why they are killing so many people, the need to end the occupation. Pierre was grateful he could connect with this soldier in a more human way.

We attended Christmas service with the Lutheran congregation. The message of the sermon was "God comes to us. We are not alone." I needed to hear that.

In the afternoon most of our team participated in the annual peace march from Shepherds' Field in Beit Sahur to Manger Square in Bethlehem. The march was led by twelve people on camels who had traveled on camels from Iraq on a peace pilgrimage to Bethlehem. I talked to one of them and learned they are trying to combine Christian faith with concern for social justice. I had a fantastic time reconnecting with a lot of people I know and talking about how to end the occupation.

December 26, 2000, Tuesday

After sleeping in Bethlehem last night, I went with Anne Montgomery this morning to see the CPT apartment in Beit Jala, a traditional Christian town just west of Bethlehem. The town has received mortar fire from tanks located in Gilo, an Israeli settlement on the hill just north of Beit Jala, built on land that has been part of Beit Jala. Some of the land for the Gilo settlement was bought from Palestinians, but much of it has been confiscated from them. The people of Beit Jala have not been permitted to pick the olives on their land on the hill below the Gilo settlement.

Palestinian gunmen have been coming into Beit Jala at night and shooting at the Gilo settlement, which brings heavy fire from the Israelis. This is difficult for the people of Beit Jala, who are not the ones shooting, but like the innocent in all wars, suffer the consequences. Team members have heard the gunmen shooting right outside the apartment.

Palestinian Christians asked CPT to have a presence in Beit Jala. In the beginning of December the team rented an apartment here, making a one-month commitment. Several nights later the apartment was hit by mortar fire, with one shell exploding inside the apartment. The team immediately got in contact with the American Consulate in Jerusalem who said he would call Israeli military headquarters. The shelling soon stopped. A week later the apartment was hit again. Things are quiet now, with no shelling in the past ten days.

Anne showed me the apartment with all the holes in the walls. The spaces that once were windows are now filled with sandbags. The Israeli military is using high velocity fragmentation bullets both when shooting into homes and into crowds. The bullets shatter upon impact, sending shrapnel in all directions. Some bullets are designed to shatter inside flesh, causing internal tearing wounds.

A German doctor living in Beit Jala was killed here in November while helping wounded neighbors. His body exploded from the tank shell that hit him. I saw the effects of these bullets inside and outside the CPT apartment. Fragmentation bullets are illegal under international law, as is shooting into residential homes.

We went on a short walk around the neighborhood, seeing holes in the street where shells hit, damage to St. Nicholas Orthodox Church, and the Catholic Church and seminary. Many of the homes have sustained a lot of damage. Most of the residents here now sleep elsewhere at night, or stay in protected rooms in basements. The CPT team stays in rooms on the other side of the apartment from Gilo, protected by two stone walls and sandbags.

CPT has tried to have two people living in the apartment. The purpose is to be present with and to stand in solidarity with people who are being bombed, to be able to give eyewitness accounts of what is happening here, and to call world attention to the situation. We also hope our presence may give some protection to the people here.

We never know the effects of our actions, but we do know the shelling of Beit Jala has stopped and we have brought news media here who have gotten the word out. We have helped make people aware of the risks people here live with every day. Through our worldwide contacts we have encouraged many people to pray for the people here.

After finishing my visit, I got a taxi to Hebron. We had to stop at Halhoul, where there was a huge mound of dirt on the road. We got out of the taxi, walked around the mound of dirt, and got another taxi into Hebron. Traveling here is not impossible but it is difficult. Much of Palestinian traffic is restricted to back roads.

The old road across from the Jabers is a good example. The exit here from the new bypass road is the one access to many of the towns and villages east of here. This is the only way, for example, to drive to Beni Naim, a town southeast of Hebron. For some people, that means an extra ten miles over extremely rough roads. Sometimes even this road is closed.

In addition to the blocked roads, it seems every day the soldiers close different roads, making each day different, and impossible for Palestinians to know which road to take on any particular day. It is a big risk to drive one's car. Sometimes soldiers simply stop cars, cut all four tires, and leave. Dianne Roe was in a taxi that was stopped and had the tires cut.

Soldiers stopped our friend, Yussef Al-Atrash, at gun-point, forced all the riders to move stones onto the road behind them to block the road, and then threw a tear gas canister into the car. It was three hours before people could get back into the car, and three weeks before the smell was gone.

When I got to Hebron I witnessed a large funeral procession for a young man killed by Israeli soldiers. I heard a fiery sermon from the mosque loudspeaker before the body was carried out in the street to the cemetery. This made the killing here more real to me.

December 27, 2000, Wednesday

Ramadan ended yesterday, so the next three days are feast days, a very special time for Muslims. This was a good day for the Jabers. Since the weather was warm, we ate out on the porch, all sitting on the floor around a common dish. It a happy day, although the family didn't have any money to spend on new clothes. I told them I don't buy new clothes for Christmas either. Because of all the suffering, the feast is a low-key affair this year. Various relatives came to visit.

December 28, 2000, Thursday

I went into Hebron to go with some of the team to Beit Sahur. As we were walking to get a taxi, we were stopped by soldiers who asked to see our passports. We got into a big discussion about their role here and the realities of the occupation. We heard the usual arguments that they are here because Israelis are under threat from the Arabs, that all the problems are caused by the Arabs. One of the soldiers said the Israelis have only two choices: either dominate or be dominated. One of the soldiers remembered me from five years ago and immediately accused me of trying to hide the knife five years ago. He wouldn't accept the way I remember the incident.

Five of us went to Shepherds' Field in Beit Sahur for a march to the Israeli military camp, just east of Beit Sahur.

There were probably 500 of us, including between seventy-five and 100 Israelis and at least fifty internationals. It was great to see Israelis and Palestinians greeting each other, actually glad to see each other. We heard there was a bombing in Tel Aviv this afternoon. I reported this to an Israeli from Tel Aviv who called his wife to check if she was safe at home. Here was a man, who was afraid of what might happen to his wife, reaching out to the people he has been told to fear and hate.

We marched past homes damaged by shelling from the military base. We walked right into the camp and began chanting, "Go home, go home, go home." We saw only a few soldiers in the distance, who ignored us. We then walked back into Beit Sahur and toured a number of homes demolished by shelling from Israeli tanks not far away, tanks we were looking at only minutes earlier. I met one Palestinian family who lives there, people I know from the congregation at Bethlehem Bible College. Their home was hit by Israeli shelling.

It was sobering to go through several of the homes: burnt-out shells, with broken china, melted glass, and charred remains of people's possessions. The walls of the houses were full of holes from the shells. We were told phosphor shells, which cause intense heat when they explode, were fired into the homes. The demolition of these Christian homes must have been deliberate. I stood for a while in one of the rooms and just cried.

After the march I spent the night in the CPT apartment in Beit Jala. It was an honor to sleep there. The night was quiet.

December 29, 2000, Friday

I awoke this morning to the sound of the Muslim call to prayer and to the ringing of church bells, all calling me to God and to prayer. How wonderful.

I got back to the Jabers and found everyone in the turnip patch, including Pierre and Rick who came out here last night after hearing of trouble here. I learned that hundreds of settlers were over at Atta and Rodeina's house last evening for lighting Hanukkah candles and prayers. After that, my Jaber home was stoned for about ten minutes. I assume this is a response to the two bombings yesterday in Tel Aviv and Gaza.

December 30, 2000, Saturday

The whole team was here this afternoon to eat maqlube with the Jabers. The Jabers keep insisting on the team coming to eat with them. Atta and Rodeina were also here. It was a joyful time.

We had a team meeting and I was asked to stay on here with the Jabers indefinitely. The team said that since this valley is a microcosm of the West Bank, it is a good place to be, both to observe and to take a stand. We continue to believe that the settlers intend to take this whole valley. If the settlers can take one house in this valley, then all the homes in this valley will be threatened. It seems to us that the Jaber home now is the most threatened home in this valley, so it is strategic to be here with this family.

It also seems that the Jaber home is a ready target anytime something bad happens elsewhere, such as Israelis being killed in a bomb attack. When something like this happens, we can expect a reaction from the settlers here. Should the current peace negotiations break down, or tensions increase, it is possible that the Israeli military could unleash the settlers.

I also am to visit other families here in the valley, building up relationships with the people here. I will be the only team member here, but the team is ready to send help at any time, and I hope to go to Hebron occasionally for worship with the team. I couldn't ask for anything better than this.

I asked about the focus for the team now in Hebron, and heard three answers: to create a space for nonviolence, to provide an alternative perspective, and to help people back in North America and elsewhere to connect with the reality of what is happening here. The team is doing daily patrols around the tense parts of the city, maintaining contacts with families in neighborhoods being shelled, and doing CSD visits with families. The team is seeking ways to be more visible in Hebron.

There are intense peace negotiations going on right now, with President Clinton wanting to accomplish something here before leaving office in a few weeks, and Israeli Prime Minister Barak needing some kind of peace deal to be able to win reelection in February. Most people seem to think the prospects for a settlement are dim. The Palestinians are in no mood to give up more than they have already given up.

This evening Arafat called for increased resistance to Israeli occupation. What does that mean? More people dying? I appreciate the commitment of the Palestinian people, their willingness to suffer and die. I hear them saying that they would rather die than live under slavery. I am amazed at both the capacity of the Palestinian people to endure suffering, and the utter futility of much of that suffering.

How I wish that all this energy could be put into a creative nonviolent movement to end the occupation. If people went out into the streets ready to die, and simply said "No more," the Israelis would be helpless to stop it. The whole world is watching. The Israelis would not dare to kill masses of unarmed people. At least not more than once. But the Israelis can get away with killing children who are throwing stones, or bombing residential neighborhoods from which there is sporadic gunfire.

The Palestinian tragedy is compounded by the pathetic leadership of the Palestinian Authority. Not only are they autocratic, having suppressed grassroots organizations, but they have been unable to articulate a strategy for ending the occupation. Brave young warriors throw stones at Israeli soldiers, many ending up as martyrs, but their energy is not directed toward any creative strategy of social change. The Palestinian leadership should be clear and open about their goals, and have a well-defined plan to reach those goals.

The means for ending the occupation are readily available. There is a just cause, an oppressed people with well-organized leadership in place, a willingness in the people to suffer, and widespread international support. Everything is in place to end the occupation except the vision to do it. How has CPT failed to articulate a vision for nonviolent change?

Some argue that because of 100 years of conflict, Palestinian society is not fertile ground for nonviolence. It is also argued that Palestine is not to be compared with South Africa because the populations here are more equal and the Afrikaners were not as paranoid as are the Israelis. Israel is a traumatized society, fighting for its very existence, it is argued. There is a real danger of plunging the whole region into war. Israel will not hesitate to resort to all-out war if threatened. As one of our friends put it, "You can frighten the Israelis, but don't scare them." Even massive nonviolent resistance could upset the delicate balance of power, threaten the Israelis, and result in war, even nuclear war.

I am not convinced that Palestinian society is not fertile ground for nonviolence. I think the vision is not there in the leadership. I also think there could be a massive nonviolent uprising, with Israeli participation, that could be sensitive to Israeli fears and not frighten Israelis. In fact, it could give Israelis a vision for getting out of this mess and point to the possibility of a brighter future.

Atta suggested that what is needed is a pilgrimage of five million Muslims from around the world to Jerusalem to pray. If unarmed, no Israeli army could stop them.

Iraqi President Saddam Hussein has offered 8,000 soldiers to come and fight with the Palestinians. They would be of no help to the Palestinians. It could only result in the deaths of more Palestinians. The Israeli military knows how to deal with foreign soldiers. But no military knows how to stop a nonviolent movement based in love and truth.

December 31, 2000, Sunday

I went to worship with the congregation at Bethlehem Bible College this morning. This time they knew about CPT since they helped bring CPT to Beit Jala. A number of the families in the congregation have had their homes hit by Israeli gunfire. I was warmly welcomed.

When I got back to the Jabers I learned that two settlers, the son and daughter-in-law of Meier Kahanne, were killed today by Palestinians. This is not good news. I wonder what the settler response will be. I decided to walk over to Atta's house and talk with the soldiers who are staying there. I told them I am living here, that I am afraid there may be trouble here tonight. I gave them a little history of what has been happening to the Jaber family.

They acted as if they didn't know much. They didn't even seem to know about all the land that has been confiscated from the Jabers. We talked about the settlers and the trouble they are causing here. They said they are neutral. They said they are staying in Atta and Rodeina's house to protect it from the settlers. One of them said he would complete his time in the military in six months and then wants to go to America to visit his family. I am glad I went to talk with them. I feel more safe now.

January 2, 2001, Tuesday

This morning I watched a propaganda show on Arab television. There were lots of scenes of war, carrying the bodies of martyrs through the streets, soldiers being blessed by imams, soldiers kissing the Koran before going to war, scenes of Hezballah in Lebanon, and frequent scenes of Al Aqsa Mosque in Jerusalem which needs to be liberated from Jewish control. It is so sad to see the Muslim people being seduced into war, and not being given the nonviolent alternative.

There is only one basic religion in the world. It makes little difference whether one is Muslim, Jew, Christian, Hindu, atheist, liberal, or conservative. The one basic religion in the world is faith in the saving power of violence, the belief that violence is the ultimate solution to any problem.[1] One can see this in most television programs, be they cartoons, westerns, or any good guy/bad guy show. When the tension mounts, when the bad guys threaten the good guys, violence is the only one possible solution.

We hear this myth repeated over and over by political leaders. Whoever our current enemy is, the enemy is portrayed as the embodiment of evil, representing the forces of chaos. We are good, and the only answer is to destroy the evil forces that threaten us. There is little hope in a peaceful resolution to the conflict.

The religion of redemptive violence is rooted in the Babylonian creation myth, in which the universe is created out of the parts of the goddess Tiamat's dismembered body. People were created out of drops of her blood. The implications of this myth are clear. Reality is basically violent and evil. Violence is in our blood. Violence is the answer to chaos. Order must be imposed on us; otherwise chaos will rule.

The creation stories in the Jewish, Christian, and Muslim Scriptures, however, affirm that the universe was created by a good God and is basically good. Justice and mercy are at the heart of reality. Evil came into the world later as a result of human decision, and thus can be overcome. Redemption is possible without more violence.

The basic worldview of most people today is that the world is evil, and when chaos threatens, violence can overcome the chaos and reestablish peace. This is the basis for military preparedness. One more bloodbath, we are

---

[1] For a more in-depth discussion of this idea, see Walter Wink, *The Powers That Be* (New York: Doubleday, 1998), 42-62.

promised, and then there will be peace. We brainwash our children with this lie.

Retaliation is a profound rejection of God. It is a denial of mercy, which according to Jewish, Islamic, and Christian teaching is at the heart of God's essence. Jesus said that retaliation must be left to God. It is not something to be taken into our own hands. Retaliation takes what belongs only to God into our own hands, and displays a profound mistrust of God. To trust in God is to give up the right to retaliate. Retaliation is also ignorant, for it leads to counter retaliation. It is a simple law of reality, that retaliation perpetuates the cycle of violence.

Violence and hate are never overcome by more violence and hate. We reap what we sow.

January 3, 2001, Wednesday

This evening Jaudi and I made a CSD visit to Samieh and Mohammed Jaber, two brothers who live nearby. Settlers came into their land fourteen days ago and destroyed 2,000 cauliflower plants and $250 worth of irrigation pipes. They went to the Israeli police who told them that they didn't care, that all this land belongs to the Israelis. Several days ago soldiers shot the tires on their car. Today they were detained for four hours before they could finally get their cauliflower to market. Two days ago their uncle's wheat field was destroyed by settlers running their jeep through it.

January 7, 2001, Sunday

Last evening at around 7:30 we saw a car with blinking lights parked on the road below the gas station. We took it for a settler car and kept watch on it. At 8:00 we heard rapid gunfire from the direction of the gas station for a minute or two. We quickly turned out the lights and hid behind concrete walls in the house. The family was terrified. What was going to happen? About five minutes later there was more gunfire. There seemed to be little I could do, but be present with the people here, pray, and document what happens. I tried to understand what was happening. There were a few soldier jeeps down on the road, one of which kept a search light on the houses across the road. Traffic kept going on the main road. The Jabers say the shooting came from settlers shooting in every direction at Palestinian homes.

As soon as it was daylight this morning I walked down on the road and talked to soldiers sitting in a jeep parked there and asked them what happened last evening. They said the car parked below the gas station last evening was a military car, and was shot at from up on the hill across the road. The soldiers returned fire. I asked if anyone was hurt and they said no. Later I walked down on the road to look for empty bullet shells, but couldn't see any. Maybe the soldiers picked them up. There was a tank parked up on top of the hill across the road, but by 9:00 it was gone.

Today municipal workers came and replaced about twenty pieces of glass in the windows here that were broken by settlers throwing stones at the house. Windows were broken on three sides of the house. There are no windows on the other side. Some of the windows were broken the second week of November, and the others were broken when settlers took over Atta and Rodeina's house the beginning of December. In the first incident, three-year-old Kokab got a piece of glass in her eye which required stitches in her eyeball.

January 8, 2001, Monday

I heard sporadic gunfire as I went into Hebron this morning. I saw a clash on the other side of the cemetery this morning. This afternoon I watched three soldiers at the end of Shuhada Street dealing with Palestinian boys who were up the hill. The road going up the hill is now closed, and littered with rocks. The boys throw stones at the soldiers, and then quickly run away. Two soldiers had their guns aimed, ready to fire, but there was no shooting.

The team asked me to be prepared to do more monitoring of settler actions here. The settlers are reported to be ready to start doing more to provide for their own security, claiming that the Israeli military is too lax in dealing with the Palestinians. That sounds scary. If the settlers close the roads or do other actions, I will observe, talk to soldiers about their attitudes toward the settler actions, and maybe try to dialogue with the settlers. This feels like taking an additional step, but I feel ready for that.

There was a settler action here today. The settlers had a memorial service down the road where two settler women were killed a month ago, and then drove slowly in a big procession past here and on to Jerusalem for a protest. The old road was closed for about an hour, with traffic backing up a long way.

This evening as we were eating supper we heard a noise which I thought was shooting in Hebron. I went out on the porch and saw a backhoe with a jackhammer pounding on the rocks on top of the wall behind the house. It was 6:45. I saw several people up on the wall, who started throwing rocks at the house, so I quickly ducked into the house. The family was terrified. I was scared too. Were the settlers going to tumble those big rocks down on the house? We made our phone calls. Jaudi called the Israeli police, but they hung up on him.

I couldn't see any soldier vehicles anywhere. Fifteen minutes later I saw one jeep go up the hill toward the settlement. Five minutes later I saw one more jeep go up the hill.

Anita and Bob called the U.S. Consulate and were advised that I should call John Davidson, who is in charge of security for the consulate. That was an interesting conversation. I told Davidson about the danger the Jaber family is living under and suggested the U.S. government do something about it, since the United States is paying for the occupation. He said his only concern was for my safety, and reminded me that the U.S. government has put out an advisory recommending that no Americans travel in the West Bank, and said that Hebron is the most dangerous place in the West Bank. He said he was not sure he had the resources to come and rescue me.

I then realized I was probably talking to a U.S. Marine. I told him I am a Christian pacifist, that I do not want to be rescued, that I want to face the same danger the Jaber family is facing, that my concern is not just for my own safety, but for the safety of everyone. He said he thought I was being foolish, but wished me good luck.

The rest of the evening was quiet.

January 9, 2001, Tuesday

At about 7:45 this morning I saw soldiers closing the old road. I decided to go over and talk to them. I greeted one of them with shalom and asked if there is a problem. He said, "No, there is no problem. The road will be closed for half a day for an operation." I wondered what that meant. It didn't sound good to me.

I walked back to the house and then saw that two tanks were across the road, and then saw two bulldozers and a backhoe. I immediately knew that meant trouble. It wasn't long before I realized that the bulldozers were going up to Atta and Rodeina's house. I immediately called the team and told them I think they are demolishing the house.

I then headed back across the road to observe. I didn't know what I could do. I walked right past the soldiers I had talked to earlier and went halfway up the hill to where a tank was parked. I started to talk to the soldiers in the tank, asking them if what they were doing is making peace.

They gave me the usual story of how the Arabs are bad and the Jews are good, the Arabs don't want peace, the Arabs rejected the "generous" Israeli peace offer, they keep killing Israelis, and if they don't stop them here they will have to fight them in Tel Aviv. They referred to the shooting Saturday evening to justify their actions. I said, "I oppose all violence," and asked them to consider why some Palestinians resort to desperate acts of violence. I pointed to Atta and Rodeina's two demolished homes, to the wall and devastated Jaber orchard, and the expanding Harsina settlement. I asked, "Is this shalom?"

A bulldozer started leveling all the ground around Atta and Rodeina's house. The backhoe with a jackhammer helped break up the big rocks. Were they leveling the land so they could more easily demolish the house? Were they preparing to expand a military camp here? The soldiers said this was development. Developing what?

I stood there alone, trying not to curse. I cried. I prayed. How ridiculous for me to stand here against two tanks, two bulldozers, and a backhoe, and maybe thirty soldiers with machine guns.

I saw Anita, Rebecca, Bob, and Pierre arrive. Pierre and Bob followed a bulldozer going south on the old road. I feared the bulldozer was going to demolish a house there, but it turned out the bulldozer started clearing a road up the hill. Anita, Rebecca, and I started walking up the hill. I saw that soldiers were still in the house, so concluded that the house would not be demolished. But the bulldozer and backhoe kept working around the house. Were they building a military camp?

A soldier told us that they are simply making a road so that Atta and Rodeina could move back into their house. They were building a road, they said, to make a clear line between Israeli land inside the circle, and Palestinian land outside the road. So what really was going on was this hillside was being confiscated and in return the Jabers can have their house. They called it a compromise. A compromise? Stealing yet more land is a compromise? Slowly, piece by piece, in contradiction to everything Israel says, we see the real intentions of Israel. They intend to take this valley. They have no intentions of leaving or turning this back to the Palestinians.

As the bulldozers worked from two directions to encircle the hillside, we had a quick team meeting to decide what to do. Should we sit in front of the bulldozers? We didn't have clarity.

I quickly went back to the Jabers, who were watching from the porch, to inform them of what we understood to be happening. When I told them of the "compromise," they sarcastically said we should thank the Israelis for being so generous.

I went back across the road. A group of about twenty Palestinians and maybe six journalists followed a bulldozer and backhoe that were above the Jaber house, but headed north along the hill instead of further up the hill. We then realized that they were confiscating even more land than we thought.

As the backhoe and bulldozer moved along a terrace, we realized that some olive trees just below the terrace were threatened by all the rocks and dirt falling down. The rest of the team went down and each stood by an olive tree, prepared to be arrested. The soldiers called the police and threatened them with arrest. Soon the backhoe was past the olive trees, and everyone moved on.

At that point both Palestinians and CPTers moved onto the terrace and were in front of the backhoe. For the next half hour we were continually confronting the soldiers. Pierre and I did some preaching to the soldiers and police. In a loud voice, I proclaimed God's judgment on this atrocity, asking whether this is shalom, whether this is what they want Israel to become, a nation of coldhearted thieves. I cried, "Shame on you, shame on Israel." I proclaimed that they must answer to God for what they are doing. Over and over, I cried out in a loud voice, "Baruch hashem Adonai (Blessed be the name of the Lord)." I know little Hebrew and it was the one phrase that I know that points to the reality of God. I wanted to remind everyone that we must answer to God. I kept referring to the Jewish Scriptures.

All of us were engaging in personal conversations with the soldiers. In addition to preaching to them, I also had a personal conversation with most of them, so I related to them on a number of levels. We certainly left no doubt in anyone's mind that we considered this confiscation to be morally repugnant. There was not a conscience that was not at least spoken to.

During this time our Palestinian neighbors were serving tea to the soldiers. Maybe these Muslims understand the message of Jesus better than do most Christians. They were saying they want peace. The Israelis accepted the tea and continued their evil.

The soldiers kept asking everyone to leave and threatening us with arrest. Slowly everyone retreated, walking a fine line between being arrested or not. At one point Pierre and Bob were sitting on the ground in front of the backhoe with about ten Palestinians and were prepared to be arrested. The Palestinians argued with the soldiers, but when the Palestinians decided to move, Bob and Pierre felt they should move also. When the Palestinians left the area around noon, we also left, feeling we had made our point.

We wonder, should some of us have been arrested? We didn't stop the construction of the new road, but we did morally confront the evil, we expressed our outrage at what was happening, we stood with the Palestinians, and maybe shared a small sign of hope. Whatever was done today is now in God's hands.

We all came to the Jaber home for food and sharing as we watched the Israelis finish their work across the road, taking more of the Jaber land. This confiscation leaves little land left for the Jabers.

January 10, 2001, Wednesday

I went into Hebron early this morning for worship. At about 7:45 we heard a loud bang, followed by rapid gunfire not far away. Bob and I went to investigate. Palestinian friends said the shooting was in the market area near Avraham Avinu. Soldiers said someone shot at a soldier there and soldiers returned fire.

We walked into the market and saw a group of about eight soldiers going through the market, ordering shopkeepers to close their shops. The commander was being really nasty, pushing elderly shopkeepers, throwing their merchandise, yelling and screaming at them. I stepped in front of him and told him to treat people with respect. He told me to shut up. I didn't shut up. I shouted at him to stop his arrogant behavior. I shouted not out of anger, but out of wanting not only him, but everyone in the area to hear and to call attention to his behavior, hoping that might have some effect on stopping the dangerous behavior of the soldiers. There were a lot of soldiers clearing the market and looking for whoever fired the shot. We walked around, observing, and standing near shopkeepers who were being harassed by soldiers. Curfew was reimposed after there being no curfew for a few days.

Two mentally handicapped men who we often see were yelling and screaming at the soldiers. We were concerned for them, since two mentally handicapped Palestinians were shot near our apartment in the last month. We explained the situation to the soldiers and watched them awhile. A Palestinian man made a disparaging reference about the two men, so I said to him, "Humme min Allah (They are from God)." The man immediately changed his attitude, and agreed that they are from God. They really are. Their absurd behavior was a prophetic word from God to the demonic powers they were resisting. I praise God for those two angels.

When I got back to the Jabers this afternoon I learned that a bulldozer and a backhoe had been here today to do more demolition around Atta and Rodeina's two demolished homes. I immediately went over to investigate. The Israelis had flattened the remains of their first two houses. I can understand that. They were probably too much of a reminder of the evil the Israelis have been perpetrating here. But they also uprooted the olive and fruit trees, ripped up the gardens, and demolished the stone terraces for their gardens. I guess I am naive. I couldn't believe what I saw. I was reminded again that we are dealing with a massive evil power. I cried out to God, "How long, O Lord, how long?" I seemed to hear an answer. Not long.

The Israeli civil authorities who were here yesterday directing the confiscation told me that Atta is their friend, that they are doing all this for shalom, that Israel never does

Atta, Rodeina, and children in front of their first demolished home, with their new third home above.

anything bad. Today they did all this devastation. Did they believe what they said to me yesterday, or were they just plain lying? I really don't know.

Why are they doing this to this family? Atta is a gentle man, a man who wants to live side by side in peace with Jews, an advocate of nonviolence. He is an outspoken opponent of racist thinking, a man of deep faith and hope. Do the Israelis consider people like Atta dangerous, a threat to their racist ambitions? I wish all those Israeli bullies I talked to yesterday could sit at Atta's feet and learn from him.

I want to share a little of Atta's story. After getting married in 1992, Atta and Rodeina built a small house on their land and in the same year received a demolition order. Their first daughter, Amooni, was born on October 23, 1993. In 1995, the Jabers paid $1,000 to take their demolition order, along with fifty-nine other demolitions orders, to the Israeli High Court. The High Court ruled in April 1995 to confirm the demolition orders. Atta and others then met with the mayor of Hebron, who contacted Yasir Arafat, who contacted then Prime Minister Peres. The press reported that Peres assured Arafat that he would rescind the demolition orders for all sixty homes. Their second daughter was born on December 8, 1995.

In October 1996, the Jabers were given a demolition order for their garden terraces. On December 12, 1996, Atta was arrested at his home for cultivating "Israeli state land." Atta was held for ten days and fined $300. On January 21, 1997, Atta and Rodeina's gardens were bulldozed and his irrigation pipes were confiscated. Israeli soldiers forced Rodeina and the two small children to stand for four hours in the cold rain and watch their gardens being destroyed. Atta was not at home. Rodeina and the two children then spent two days in the hospital from exposure to the cold.

I first met the Jaber family on March 5, 1997. Soldiers had come to the house that morning and had given the family two hours to remove everything from the house before it would be demolished. Atta asked the soldiers where he should take his family. "We don't care. You can live in the sky," the soldiers replied. I helped remove their possessions that day, but the bulldozers never came, apparently because of pressure the Israeli military received to stop the demolition.

Rajeh, their first son, was born May 4, 1998. At noon, on August 19, 1998, 140 Israeli soldiers and two large bulldozers arrived at the house. The soldiers physically removed Rodeina and the three children from the house, banging three-year-old Dalia's head against the wall. Atta arrived at that point and argued with the officer in charge. Extended family members came to protest, everyone of whom was beaten by the soldiers, with twenty-one being beaten so severely they had to be treated at the hospital. Rodeina was beaten in the face. Atta's mother, Amni, had a broken arm, and Nihaad's hand was broken. To keep more people from being injured, Atta asked everyone to allow the soldiers to demolish his house.

The extended family and community rallied around the family, donated work and materials, and built a new unfinished house in five days. As Atta puts it, "It wasn't much, but it was a place to live." On September 10, a bulldozer came and demolished Jaudi's beautiful sculptured orchard. On September 16, twenty-seven days after the first demolition, one bulldozer and about eighty soldiers returned and demolished the second house. Here is the story in Atta's words.

> They demolished the new house, again without presenting me with any demolition order and without giving me any time to contest the demolition. I held my five-month-old son, Rajeh, out to one of the officers. "Take my baby to live with your family. I can't take care of him without a home." He held Rajeh for one moment and got angry. He hit me in the head. He put his hands on my neck and began to strangle me, causing internal injury. The soldiers brought me to the tent that we had set up after the first demolition. As I

bent down to pick up my daughter, one soldier hit me in the back with the butt of his M-16. Another kicked me in the face and broke my nose. A third hit me in the shoulder with either an M-16 or a billy club. I fell to the ground and they continued to kick me.

Finally they dragged me to a police jeep and arrested me. At the police station I was given a cursory examination by a Civil Administration doctor. He pronounced me healthy even though I could not stand under my own power and had difficulty breathing. The next day I was transferred to another prison where I was held for four days. On the fifth day I was given a hearing. I was formally charged with speaking rudely to a soldier, interfering with the duties of a soldier, and "assault by infant." The judge ruled that I should be held for six months and fined $2,500. I was returned to my cell, still in bad health. On the eighth day they finally took me to Kiryat Arba hospital. There the doctors decided that I needed immediate medical attention. But I was returned to my cell. On the twelfth day after the demolition I was released. I was fined $400 and my six-month sentence was suspended for three years.

For four months the family lived in a Red Cross tent beside the demolished homes. In January, with the family sick due to the cold and rain, they moved to an apartment in the Old City of Hebron. Atta was unable to work for eight months because of his injuries.

In October 1998, Atta received a call from Nomi Betser, an Israeli woman who had read the Jaber story in the *Ha'aretz* newspaper. She apologized to Atta for what had happened and promised to work to get a permit for him, to build a third house. On April 15, 1999, Atta received a call from the Israeli Civil Administration. They offered to help him get a permit for a third house and suggested that Atta draw up plans and apply for a permit.

Atta made the plans and maps and applied for a permit. In October 1999, Atta received a call from the Civil Administration to meet him at the building site. They came and informed him that not only were his maps incorrect, but also that the land didn't even belong to him. It was Israeli land, he was told. On December 24, 1999, his application for a permit was refused. Five days later, they signed the maps and said they would give a permit. The next day they refused to grant a permit. With the help of Nomi Bester, Israeli peace activists, and a lawyer, negotiations continued. On February 1, 2000, in a meeting with Atta, Arik Ascherman, and the lawyer, Atta again was told he was not the owner of the land, and could not build without proof of ownership.

On April 15, 2000, the Civil Administration said that since this was a hardship case, they would make an exception and grant Atta a permit. An agreement was made with his lawyer, and Atta started building the same day. Ten days later, Civil Administration people came and said Atta had to stop because he was building at the wrong place. Atta stopped. Ten days later Atta was given permission to continue.

On May 3, Civil Administration people came and arrested Atta since he had not stopped work. Atta thinks this happened because of pressure from the settlers because he was working on the Jewish Sabbath. Atta was released after one hour. The next day, May 4, soldiers stopped the concrete mixer trucks from delivering concrete for pouring the roof. Nomi Bester and Atta's lawyer contacted authorities and got permission for pouring concrete to continue.

On June 30, the mayor of Kiryat Arba came to the house. Atta welcomed him and offered him tea. The mayor said he wanted to see what Atta was doing. Soon over fifty settlers arrived and started to vandalize the house and destroy building supplies. Police came and watched settlers destroy property. Atta says they did about $300 worth of damage. Between seventy and eighty family members and neighbors came to defend the house, but Atta asked them to move away. Officers gave settlers five minutes to leave, and the settlers left. Atta was told he had to stop work for two weeks. Then two more weeks. On August 1, Atta was given permission to continue work.

Nomi Bester, Jeff Halper, Arik Ascherman, Kate Aleiza, Harriet and Amoz, Peace Now, Bat Shalom, Rabbis for Human Rights, and many other Israelis stood up for the Jabers and helped pressure the Israeli government to do right by the Jabers, and found the money to build the house. There was no further trouble at the new house until December 8. Atta's suffering has only seemed to strengthen him.

January 11, 2001, Thursday

I have been inwardly groaning, crying out to God for an end to this evil. What can I do? I decided to fast today. I am sure this evil will not be overcome without much prayer and fasting.

January 12, 2001, Friday

Early this morning Abdel Jawad asked me to go over to Atta and Rodeina's house to see if there were any soldiers there. Atta heard that they had left and that he can move back into the house today. I quickly ran over to the house and found it empty, ran back, and informed the family of the good news. Abdel Jawad called Atta, who asked me to go over to the house and stay there to protect the house until he could get there. I came over to the house with a deep sense of awe and feeling honored to come into this house. I am on holy ground. I feel unworthy to come into this holy place, feeling I am invading the privacy and sanctity of Atta and Rodeina's home.

It was shocking to come into the house and see the devastation left by the settlers and soldiers: the broken walls, the broken stones, the Hebrew graffiti on the walls, the burned possessions, the trash left behind, and the bulldozed mess outside. Even the family picture album was destroyed. My mind is too small to comprehend the depravity that caused this. The Israelis apparently did not realize that they were on holy ground.

My response was to cry. For at least fifteen minutes I cried, releasing a lot of emotion and pain that has been building up in me over the past weeks and the past years of relationship with the Jaber family. But my crying was more than that. I walked from room to room, shrieking and screaming. It felt as if I were exorcising demonic spirits from the house, like I was cleansing the place of the evil which has been manifested there. This time ended with a time of going from room to room, praising God. I felt a deep peace and joy. Yesterday I wanted to fast. No fasting today. I want to celebrate. I sense a spiritual victory here.

I am trying to comprehend what is happening here. It seems like the Israelis are saying, "Okay, we let you back into your house, but we are going to let you know that we are still in control, and you had better be submissive." Pierre suggested that in demolishing the gardens and fruit trees, the Israelis wanted to erase every living thing that existed here that is a reminder of what the Israelis have done here in the past. Erasing the evidence is not the same as repentance. As I walked around the house I saw a number of garden plants that survived the bulldozer tracks. They are living witnesses. What is clear is that all the Jaber land across the road is confiscated land, except for the house, around which the new road sets the clear boundaries.

I am worried about tonight. It will be Sabbath, and the settlers may be angry that we are in the house.

January 14, 2001, Sunday

It has been quiet here. Last evening Atta and I spent time in his house in case settlers wanted to cause trouble. He was especially concerned that something could happen at the end of Sabbath. I felt a lot of fear, but was ready to face the settlers.

There were soldiers down by the road most of the

evening. I realized that I have very conflicting attitudes toward the Israeli military. Last evening we felt we were more safe from settler attack with the military present. Yesterday two soldiers came by Atta and Rodeina's house to survey the damage done to the house by settlers and soldiers. They were very polite. But sometimes the military aids and abets settler rampages. Other times the soldiers come with bulldozers to destroy. Sometimes they kill, sometimes they protect.

The roads were open to Bethlehem this morning. When I came back to Hebron, I saw a clash beginning on Shuhada Street. About a dozen youth were throwing stones with slingshots toward soldiers some distance away. About a dozen journalists were there with their cameras, waiting for a clash to begin. Shortly before this there was a funeral procession for a youth killed there two days ago. Yesterday, I saw on TV the body of this youth being dragged through the street by the soldiers who killed him. The team learned from eyewitnesses that the body was dragged to Beit Hadassah where settlers kicked and spit on it. They celebrated his death by dancing on the street and giving candy to the soldiers who had killed him.

More youth were ready to be martyrs today. I waited awhile and visited with my journalist friends who had filmed the killing two days ago. The soldiers didn't seem to want to respond, so there was no clash. I left when the journalists left. The whole scene seemed senseless to me. I understand the anger, but wish it could be directed in some creative way. This was the very spot where two years ago CPTers stopped soldiers from shooting nonviolent protesters. Today, it did not seem like holy ground.

This evening at dusk, Atta wanted me to walk with him over to Rodeina's brother's house where she was this evening. Several families were gathered around a fire, so we joined the circle, and were served maqlube. I thought of the people who lived here thousands of years ago, of Abraham and Sarah, and David who tended sheep in these hills. These are simple farmers, who are gradually losing their land. They agonized about the land they lost last week, saying they have nothing against Jews. They just want to live in peace and have a sense of security. I could sense, however, that they have a lot of resentment against Jews. They said all they can do is look to God for help.

I learned the Israeli military today confiscated the hill behind Fayez and Hudda's demolished house. When will it ever end?

January 15, 2001, Monday

This evening Jaudi and I visited the Yusef Jaber family. They received a demolition order on their house about ten days ago. Their first house was demolished in 1985. These are simple farmers. They can't afford a lawyer. They are simply vulnerable. Their house was built ten years ago. Why are the Israelis issuing a demolition order now? What is happening here? Has Israel given up on peace and is now ready to get tough with the Palestinians? Are we facing horrible days ahead?

Each evening we keep watch in case settlers decide to cause trouble. Both last evening and this evening there were two settler buses down by the road. Last evening there were soldiers with them, and they closed the road for about half an hour. This evening we didn't see any soldiers. The settlers blocked the road for just a short time.

I am concerned about what is happening to my attitude. I am beginning to accept as normal that every day tanks rumble past the house here, that there are soldiers everywhere, that there are curfews, that people are being killed every day, that some roads are not for Palestinians. The occupation, racism, and oppression are beginning to seem normal. I am no longer shocked by these things. But these things are not normal, they are not God's intention for the world. They are curses we have brought upon ourselves.

This afternoon I observed a demonstration in Hebron by an Israeli peace group called "The Four Mothers." The group was started by four mothers of Israeli soldiers killed in Lebanon, and called for the withdrawal of Israeli troops from Lebanon. The group had a major influence in turning Israeli public opinion against the occupation of southern Lebanon. About seven Israeli women, some of them mothers of killed soldiers, were in Hebron today to call for an end to the occupation here. After meeting with Palestinian leaders, the group attempted to march on Duboyya Street from the Palestinian controlled part of Hebron to the Beit Hadassah settlement. Anita, Anne, and Rebecca accompanied the group.

They were stopped by Israeli soldiers when they got to the Israeli controlled part of Hebron. That was an interesting confrontation. The mothers brought with them a considerable amount of moral authority, which confronted the authority of the military. With TV cameras rolling, the women confronted the soldiers. It appeared that the women were telling the soldiers what the soldiers needed to hear. I saw what looked like shame on some of the soldiers' faces. I wish I could have understood the Hebrew conversations. There must have been twenty-five soldiers there to stop these women who were carrying signs shaped like a hand seen on stop signs, with the words "Stop the occupation" in English and Hebrew.

As some women argued with soldiers, other women simply walked around the soldiers, ignoring their orders to stop. Soldiers then had to move in front of the women. The march slowly proceeded in this way before it was stopped by reinforcements and two jeeps blocking the street. I wondered if the women would be arrested, but they never quite crossed that line.

Wow! Israeli mothers coming to Palestinian territory to call for an end to the occupation. Some call them traitors. When we call for an end to the whole system of domination we can expect to be called traitors by those whose loyalty is to that system.

This evening the whole family watched the news and watched settlers go on a rampage, setting fires, breaking windows, destroying property, and shooting at Palestinians, while Israeli soldiers watched. We saw Palestinians screaming in horror. The Jabers became quite upset. They have been through this. They understood. I didn't know what to say.

January 17, 2001, Wednesday

I spent much of the day with Atta at his house. We stayed until after sunset and came back across the road to his parents house. The house needs a lot of work before they can move back into it. Atta estimates there is $3,000 of damage to the house and loss from tools and supplies stolen by the settlers and soldiers. We also examined more closely the damage done by the bulldozers. They pushed the topsoil from one of his gardens unto the rocks right behind his house. Why?

Three-year-old Kokab got the stitches taken out of her eyeball today.

January 22, 2001, Monday

I have been accompanying Atta some evenings when he wants to visit neighbors after dark. He apparently feels more safe when I am with him. Everyone here feels a lot of fear of the settlers, and for good reason. I share that fear, but consider it an honor to be able to share the danger these people live under every day.

This evening we went to see Monsur Jaber, the thirteen-year-old boy shot in the stomach by settlers when they went on a rampage here on December 9. He was hospitalized for thirty-six days in Jerusalem, part of the time in critical condition. He is home now, but having problems. He showed me his huge scar from where doctors cut him open to repair all the damage from the bullet which went into him from the front and out the back. It was an honor to spend time with this family.

January 30, 2001, Tuesday

Things have been quiet here the past two weeks, with things slowly becoming a little more "normal." There has been less shooting, the roads are slowly being opened, and the curfew which lasted ninety-five days has been lifted. But there are still clashes and people are still being killed.

I have not seen the big victories I had hoped to see here. Just because I haven't seen them doesn't mean they haven't happened. I have seen some signs of victory. The harassment of the Jaber family has mostly stopped, Atta and Rodeina have their house back. God is working in the Jaber family. Palestinians and Israelis continue to come together, and by faith I see the occupation coming to an end.

What will happen here? Will the stalemate, the oppression continue? Will there be a peace agreement? If so, will it be implemented? Will there be a new dawn of peace for Israelis and Palestinians? Will the people of Hebron be given back their lives and their future? Or will the conflict escalate, with more killing, more hatred, or even all-out war? I see few signs of hope. Everywhere I go I see new settler roads being constructed, new settlements, massive expansion of settlements. It seems clear that Israel is not preparing to leave here. They are digging in. It is hard to believe that peace talks going on now are real.

As I reflect on the situation, I feel strongly that I don't want either side to win this war. I don't want the Israelis to win. The occupation must end. Israel's reliance on military might and oppression must be brought to an end.

Never before has Israel been as strong militarily as they are today, but never before has Israel been so insecure. Military might does not bring security. But I also do not want an Islamic military victory. That would be bad for Islam. It would only encourage Muslims to trust in guns for salvation and follow the example of the Israelis. I don't want the oppressed to imitate the oppressors. I am praying for another victory, the victory of God's Spirit in which there are no victims, no losers, no new oppressors, but rather the dawn of a new reality. Unless this nightmare is defeated non-violently, the victory will not be sweet.

The people who are in power are in power because they are not afraid to kill. The only human force that can overcome that oppressive system is people who are not afraid to die.

I do not know the future. I can only affirm my hope in the goodness of the universe, and trust the evidence I have seen of God's redeeming and saving work here. I trust the powers of oppression will be overcome, that swords will be beaten into plowshares. Come Lord Jesus, come.

As I leave Palestine, the fruit trees are beginning to bloom. That is a promise of another harvest, a sign of God's continuing mercy.

January 31, 2001, Wednesday

I said good-bye to the Jabers this morning. It was hard to leave my family. They have even given me a Palestinian name: Jaber Iben Jaber.

As a farewell to me during our team worship this morning, Rebecca washed my dirty feet. I don't like to have my feet washed. I want to be the one washing others' feet. But I need to learn humility. I need to learn to trust God.

At about 2:00 this afternoon we heard a loud boom which sounded like a sonic boom. Soon we heard soldiers announcing curfew. We all quickly went out on the street to observe and to give protection to shopkeepers as they were putting their things away. There were soldiers everywhere, ordering people to close up and leave. Some of this was rather nasty, and I confronted quite a few of the soldiers with their nastiness. One soldier was both ordering the people to leave the market and blocking the exit. I confronted him, and he soon allowed the people to pass by. We have learned that often these soldiers are not following orders. They are simply being nasty, and will back down when confronted.

Settlers watched as the soldiers did their work. I saw Noam Arnon, greeted him, and listened to him telling me how threatened the settlers are, how the Arabs want to kill the Jews, how you can never trust an Arab. It was word for word what I hear about Jews from Palestinians.

As soon as things quieted down, I left Hebron for my journey home, with a fresh reminder of the intensity of the struggle in Hebron.

Postscripts

The Palestinian Tragedy Continues

Khalid M. Amayreh,
Journalist and Islamist leader

I'm writing my impression of Art Gish's testimonies at a time of great stress as the Israeli occupation army has effectively reduced the entire West Bank into a giant open-air prison. Palestinians can't move from one locality to another, and in some cases, such as in Hebron, they can't even move within the same town.

In Ramallah, twenty kilometers north of Jerusalem, the Israeli army carried out draconian measures reminiscent of medieval times, like digging up deep trenches and placing huge piles of earth outside most Palestinian towns and villages. Even small country hamlets are hermetically closed by concrete slabs or army roadblocks, which are often manned by trigger-happy soldiers.

The siege is being enforced with conspicuous vindictiveness and harshness, and the results are catastrophic. So far, a score of patients, who were being transferred to hospital, succumbed to their illnesses as Israeli soldiers guarding roadblocks refused to allow them to proceed to hospitals "because the area is a closed military zone." Even pregnant women are routinely refused access to hospitals, and are forced to give birth inside their cars or in the open air, with occasionally tragic consequences.

Some Palestinians were beginning to refer to their

besieged towns as "concentration camps." The description may be exaggerated, but the suffering, the narrow horizons, the claustrophobia are far from being unreal.

Hebron always takes more than its share of suffering and oppression. A few days ago, Jewish settlers celebrated a religious holiday called Purim. They dressed up like Baruch Goldstein, the settler who in 1994 massacred twenty-nine Palestinians praying in the Ibrahimi Mosque. Once again they rampaged through Hebron's Old Town, attacking Palestinians, vandalizing their property, and shouting, "Death to Arabs."

The settlers, some drunk, fired into the air, ostensibly in a gesture of defiance to the Palestinians. They also pelted pedestrians with stones and empty bottles in full view of Israeli soldiers who had orders to "let the settlers have a good time undisturbed."

Following the wanton gala, the Israeli army reimposed curfew on the Palestinians, leaving the settlers strolling the streets rather gleefully, while the Palestinians were locked indoors. Indeed, the Palestinians of the Old Town, estimated at twenty-five to thirty thousand, have been under an intermittent curfew ever since the breakout of the Intifada or uprising on September 28, 2000.

The Israeli army claims the curfew is imposed "for security reasons." But Palestinians contend the real reason is the Israeli desire to "clean" the old town of non-Jews, a process that is expected to be stepped up, especially after the ascendancy of Ariel Sharon to the helm of power in the Jewish state.

In fact, the testimonies Art makes in his book, characterized more by honesty and veracity and maybe less by scholarship, provide a firsthand description of a harsh situation that I have described as "transcending reality." Art's testimonies and reflection seem to be very sincere and genuine. Sometimes I, as a Palestinian, feel Art's impressions even understate reality.

Nonetheless, I hope his work can be an eye-opener for those Americans who have long been misled by Israeli-Zionist propaganda that succeeds in clouding the truth about the Palestinian-Israeli conflict.

Finally, a word to Jewish readers. I believe you should speak up against the inequities that are being done in your names. Judaism, I understand, can be encapsulated in two or three phrases: "You shall not murder, you shall not lie, and you shall not do unto others what you wouldn't want others to do unto you."

Frankly, the way Israeli soldiers and settlers have been behaving toward the Palestinian people, including innocent civilians and children, constitutes a stark contradiction to your sublime values. This is sad and lamentable. I hope you can do something about it.

—Dura, Hebron
March 12, 2001

In His Steps Today

Rabbi Arik W. Ascherman,
Executive Director, Rabbis for Human Rights
(http://www.rhr.israel.net/)

In the late nineteenth century Charles Sheldon wrote *In His Steps*, a novel about a pastor with the radical idea that Christians ought to act as they think Jesus would. The 1956 Moody Press edition claimed that *In His Steps* had sold more copies than any Christian book next to the Bible. I am not sure that I fully agree with Charles Sheldon's understanding of how Jesus might act. However, from my outsider's perspective as an Israeli Jewish rabbi, it seems to me that the work of Art Gish and his fellow Christian Peacemakers is today's real-life application of *In His Steps*.

CPT has placed itself in the seething cauldron of Hebron. Even in comparison with other areas in the Occupied Territories, I can think of only one other area which even comes close to Hebron in terms of settler violence and fanaticism. I can barely imagine the terrible challenge of maintaining optimism, humor, love, and centeredness living in such a reality on a daily basis.

Art Gish's words alternatively make me cringe and feel angry at the evils being committed in my name, defensive or upset at what sometimes seems a lack of appreciation of our situation as Israelis, or inspired and awed by Art's wisdom, courage, and vision. Ultimately, I am encouraged and strengthened as a person of faith to know that we share a religious vision of faith-based activism seeking to bring about a world which actualizes the teaching of the book of Genesis that all human beings are created in God's image.

As I write nine months into the second Intifada, such a vision is more important then ever. On both sides, hatred, anger, fear, and trauma reign as the number of Jewish and Palestinian victims grows day by day. Even many progressive Israelis have been taken aback by the level of Palestinian violence, rendered incapable of confronting our violence. Seeing the Palestinian rejection of former Israeli Prime Minister Ehud Barak's proposals at Camp David as proof that Palestinians are not truly interested in peace, they do not take responsibility for the land confiscations, home demolitions, tree uprootings, and unfair water allocations which pushed the Palestinian streets toward Intifada much more than the state of negotiations in a peace process they no longer believed in. They forget the teaching of Pirke Aboth (Mishnah), "The sword comes into the world because of justice delayed and justice denied." Disillusioned and bitter because of this quiet war of human rights violations which continued even as leaders negotiated, most Palestinians do not see that violence is morally unacceptable and strategically counterproductive. They see all Israelis as their enemy, rejecting the possibility of cooperative nonviolent struggle. We must rekindle our ability to find the spark of God in every human being which render human rights violations, mass generalizations, and violence an affront to God.

Finally, Art's book recalls to mind the teaching in the Rosh ha-Shana tractate of the Talmud that we must act as if life is a set of perfectly balanced scales. On both the personal and the cosmic level, the most minor and seemingly insignificant act on our part may be the one that tips the scales one way or the other. Today when causes for optimism here are so few and far between, such an understanding is necessary to sustain us. It is clear that Art lives his life in this way. It is my hope and prayer that Art's words will inspire you to do the same, whether or not your life's journey brings you anywhere near the Middle East. May each of us find our way to tip the scales, acting as God's partners in the work of Tikun Olam (Social Action), the ongoing task of creating a repaired and sanctified world.

—Jerusalem
July 4, 2001

The Power of Love and Compassion

Nora Arsenian Carmi,
Armenian-Palestinian Christian
Sabeel Ecumenical Liberation Theology Center
(http://www.sabeel.org/)

"Finally, all of you, have unity of spirit, sympathy [compassion], love for one another, a tender heart, and a humble mind. Do not repay evil for evil or abuse for abuse; but, on the contrary, repay with a blessing." —*1 Peter 3:8-9a*

During the final worship service of the Alternative Assembly organized by Sabeel Ecumenical Liberation Theology Center in the Chapel of the Notre Dame Jerusalem Center on February 24, 2001, the unusual distribution of a stone to each of over three hundred participants moved many to tears. These stones, remains of demolished homes in Hebron, were collected by Christian Peacemaker Team members Anita, Bob, Diane, and Jamey. Each stone, a symbol of the ongoing injustice in the Holy Land, urged the worshipers to commit themselves to "roll away the stone," the Israeli Occupation, the big boulder obstructing peace.

Once again, CPT was making an important statement by using the nonviolent action strategy that they had first brought with them into our country almost six years ago. From the moment in 1995, when the Christian Peacemaker Teams stepped into the lives of members of Sabeel and the

Palestinian congregation of St. George's Episcopal Cathedral, an important relationship began to flourish between the indigenous Palestinian Christians and these dedicated Western Christian men and women who had chosen to follow the "Way" in the remote occupied West Bank town of Hebron, known in Arabic as al-Khalil (the friend).

We knew little then about CPT, but ever since that encounter, we awaited our Sunday meetings with anticipation. As we gathered eagerly to hear the stimulating Sunday sermon of Dr. Naim Ateek, followed by a challenging discussion hour, we would look forward to seeing the beaming smiles of the red-capped and red-banded men and women who braved bad weather and curfews to arrive in Jerusalem and shared the latest information on the situation in Hebron.

The experiences and stories they related would not necessarily appear in newspapers or on televisions, which do not explore the depth of the presence and role of nonviolent intervention in a sea of antagonism between a handful of the occupying Israeli settlers and a majority of Palestinian Muslims under occupation.

Why would five or six unarmed peace-loving North Americans risk their lives in a situation of conflict? What could they achieve when we, their local compatriots (in God's kingdom of justice and peace), did not dare to venture into that hot spot? According to Art Gish's introduction to this book, "out of their faith, they had chosen to confront evil and injustice by making themselves vulnerable to evil."

Anne, Art, Cliff, Diane, Gene, Jeff, Kathleen, Marge, Pierre, Sarah, Wendy, and later, Anita, Bob, Grace, Jamey, and Natasha (I hope I have not forgotten anybody) all presented us with a new way of putting Christianity into practice. This was a new way (sabeel), a live witness, and a tangible interpretation of the gospel being put to the test.

I want to point out the lessons I, as a Palestinian Christian, have learned from the CPT during the past six years of our mutual interdependence. But first, with love and gratitude, I as a member of Sabeel recall some memorable and touching banners that adorn the walls of our center: "Getting in the WAY," painted for the Sabeel 1996 international conference. "Truth and Justice," "Remembrance and Forgiveness," and "Liberation and Healing" for the 1998 conference. The latest banner, "We are brothers, we are sisters, together we stand for justice," prepared for our latest Alternative Assembly, February 2001, will need a special wall!

When members of the CPT were deported or arrested for daring to expose the oppression, we Sabeelers felt the added pangs of injustice stabbing all those who stand against the structures of domination and who "are willing to speak truth to power and call oppressors to repentance" (Art Gish). Thus with deep humility, some of us participated in the 1997 Lenten fasting of the CPTers as a sign of protest against home demolitions. With greater joy, we shared the thanks-giving worship that ended this trying period, after which we completed the fellowship by breaking the fast together.

This daring decision has borne fruit, and many North American families have adopted Palestinian families in Hebron. Better still, a joint Palestinian-Israeli-International Committee is working against home demolitions and rebuilding homes each time they are destroyed.

When Sabeel moved to its present quarters, and Ateek retired from St. George's, the link between the two groups per-sisted and became stronger. Once again, we looked forward to the CPT presence, this time at our Thursday noon communion services. As one delegation has followed another, a silent part-nership developed. Now it is only natural that we pick up the phone to inquire about the safety of our CPT brothers and sis-ters every time the TV flashes scenes of violence in Hebron (and lately in Beit Jala, where Anne and Pierre tried to medi-ate during the last Intifada). Nor will we forget Anne's valu-able worship prayers for conferences and the Contemporary Way of the Cross, as well as Anita's and Bob's sound advice in organizing and mobilizing nonviolent marches.

The CPT model of resistance has taught us that—

• To accept God's call to follow the "Way" involves the willingness to risk one's life for others. This means to adapt one's lifestyle to a foreign culture and environment and to bear the anger and insults of those we are trying to help.

• Not to diminish or minimize the impact of any form of peacemaking. True peace is not dictated by politicians or official signatures on papers. It is a long process of interactions between human beings, on the grassroots level, whereby the one meets the other, when both parties face and accept responsibilities, acknowledge and rectify injustices, and together work to remove hatred and replace it with a concrete translation of "love your enemy" in practice. The CPT has been able to unmask the hidden humanity of some of the soldiers and yes! even settlers. It may be only a seed that has been planted, but the seed will grow!

• Not only has the CPT been able to break through the hard barriers separating enemies, but some of the dedicated women have also been instrumental in resolving social problems such as violence within the family or gender issues within the Palestinian community.

The CPTers have not *yet* been able to influence the policy of their own governments. The power of love and compassion can be truly fruitful when decision makers become truly honest brokers, enforcing measures necessary to secure a just and lasting peace, which will undoubtedly lead to reconciliation.

In his introduction, Art Gish clearly defined the CPT mission: to learn, talk, listen, and understand. The CPTers dared to speak out, and for that we are grateful. Let us pray together, for in Art Gish's words, prayer "is a source of strength and courage to act in calmness and love."

—*Jerusalem*
April 10, 2001

GOLAN
HEIGHTS

Sea of
Galilee

Haifa

Nazareth

Mediterranean
Sea

Jenin

Nablus

Jordan River

JORDAN

Tel Aviv

WEST
BANK

Ramallah

Jericho

Jerusalem

Beit Jala

ISRAEL

Bethlehem

Gaza

Dead
Sea

GAZA
STRIP

Hebron

N

W   E

S

0   MILES   25

297

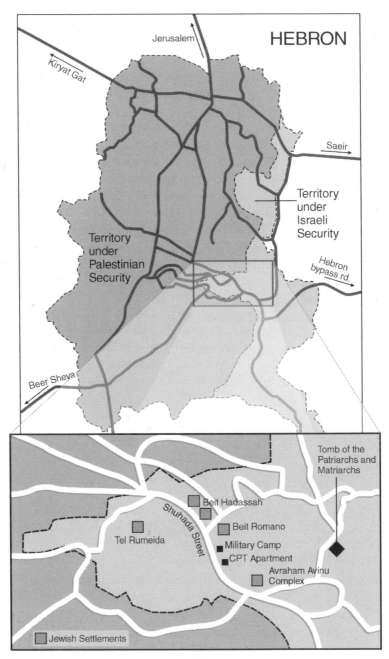

HEBRON

Jerusalem

Kiryat Gat

Saeir

Territory
under
Israeli
Security

Territory
under
Palestinian
Security

Hebron
bypass rd.

Beer Sheva

Tomb of the
Patriarchs and
Matriarchs

Beit Hadassah

Shuhada Street

Beit Romano

Tel Rumeida

Military Camp

CPT Apartment

Avraham Avinu
Complex

Jewish Settlements

Glossary

Amir, Ygal. The man who assassinated Prime Minister Yitzak Rabin.

Avraham Avinu. One of the small settler enclaves in the old city of Hebron.

Bantustans. The name given to areas in South Africa in which the apartheid government gave limited self-government to blacks.

Beit Hadassah. One of the small settler enclaves in the old city of Hebron.

Beit Romano. The settler yeshiva school in the old city of Hebron.

Cave of Machpelah. The traditional burial place of Abraham and Sarah, Isaac and Rebekah, and Jacob and Leah.

Druze. The people of a religious sect whose roots are in Islam. The Druze people live in southern Lebanon, Syria, and northern Israel.

Fatah. A major faction of the Palestine Liberation Organization (PLO). Yasir Arafat is the leader of Fatah.

Goldstein, Baruch. The Israeli settler who massacred twenty-nine Muslims as they prayed in the Ibrahimi Mosque in Hebron in February 1994.

Hamas. A Palestinian Islamic cultural and political organization, sometimes involved in violent acts against Israel.

Hebron Solidarity Committee. A group of Israeli peace activists concerned about peace and justice in Hebron.

Ibrahimi Mosque. Built over what is thought to be the Cave of Machpelah. The building is now half mosque and half synagogue.

ICAHD. Israeli Campaign Against House Demolitions.

Intifada. The widespread Palestinian uprising against Israeli occupation. The uprising began in December 1987 and lasted about seven years.

KACH. A group of followers of Rabbi Meir Kahane, identified by Israel as a terrorist group.

Kaffiyeh. An Arabic head scarf worn by men.

Kiryat Arba. A large Jewish settlement on the eastern edge of Hebron.

Ma'ale Adumim. A large settlement of about 20,000 people located east of Jerusalem.

Maqlube. A traditional Palestinian chicken-and-rice dish.

Oslo Agreement. The agreement between the Israeli government and the Palestinians, which was concluded with the historic handshake between Yitzak Rabin and Yasir Arafat on the White House lawn in September 1993.

Palestinian Authority. The Palestinian government headed by Yasir Arafat.

PLO. Palestine Liberation Organization, the umbrella Palestinian organization headed by Yasir Arafat.

Salaam alykum. A common Arab greeting meaning peace be unto you.

Shabbat shalom. A Hebrew greeting used during Sabbath, wishing a peaceful Sabbath.

Settlements. Israeli housing developments, actually towns, built in the West Bank and Gaza.

Tel Rumeida. One of the small settler enclaves in the old city of Hebron.

TIPH. Temporary International Presence in Hebron. European observers working in Hebron.

West Bank. The Palestinian area west of the Jordan River, referred to by Israelis as Judea and Samaria.

Yeshiva. A Jewish religious school.

The Author

Arthur G. Gish has been active in peace and social justice work for over forty years beginning with work as a conscientious objector with Brethren Volunteer Service in Europe (1958-60). He participated in the Civil Rights Movement in the sixties, and has opposed United States involvement in every war since his youth.

Born and raised on a farm in Lancaster County, Pennsylvania, Gish was reared in the Church of the Brethren. He and his wife, Petty Faw Gish, are members of New Covenant Fellowship, a communal farm near Athens, Ohio.

Gish is the author of *The New Left and Christian Radicalism* (Eerdmans, 1970), *Beyond the Rat Race* (Herald Press, 1972), and *Living in Christian Community* (Herald Press, 1979).